P9-BYJ-657

THE ROAD TO
SLEEPING DRAGON

*In Manchuria: A Village Called Wasteland and the
Transformation of Rural China*

*The Last Days of Old Beijing: Life in the Vanishing
Backstreets of a City Transformed*

THE ROAD TO
SLEEPING DRAGON

Learning China from the Ground Up

MICHAEL MEYER

BLOOMSBURY

NEW YORK · LONDON · OXFORD · NEW DELHI · SYDNEY

Bloomsbury USA
An imprint of Bloomsbury Publishing Plc

1385 Broadway   50 Bedford Square
New York   London
NY 10018   WC1B 3DP
USA   UK

www.bloomsbury.com

BLOOMSBURY and the Diana logo are trademarks of Bloomsbury Publishing Plc

First published 2017

ISBN: HB: 978-1-63286-935-7
ePub: 978-1-63286-937-1

LIBRARY OF CONGRESS CATALOGING-IN-PUBLICATION DATA

Names: Meyer, Michael J., 1972–
Title: The road to Sleeping Dragon: learning China from the ground up / Michael Meyer.
Description: New York: Bloomsbury USA, 2017. | Includes bibliographical references.
Identifiers: LCCN 2017007486 | ISBN 9781632869357 (hardcover)
Subjects: LCSH: China—Description and travel. | Meyer, Michael J.,
1972—Travel—China.
Classification: LCC DS712 .M495 2017 | DDC 951.06/12—dc23 LC record available
at https://lccn.loc.gov/2017007486

2 4 6 8 10 9 7 5 3 1

Typeset by Westchester Publishing Services
Printed and bound in the U.S.A. by Berryville Graphics Inc., Berryville, Virginia

To find out more about our authors and books visit www.bloomsbury.com. Here you will find extracts,
author interviews, details of forthcoming events and the option to sign up for our newsletters.

Bloomsbury books may be purchased for business or promotional use. For information on bulk purchases
please contact Macmillan Corporate and Premium Sales Department at specialmarkets@macmillan.com.

For Frances

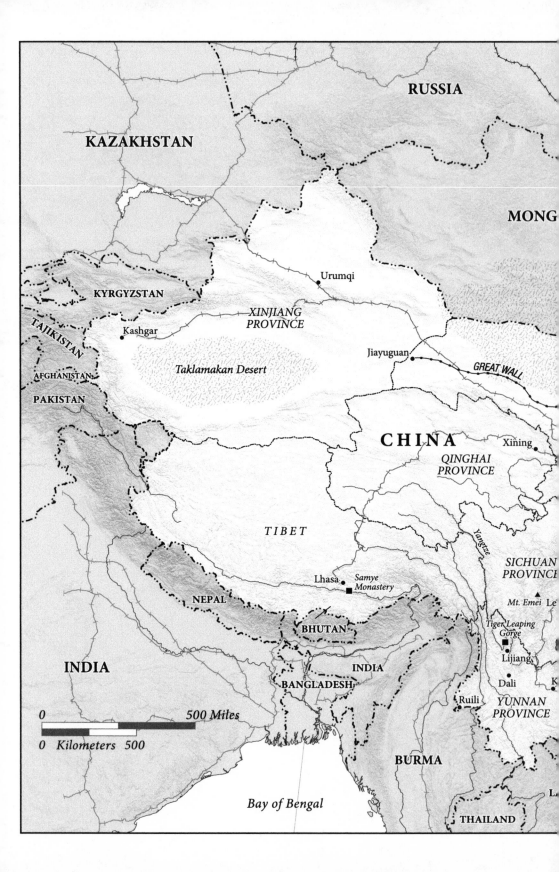

Contents

Author's Note   XV

CHAPTER 1   A Plunge into the Middle Country   1
CHAPTER 2   On the Stall-for-Time River   21
CHAPTER 3   Every Village Faces the Sun   39
CHAPTER 4   Sinking In   58
CHAPTER 5   Parting the Cloud of Compassion   70
CHAPTER 6   Far and Away in Tibet   86
CHAPTER 7   Tomorrow Will Be Even Better
              (but Today Things Will Just Get Worse)   99
CHAPTER 8   Thought Liberation   110
CHAPTER 9   Beijing Spring   126
CHAPTER 10   Meet the Parents   149
CHAPTER 11   Signposts   169
CHAPTER 12   Three Protests   179
CHAPTER 13   Arrivals and Departures   194
CHAPTER 14   Digressions on the New Frontier   209
CHAPTER 15   Countdown Clocks   229
CHAPTER 16   Defending the Ghosts   240
CHAPTER 17   Learning to Speak Olympics   250
CHAPTER 18   The Road to Sleeping Dragon   264

CHAPTER 19   "One World, One Dream" One Year Later   270

CHAPTER 20   A Trans-Siberian Exit   277

Acknowledgments   285

Notes   287

THE ROAD TO
SLEEPING DRAGON

It is nothing to start a journey, but it's hard to end one.

—From the classic Chinese novel *A Journey to the West*

Author's Note

Sometimes to see a place clearly you first have to leave. This is my third book set in China, and the second written while living, on separate occasions, in London, where history is always close at hand. The shelves of Charing Cross Road bookstores sag with guidebooks covering the capital's food, art, architecture, statues, shops, tea, writers, war, buses, churches, jewels, Jews, flowers, ghosts, and "secret open spaces." The longer you stay in London, the more you realize how little of it you've seen—despite the fact that in 1666, most of the city burned down.

Chinese cities are different: the longer I lived there, the more aware I became of what I could never see, because in China progress often looks like destruction. In London you can drink a pint at the Thames-side pub where Samuel Pepys watched the Great Fire. In Beijing, it is surprising to find your favorite dumpling restaurant still standing after one year has passed, let alone 350.

Unlike *The Last Days of Old Beijing* and *In Manchuria*, this is not a book of reportage but rather of mostly chronological impressions, of lessons learned over time. Although my understanding of China has deepened over twenty years, I can't pretend to be a "foreign expert," as my work permit alleged. I did not fall in love with China at first sight; the place bewildered me. I arrived knowing very little about the country and unable to speak a word of its language. In this, I resembled the students, job seekers, and travelers who write me asking how best to study Chinese and how to "learn" China.

I was given advice there, constantly. In the West you greet someone by asking how he or she is doing; in China you begin by informing the person what they should be doing: eating more, paying less, dressing warmer, getting married, or taking a different path and living "free and far from the dust of the normal world." A man holding a clucking chicken advised me to do that, moments after I had boarded a public bus in rural Sichuan.

Partings were equally instructive: people sending me off customarily said, "*Màn màn zǒu.*" Go slowly. When food arrived I heard, "*Màn màn chī.*" Eat slowly. While studying a map, admiring old photos, or wandering a temple, I was told, "*Màn màn kàn.*" Look slowly.

Go slowly, eat slowly, look slowly. Often the people suggesting this were themselves in an enormous hurry. The faster China accelerated, the more urgent the mantra became.

I repeat the phrase now because it is also encouraging, in the middle of a long journey, to pause and consider how far you have come.

—Spring 2017

CHAPTER I

A PLUNGE INTO THE
MIDDLE COUNTRY

I AM AN UNLIKELY answer to the question, asked anxiously by a Chinese
writer in 1935: "Who will be China's interpreters?" Sixty years later I
arrived by accident, after rejecting six other countries from the Peace Corps.
I was fluent in Spanish, and applied after a short stint volunteering at the
Texas-Mexico border with the United Farm Workers, hoping to be sent to
Latin America. The Peace Corps offered Turkmenistan, Vladivostok, Sri
Lanka, and Kiribati. "It's not Club Med, it's the Peace Corps," the recruiter
finally snapped, after I declined to spend two years in Mongolia or Malawi.
"You don't get to choose."

Months passed, until one late-spring day the phone rang in the English
classroom in Madison, Wisconsin, where I was student teaching. My turf-
warring Comp Ed ninth graders had been ordered to attend an assembly
optimistically titled "We're All in the Same Gang." I warily picked up the
receiver, expecting the vice principal to yell that the students in the local
branch of the Gangster Disciples were rejecting the suggestion. Instead, I
heard the voice of the all-but-forgotten recruiter, who pronounced a single
word with great finality: *China*. It sounded like a sentence, although really
it was a reprieve.

"I didn't know Peace Corps was in China," I said, twirling the phone
cord, stalling for time. In fact, the program had just tenuously begun, after
its planned 1989 start was shelved following the crackdown on the nationwide demonstrations centered at Tiananmen Square. I was seventeen then,
and when I heard of the bloodshed via my Beetle's radio, I pulled to the

road's shoulder, and—completely out of character—burst into tears. I didn't know any Chinese people personally, had never read a book by a Chinese writer, and could not have found Beijing on a map. But suddenly a world event had punctured my bubble of enormous teenaged self-regard. Six years later I knew little about the country beyond the Great Wall, pandas, one billion people, fortune cookies, and the indelible image of a man standing in front of a tank.

In 1995, China was more of a pariah than a hot travel destination, academic subject, or journalist beat. The country's ascent looked far from guaranteed; what looked preordained was its demise. One-third of China's population lived in poverty. The average Chinese worker earned only $500 each year.* Permitting the Peace Corps to send English teachers coincided with China opening its doors to the wider world and its markets. Still, there were limits. When Chairman Mao held power, Chinese propagandists had condemned the Peace Corps as a "tool of American imperialism." Rather than change its verdict, the current regime simply changed the program. "Officially," the recruiter said, "you'll be called a 'U.S.-China Friendship Volunteer.'" He paused, and through the phone line I heard the rustle of papers. "I don't know how to say it in Chinese."

I couldn't speak the language, either, of course. I didn't even know how it sounded. Not only was I wrong about fortune cookies—they're from California by way of Japan—I couldn't even use chopsticks. But this was it: Peace Corps' take-it-or-leave-it final offer—China.

I was flat broke. Except for a calico named Barky that could not meow, I was single. I drove a failing black Crown Victoria that my students often mistook for a narcmobile, scattering like pins when I bowled into the school lot. I liked them; I had the patience, thick skin, and sense of humor for the job, and believed the best way to "empower" kids was to teach them to read and write at grade level by year's end. The veteran teachers smirked at my rookie enthusiasm and shoulder-length hair, but praised my knack at reaching "troubled" teens. Nevertheless, to earn my certification

---

*In the next twenty years, the number would soar to $8,000. Even as the economic divide between urban and rural areas widened, by 2012 the overall rate of people living in extreme poverty (on less than $1.90 per person per day) fell from 88 percent to 6.5 percent over three decades, per the World Bank.

I was paying full tuition to teach full time for free, and had no job prospects. The Internet was nascent and smartphones were a dream; I fed myself working graveyard shifts as a relay operator between deaf and hearing callers, and by writing reviews for the two city newspapers of cassettes mailed by record labels promoting new bands such as Radiohead, Green Day, and Oasis. In two weeks I was turning twenty-three; in a month I would graduate. What then? Slink back, unemployed, to my parents in Minnesota? Or hang up the phone, drive that Saturday to the Madison airport, meet the FedEx envelope from D.C., sign the federal forms and waivers, and do as the voice commands? *China*. It's not Club Med, it's your life. You don't get to choose.

Six weeks later I handed the grim border agent the tissue-thin form that asked arriving passengers if they had "mental confusion" or psychosis (manic, paranoid, or hallucinatory). A connecting flight landed in China's southwest, where I would be posted as an English instructor at a teacher-training institute located on a dead-end dirt road at the bend of a polluted river whose name, Tuo, sounded like the spitting that scored Sichuan's streets. The province was one thousand miles from Beijing, but really a world away in terms of development and engagement with the West.

Yet some things felt familiar, if incongruous. In Chengdu, the provincial capital where I would go through two months of preservice training, the bleached pate of the city square's Mao statue glowed from neon billboards at his back, telling us PERSIST IN REFORM AND OPEN POLICY and also to DRINK PABST BLUE RIBBON. The beer originated in Wisconsin, the state I had just put seven thousand miles behind me. The local brew, Blue Sword, used the same colors on its label, and tasted just as flat, but came in twenty-ounce bottles that cost the equivalent of 25 cents, half the price of a bowl of cold hand-pulled noodles topped with fried peanuts, jade-green spring onions, red chili oil, and white sugar. This colorful dish was a vibrant upgrade from the ramen-brick penury of student teaching. Whatever hardships awaited in Sichuan province, bad food would not be one of them.

The Peace Corps worker who had met my volunteer group of seven men and seven women at the Chengdu city airport asked if we had any fears, beyond contracting mental confusion. A few people did fret about the famously spicy cuisine, others asked if their mail would be opened, but most were apprehensive about the squat toilets. "Bus plunge," I said, to laughter. But I wasn't joking; a childhood of reading the brief but ubiquitous news stories in the *Minneapolis Star Tribune* convinced me that this was a real danger in the developing world. That summer's headlines included:

7 DEAD AFTER SCHOOL BUS PLUNGES INTO RIVER

6 DEAD AFTER BUS PLUNGE

4 DIE, 7 HURT WHEN BUS PLUNGES FROM BRIDGE

The last story, one paragraph long, reported such details as "Firemen could not reach passengers trapped inside the wreckage until three cranes arrived to lift it off the ground. They arrived too late." The cranes always arrived too late.

During the Second World War, American pilots ferrying supplies over the Himalayas—the Hump—landed at the Chengdu airfield to support China's defense from Japan. Fifty years later the facility's concrete lump of a terminal looked little changed. Over the next two decades it would be rebuilt and become the nation's fourth-busiest airport, handling 42 million passengers annually, but on this July day in 1995 we all but had the building to ourselves. Our bus rolled along a two-lane unlined strip of tarmac that looked indistinguishable from the runway and whose color matched the overcast sky. I stared at the Pepsi billboards sprouting from fields thick with rapeseed and wondered where everybody was. A lone farmer pedaled a heavy black bike against traffic (our single bus). The oldest member of our group, a fifty-five-year-old U.S. Coast Guard veteran called the Captain, proclaimed sarcastically, "Behold, the teeming masses of the Orient!" The Peace Corps trainer lectured us to never use that outdated term.

The rest of the group was in their twenties, and conversation moved on to how much their Teva sandals cost (*Too much*), if Chinese shot pool (*Yes*), and whether volunteers could date the "Host Country Nationals" (emphatically *No*). Six of these people—nearly half of the group—would drop out before our two-year commitment expired. In Corps-speak, quitting is ominously called "early termination." I was surprised we were permitted to leave; the application process had taken a year, but ET'ing was instantaneous: sign the forms, accept the plane ticket, and by week's end you'd be home, unstrapping your Tevas and realizing that those tan lines were actually drawn by diesel fumes and dirt. No wonder the Chinese wore sandals with socks.

I would stay, but from the start, I thought I was even less likely than the Captain to make it. He left after fifteen months. I began an unexpected engagement with China that has lasted more than twenty years.

The volunteers took turns identifying a skill they each possessed that they thought might help the group. One woman, from Alaska, said she could wring, pluck, and cook a chicken. The Captain brought a mimeographed copy of a POW survival manual—*Why Men Live or Die!*—and said he could strip and assemble an M16 rifle blindfolded. Three volunteers said they played acoustic guitar. I provided protection: if anything went wrong, I told them, it would happen to me first. I was accident-prone, skilled at being in the wrong place at the wrong time, always putting my foot in it—like now, as I nodded at the Peace Corps trainer, who glowered and assured volunteers that China was a very safe country.

Later, I learned that editors laying out newsprint often pulled bus plunge stories off the wire to plug holes on the page; public transport appears to be much safer as newspapers move online. But in early-Internet 1995, I remained certain that buses couldn't stop hurling themselves off cliffs, down embankments, and into rivers. Even the state-run *China Daily* reported them: AT LEAST 38 DEAD AFTER BUS PLUNGES INTO RAVINE. I silently vowed to steer clear of ravines. But Sichuan province, set deep in the southwest against the Tibetan plateau's mountains, had many, formed in part by the four rivers, including the Yangtze, for which it is named. Sì = four; chuān = river.

That was one of the first lessons in Peace Corps training, which was helpfully heavy in language instruction. For four hours each weekday morning, I studied Chinese, or zhōngwén, also called hànyǔ (Han language), after the ethnicity that forms 92 percent of the population. The term is misleading: Han speak seven "dialects," and some, such as Cantonese, are mutually unintelligible, although they use the same writing system. A linguist famously observed that asking the question "Do you speak Chinese" is akin to inquiring, "Do you speak Romance?" The country's other 55 official ethnic groups speak at least 130 other languages, including Tibetan. I pictured the country as homogeneous, but geographically China is as big as Europe, with an even larger diversity of tongues. Five are represented on its paper currency, where "The People's Bank of China" is written in Chinese, Mongolian, Tibetan, Uighur, and Zhuang.

On the mainland, studying Chinese means learning Putonghua, "common speech," a lingua franca based on the northern dialect promulgated since 1955, shortly after the Communists took power. In English it's more commonly named Mandarin, from the Portuguese word for minister, a term coined by sixteenth-century Jesuit missionaries to describe the "official speech" used throughout the multilingual Chinese empire.

Although Mandarin was added to the country's constitution in 1982— "The state promotes the nationwide use of Putonghua (common speech based on Beijing pronunciation)"—one-third of Chinese citizens, at least 400 million people, do not speak it. Chairman Mao didn't, nor did two of his successors, Deng Xiaoping and Jiang Zemin. (Xi Jinping, raised in Beijing as an official's son, is said to be the first paramount leader to speak "properly.") In the run-up to the fiftieth anniversary of its introduction, China's education ministry lamented that of the 70 percent of the population that did use Putonghua, "only one in ten could speak it articulately."

In the humid Peace Corps training classroom, the flop sweat pooled as I struggled to distinguish Putonghua's four tones—five, if you count the neutral tone, used on sentence-ending particles, such as *ma*, which indicates you've asked a question. My teacher ran me through a drill familiar to many beginners, repeating "mother" (*mā*), "hemp" (*má*), "horse" (*mǎ*), and "curse" (*mà*). And then I would exit the classroom, and for the next twenty hours hear a faster, organic, and, to my ears, more beautiful Chinese. Sichuanese uses tones, too—it flips the second and fourth tones, making a mirror image of Putonghua—but otherwise sounds like a sibilant slur compared to Mandarin's sober propriety. *Duōshǎo qián* (How much does it cost?) becomes *Hàoduóqiàn*; *Bùzhīdào* (I don't know) is *Buxiàodei*; "What are you talking about?" transforms from *Nǐ shuō shénme?* to *Suósènmenǐ?* or, more commonly, a simple *Sázi?* (What?). Walking around with pricked-up ears I also learned expressions about dogs and melons that my reserved teacher, after bursting into surprised laughter, explained were local profanities.

Mr. Li was a chalk-dusted middle-aged man with a dry sense of humor whose favorite English expression was "That is a hot potato," which he carefully mouthed as if one were scalding his tongue. He spoke Chinese this way, too, which made his lessons easy to follow. Mr. Li wrote on the blackboard in characters but also in *pīnyīn*, the romanized "spelled sounds" Chinese schoolchildren learn before or alongside formal instruction in characters. "China," written on the Mainland in characters as 中国, becomes Zhōngguó. Although the word's etymology is nuanced, derived from an empire that saw itself at the nexus of civilization, my beginner's brain translated its components literally: *zhōng* = middle; *guó* = country. Many Chinese nouns are compounds that snap together like linguistic Lego bricks. To this day, I still think of train, *huǒchē*, as "fire wagon" and soda, *qìshuǐ*, as "fizzy water." I came from Měiguó, the "beautiful country," coined in the nineteenth century, an era when Chinese sailed east to the California gold rush. San Francisco's name dates from that time: Jiùjīnshān, "Old Gold Mountain." From expletives to place names, this was a beautiful language.

I lived in the Middle Country. That seemed fitting, given the transformation that was taking place, shifting the nation from what it was to what it was going to be.

The dust and humidity led me to a barber, who complained about something while chopping my hair above my ears. Or maybe he was cheerful and exulting about love: I heard a stream of palatal *zh* and *sh* and back-throaty *r*'s that sounded nothing like the trilling, tongue-kissing-teeth exuberance of Spanish. You rode Spanish from the handlebars; you steered Chinese from far back on the seat or even sitting on the rear fender. If I wasn't speaking English, my brain told me it was time to switch to Spanish, and for the first month in China I often insensibly blurted out perfectly fluent Spanish to people such as the barber as he tilted my head back and aimed a rusty razor at my throat. "Be careful," I wanted to say, but instead of "*Xiǎoxīn*," out popped "*Ten cuidado*." The barber nodded and began slicing away.

As he chatted, I grabbed hold of words I knew from the stream of ones that were still unintelligible, a slippery exercise akin to trying to sing along to "Louie Louie." Still, learning Chinese felt easier than beginning Spanish. It lacked gendered nouns, conjugated verbs, and endings changed by tense, and followed the innate basic grammar of subject + verb + object. Present: I (*Wǒ*) ride (*zuò*) the bus (*gōnggòng qìchē*). Future: I will ride the bus: *Wǒ huì zuò gōnggòng qìchē*. Wry Mr. Li also taught me to say *Wǒ xīwàng tā bù huì zhuìluò*. I hope it will not plunge. Fittingly, that last word had two falling tones; my lower jaw plummeted when saying it.

I Sharpie'd phonetic transcriptions on my whiteboard-smooth inner forearms to practice outside class. Ordering in a restaurant saw me flexing like Spider-Man about to shoot his web. Then I ploddingly read the words for pork-stuffed dumplings and hollow-heart greens, scribbled from wrist to elbow. Self-sufficiency was my goal, so I focused on speaking over reading and writing, a trade-off that I later regretted.

I also learned how to use chopsticks; forks had always been set at Minneapolis's Great Wall restaurant, whose menu items suddenly felt tame and domesticated. Instead of gumming egg rolls, watercress, and chicken chow mein, in Sichuan you grappled with "tiger skin" peppers, "bear paw" tofu, and flash-fried ground pork and chilies over cellophane noodles, or "Ants Climbing Trees." The more mundane the ingredients, the more embellished the dish's name.

My teacher said that the transliteration of my surname—Mài'er—sounded like Sichuan slang for "a son sold in the marketplace by his parents." I liked that, but with a menu writer's élan he rebranded me Méi Yīngdōng—Heroic Eastern Plumblossom. I winced when writing the characters inside the little green foreign residence permit booklet I'd be required to carry for the next two years. I preferred Sold Son, but was trained to do what I was told, to see every encounter as a cultural minefield where one false step could detonate U.S.-China relations. The Peace Corps instructed us to just say yes lest "our Chinese hosts" lose face. Agree to taste every offered dish, even boiled chicken feet; nod at each inquiry and invitation; drink to every toast. Never ask a fellow squatter for toilet tissue (carry your own); never ride a motorcycle (too dangerous); never date a local (too sensitive). Otherwise, say yes, say yes, say yes.

Six weeks after arrival, in hot, cicada-scored August, the teachers ordered us away from campus for a night to practice our Chinese "in the field." I wanted to travel north to the world's largest panda preserve, located in a valley enticingly named Wolong, "Sleeping Dragon." The narrow road to pandas snaked twelve hours through deep mountain gorges. Plunge potential notwithstanding, the infrequent bus service meant I couldn't make it there and back in two days.

Instead, I queued between cattle bars at the cavernous Chengdu station and felt a surge of accomplishment in buying a train ticket without reading my ink-bruised forearms. I picked Yibin, a Yangtze River port located seven hours south. I loved trains, and had never been on a Chinese one, so the journey, not the town, was my true destination. Only one-way tickets were sold back then, so I planned to ride the rails during daylight, disembark in Yibin, look at the Yangtze, and buy a ticket for the overnight train that returned to Chengdu.

The train did not disappoint. This was the end of the era when steam engines in China still chugged on some lines, and the journey on hard, shared L-shaped benches was a rolling town square, soon to be replaced by the hushed, individual airplane seating of high-speed carriages. The trip felt more like a voyage than a ride: as the train cut through the flat, farmed landscape—as unchanging and unnoticed as open ocean—passengers chatted and shared dumplings and smoked and sang and cracked sunflower seeds and argued, and one handed me her plump baby to bounce on my knee. Kids scampered up to yell "Good morning, teacher!" in English. They didn't know that I was a teacher; it was the one sentence they remembered from school. In Chinese they politely called me *shūshu* (uncle). We discussed the train's size and speed and what foods we liked and hated, and I was happy to keep conversational pace with the children, even as they corrected my pronunciation until the train reached the end of the line.

When I asked for a return ticket in Yibin, the clerk said my least favorite Chinese word: "*Méiyǒu.*" My Sharpie'd arm once displayed it as MAYoh—"Not have." After each entreaty—a standing-only ticket; a ticket to another northerly town—the clerk repeated *méiyŏu* with emotionless finality. Sensing I would be stuck in this humid, cement-colored city with little money and even scanter Chinese, the word sounded as chilling as Poe's raven-squawked "Nevermore." I had come to China without a credit card or pocket money—or even a camera—and had to subsist on Peace Corps' monthly salary of $120. Even if there had been an airport or a driver to hire, I wouldn't have been able to pay my way back to my bed in Chengdu.

"I need a ticket," I pleaded, adding the phrase Chinese commonly invoked to persuade foreign guests: "It's for our friendship."

"*Méiyŏu*," the clerk repeated, unmoved.

"I'm a U.S.-China Friendship Volunteer."

"Take the bus. It leaves at sunrise."

I had miscalculated terribly. There were no train tickets, and only one hotel in town was allowed to take foreigners. The reform-and-opening-up policy transforming China's coastal economy had yet to trickle upstream to this river-fogged town, whose vaporous air smelled like the 104-proof *báijiŭ* (grain alcohol) being distilled in its largest factory. Even the clouds above it looked hungover.

I trudged down People's Road to the hotel, averting my eyes from the pedestrians who froze in their tracks, and bicyclists who stopped pedaling. They did not call me "uncle," they called me *lǎowài*, the Chinese slang for "foreigner" that literally means "old outsider." In training, I had been told to ignore people who yelled the word: imagine a kangaroo wandering through your hometown; wouldn't you gawp too? No, I thought now, I would not taunt the creature by yelling, "'Roo!"; I would help it find a train ticket. The road turned, leading to a crumbling concrete bridge. The Yangtze—called the Cháng Jiāng (Long River) in Mandarin—banks east in Yibin. Before this turn, its upper reach, which I stared at from the tired bridge, was called the Jīnshā, or Golden Sand River. The water looked brown and torpid. At my back, I heard voices mutter *lǎowài*. This wasn't fun. I wanted to hop back on the train.

The state-owned hotel's lobby was not quite as large as Tiananmen Square. When I spun out of its revolving door, the staff did the kind of eye-popping double take I had only seen in black-and-white comedies. In China, a foreigner gains an enlarged sense of self; you are constantly reminded how *present* you are. The hotel workers looked me over from the shoes up. In a developing land where people still walked long distances, quality footwear attracted great interest, especially before coastal factories started cranking out Nikes. The concierge said I was the first foreigner he had ever checked in.

I was lucky he let me stay, as I had forgotten to bring my passport, a requirement to register as a guest. The concierge thumbed my little green residence permit booklet and laughed. "Heroic Eastern Plumblossom!" he snorted. "That's a girl's name." Which made me feel sorry for that girl, wherever she may be.

The hall attendant who guarded the room keys opened the door to one whose clammy walls made a gallery of smashed roaches framed by shoe prints. Next door, a karaoke hall pulsed with the sound of wounded hearts bleating Karen Carpenter's every "sha la la la la" as if it were their last. When I stepped into the shower the next morning, I looked up to an open pipe, pointing straight down. The water hit my head fast and cold.

I arrived at the bus station with swollen, sleepless eyes. A billowing black balloon crowned each vehicle, making it look ready for liftoff. The bag held natural gas, a cheap way to fuel the engine, the driver said, offering a cigarette and lighting his own. So our plunge would end in a movie-perfect fireball. I didn't smoke, and tucked the butt behind my ear, just as Peace Corps training had instructed. *Always be polite. Don't make others lose face. Just say yes.*

"You're going back to Chengdu?" the driver asked. "Get on my bus. I'm going to Mount Emei. You'll be there by four." That was eight hours away. "You can catch a bus onward and be back in town for dinner." Mount Emei is one of China's four sacred Buddhist peaks, historically seen as a place of enlightenment. Pilgrims, I knew, were often plunge victims, since their destinations often perched perilously far from flat roads. But the passengers on this bus looked like they were heading back to school and work, not to a temple. So far I had made only three mistakes: assumed a return train ticket existed, failed to bring enough money, and traveled without my passport. Full of wary hope that the worst was behind me, I stepped aboard.

"Please sit down," a young man said in English from the front seat behind the driver. He wore stonewashed shorts decorated with replicas of $100 bills. Benjamin Franklins smiled from his lap. "My English name is Franklin, my foreign friend."

Franklin studied at the local teachers college. His introduction exhausted most of his English. I tried Chinese. When the bus rumbled awake five minutes later, we'd run out of things to say. Franklin looked out the window.

Thirty minutes after departure, the bus broke down. The driver stopped, opened the engine compartment beside his seat, and stared into the smoke, calmly prodding while passengers coughed. After this repair, the bus sped along a two-lane cement road threading ripening rice paddies. The view showed no billboards, no buildings, and few people. The Sichuan countryside looked beautiful from a passing window; eking a living from it looked much less alluring.

Out the windshield I watched as a man up ahead fell off his steel-frame bicycle. The driver pulled hard on the wheel, sending us gasping and leaning, then pulled hard the other way, straightening out, avoiding the man and heavy bike and not once tapping the brake pedal.

Only a line of thin baling string a little later could stop him. Tied between dried bamboo stakes, the barrier marked where a flash flood had washed away a section of road. The driver spied it from a distance, slowed to toss cigarettes to the repair crew, then swung the bus into a field of golden rapeseed, bumping along two ruts.

Franklin laughed nervously. I scanned the horizon for danger.

But there were no ravines here; the bus bounced along furrows, honking at farmers harvesting the bright yellow blossoms from the table-flat fields. The afternoon slipped away; I would not reach Mount Emei, let alone my bed in Chengdu, by dark. I worried whether I had enough cash for another hotel room, but remembered another admonishment from training: *It is rude to count money in public.* Since landing, I had sat through six weeks of cultural classes that were variations on the theme *Never Offend.*

I was a six-foot-two-inch rake whose strongest muscle was my mouth: at college I once talked down a mugger pressing a knife against my gut, and twice lost fistfights after telling off racists. I never felt big, but in China my size usually made me the largest person in the room. On this bus I was a head taller and two weight classes above the other riders. Yet, with my kindergartner's vocabulary and dependency on others, I was also the smallest person there.

I can still feel my heart racing as the bus slowed. Three young men stood at the edge of a rapeseed field. One held an open glass bottle half filled with clear liquid that I knew wasn't water. Our draining momentum brought an increase of dread. *Keep going*, I thought. *Keep going keep going keep going*. The bus stopped. The driver's sidekick, a conductor who sold tickets and let people on and off, reached up and removed the screwdriver that dead-bolted the hinged door.

The three men staggered on board, then yelped at the sight of a foreigner. They leaned into my face, laughing sharp and drunk and mewling "Hello" with fermented breath. Franklin turned to the window. I swiveled to see the entire bus looking anywhere but at the three men. One wore a black shirt, one wore a white shirt, and one was bare-chested. A large knife dangled from each of their belts.

I froze when the word *lǎowài* barked from their lips. The word was a daily, often hourly annoyance, but this was the first time I'd heard it spat with such malevolence. I tensed, muted and still. The bus lumbered on. The conductor stood by the door, silent. The driver's thin shoulders hunched forward. The shirtless man knelt and blew into my ear.

Black Shirt said, in singsong English, "Hello-ARE-you-AN-English-FELLOW?" Where had he learned that? I laughed, softening. "I'm American," I answered in Chinese. *Wǒ shì měiguó rén.*

He raised his thumb. "Very good!" He chugged from the bottle and offered me a swig. He leaned close and asked more questions, which I couldn't understand. "*Tīng bù dǒng,*" I responded, words meaning I hear (*tīng*), but don't understand (*bù dǒng*). I leaned on Franklin, who leaned harder against the window glass, but still the man came, repeating the questions louder in my ear. The other passengers stayed silent. I stared ahead.

Suddenly, from behind, the conductor demanded their fare. White Shirt pushed him away. The bus driver glanced back but kept steering. Black Shirt, now kneeling beside me, held his eyes on mine.

Over his right shoulder I watched an elderly passenger rise to tap his back. The old man spoke too quick and harsh for me to understand.

White Shirt, standing beside him in the aisle, responded by smashing the liquor bottle over the old man's head. Blood, booze, and glass splattered our faces.

Black Shirt turned from me to pummel the old man's slumping body.

This is where I should have done something. Instead I sat terrified and mute.

White Shirt shoved the old man to the floor. Then he wrapped his hands around my neck and started to squeeze. In the aisle, Shirtless kicked the prone old man. Black Shirt unsheathed his knife.

Franklin pushed me away and then clambered over the seat onto the grandmother behind us. The other passengers surged to the back of the bus. Just as I pressed a forearm into my assailant's chin, I saw the conductor remove the dead-bolt screwdriver from the door.

One quick stab between the shoulders brought down Shirtless from behind.

As if cued, the bus driver slammed on the brakes, causing Black Shirt to pitch forward and fall. White Shirt still clenched my throat. My free hand could not release his tightening grip.

The driver unscrewed the metal gear stick from its floor housing, raised it above his head, and brought it down as if driving a railroad spike. I heard the sharp crack of breaking ice. The hands around my throat loosened, then fell.

The bus went silent. And then came the sound of shattering glass. Frenzied Black Shirt and bloodied Shirtless had jumped off the bus after it stopped and started pelting the windows with rocks they plucked from the dirt road. I ducked the shards. White Shirt's body slumped beside me in the aisle.

The fusillade ceased. I peeked over my seat and met tufts of black hair and pairs of brown eyes doing the same. Sitting up, the view showed we had made it to a village; this was why the driver had kept going when the violence began. I looked out one side of the bus and saw police officers in olive-green shirts running to where a circle of village men pinned Black Shirt and Shirtless to the ground.

I had never met Chinese police, and guessed it was not a pleasant experience. I also realized that forgetting to bring my passport was about to become more than an inconvenience. My left leg spasmed from adrenaline. Villagers ringed the bus, pointing and staring and murmuring *lǎowài lǎowài lǎowài.*

"Please," a voice asked in slow, gentle Chinese. "Get off the bus. Come with me."

The man pointed at his arm patch, where I recognized the characters for PUBLIC SECURITY.

Another cop grabbed White Shirt's inert body by the ankles. His wounded head thudded slowly down the bus steps.

"Please," the officer repeated.

Since arriving in China the previous month, my reading outside of language lessons consisted of Cultural Revolution and Tiananmen Square memoirs. Exiting the bus seemed tantamount to erasure. I would walk through the gates, up the station driveway, and then slowly fade from view. I heard the sound of the body being dragged away.

"*Wǒ hàipà.*" I'm afraid. My teacher had taught the phrase in a lesson not about violent crime—of course, China didn't have any, officially—but about politely refusing the throat-closing extremes of Sichuan's spicy cuisine.

The officer realized he had a situation. Out the windshield I saw the old man, the driver, and the conductor waving encouragement from the driveway. My leg jackhammered from fear. Two more officers boarded the bus. "Foreign friend," one urged, in halting English. "Please."

I pointed at Franklin. "Can he come?"

Franklin's face said: *This is what happens when you practice English with a foreigner.*

The police led us up a pitted concrete driveway through unlocked metal gates. We entered a courtyard bordered by one-story buildings with barred windows. Slumped silently in the dirt, hands lashed to the poles behind their backs, sat Black Shirt and Shirtless. The other body was nowhere in sight.

The driver smoked at a desk inside, facing a seated officer. He looked as unfazed as earlier that day when he avoided the fallen bicyclist on the road. The men nodded wordlessly when I entered, as if I had just popped in for a chat. I sat next to Franklin on a slatted wooden bench. "Tea? Cigarettes?" a cop asked. I watched the driver smile as he spoke. The listening officer smiled as he took notes scratched onto onionskin paper with a steel-nib pen. The old man stepped inside with a large white bandage taped in the shape of a plus sign to his head. I was in a country I knew nothing about, in the hands of people I couldn't fully understand.

Then the screaming started. The howls collapsed into sobs and rose into howls again.

"The bad men," Franklin explained.

The driver kept talking. I understood nothing. The conductor gave his account to another officer in another room. Suddenly I feared that our retellings wouldn't match. The smart play was to blame the *lǎowài*, board the bus, and drive away, leaving me behind. For the first time in my life I accepted an offered cigarette. The Red Plumblossom tasted nothing like its name, but after the third one my leg finally stopped bouncing.

Outside all had gone silent, but then came more screams.

Through the barred windows I watched a white Toyota Land Cruiser arrive. The doors discharged plump men wearing white dress shirts belted into navy slacks. I thought: *I'm in trouble.* The last person out of the vehicle, a thin young man in street clothes, handed me a card that said, in English, OFFICE OF FOREIGN AFFAIRS. In Chinese he announced: "I am an English teacher!"

Switching to English, the man said he taught middle school. We were pre–cell phone, but the Chinese countryside is a network wired by word of mouth. On this Saturday afternoon the English teacher had been leading supplementary classes as his students' parents harvested their crops. The Land Cruiser scooped him up mid-lesson and raced across the fields. His head, the teacher said, rubbing it theatrically, was sore from bumping it on the roof. I was the first foreigner he had ever met, and he wore the thrill on his face.

The teacher led me to a room where a group of green-shirted officers stood around a polished mahogany table. It was the nicest piece of furniture I had seen in Sichuan, made all the more incongruous by the barred windows and dirt courtyard outside. "This is the interview room," the teacher explained. He meant "interrogation." The button-down Foreign Affairs cadres passed around my little green residence permit booklet, noisily riffling the pages. I waited for a joke about my Chinese name, but it never came. Instead I heard, "*Tā méiyǒu hùzhào.*" That needed no translation: He doesn't have a passport.

"Who are you?" a man demanded.

"I'm a U.S.-China Friendship Volunteer."

"A what?"

"Peace Corps," I confessed.

His face remained unchanged.

An officer motioned for everyone to sit and asked: What did the suspects look like? What had they done to me? Would I like some watermelon?

A cop carefully placed plates of pink triangles on the table. I told the story to a slurping audience. An officer read back my statement in Chinese, which the teacher translated aloud into English. I nodded. Next, the officer said he would read the driver and conductor's statements aloud. I tensed at hearing *lǎowài*, not understanding the verb that followed. *Provoked? Killed?* What had the foreigner done? Inwardly, I knew: he impulsively agreed to teach in China for two years; he overeagerly set off to practice Chinese on the road; he foolishly assumed he could purchase a return train ticket.

But what did the police suspect?

The teacher sucked on a watermelon slice between short bursts of translation. Finally, he said, "All three statements are the same. You can leave."

A policeman instructed me to sign each page of the transcription. In Chinese, I wrote Heroic Eastern Plumblossom with a steel-nib pen on five pages of thin paper—tearing only three of them—and pressed my red-inked thumbprint over the characters.

"What's going to happen to the two men?"

The teacher translated the reply: "They will be punished."

"How?"

"The police have decided that the criminals will be beaten until you are satisfied justice has been achieved." What a sentence! The teacher repeated it, ensuring that I understood.

We had been inside past sunset. In the dirt courtyard, under the halo of a moth-clotted floodlight, Black Shirt and Shirtless sat bound to the pole, faces blurred by blood and snot. With a skipping start as if he were taking a penalty kick, a policeman darted forward and planted his loafer into Black Shirt's face.

Flinching, I said quickly: "I am satisfied justice has been achieved."

The officer motioned toward the open gate. He smiled, waved theatrically, and in English said, "Bye-bye."

The bus waited, quiet and dark. In his seat, the driver snapped awake and tossed me the smokes. He was out of Red Plumblossoms; these were Famous Dogs, whose package showed a mirthful, panting spaniel. I passed the pack to the old man, whose bottle-lacerated head shone from ribbons of new white gauze. Franklin gestured for me to sit beside him. Only this time he greeted me in Chinese.

The bus stirred and started. The damp night air rushed through the smashed windows. Passengers heaped padded cotton jackets atop me. They held my shoulder and smiled and praised my Chinese and said America was good, and China's friend. "We are friends," they said. As unsure as I had felt at the police station, perhaps the police and passengers had, too. The officers had ignored my absent passport and lack of any contact numbers and called for a middle school teacher to interpret at a crime scene. Over the hours, the driver and conductor had retold what happened while a bus full of passengers waited in the dark.

Rolling at last toward our destination, I felt charmed. Then a fellow rider stressed that the attackers were Yi, an ethnic minority. "They are not Chinese," she said. By which she meant Han, her ethnicity. So China had racism, too. I didn't have the words to respond, just as in training I dared not question the party line that China's fifty-six "nationalities," as the country called its ethnic groups, lived "hand-in-hand" in socialist harmony. Later I learned that, as with most propaganda, Chinese didn't challenge such slogans; they ignored them. Now, however, the driver answered for me, shouting that of course the men were Chinese—didn't China have bad people, too?

Playing peacemaker again, the driver asked if I liked to sing. In training, I was compelled to learn a popular Sichuan folk song whose first line I belted now:

Pǎo mǎ liū liū de shān shàng. The mountain streams with running horses.

Laughter filled the bus, and the second line rang out strong from many throats. *Yī duǒ liū liū de yún yo.* A piece of cloud whisks across the sky.

I forgot what line came next, so I waited for the chorus:

Yuè liàng wān wān/ The crescent moon shines upon/

Kāngdìng liū liū de chéng yo. Kangding city.

The bus sang it together, from the start: "The mountain streams with running horses. A piece of cloud whisks across the sky."

The dark bus drifted across the night.

The Mount Emei bus station staff stared wide-eyed as the smashed vehicle pulled in. The passengers said *zàijiàn*—good-bye—while Franklin, the driver, and the old man with the bandaged head argued over the best place to leave me for the night. I said I didn't have much money. They argued some more.

They woke a guesthouse clerk, paid for a room, and escorted me to the door. The old man made sure the shower had hot water, holding his hand under the tap until it glowed pink, then drying it on the gauze taped to his skull. Franklin filled the tin tea thermoses at the hallway samovar. The driver lit the room's mosquito coil. The clock said 12:20 a.m. I closed the door and fell on the bed. My hair softly crunched from dried blood that was not mine.

I stepped into the shower to sluice away the day. Five minutes later, a knock. I opened the door in a towel.

"You haven't eaten all day! Come, come, come! Our treat! Fish! How's fish? Get his shorts! Dry him off! Get his shoes!"

We prowled the silent streets in the wounded bus, whose deflated gas bag sagged over shattered windows, before parking in front of a closed roll-up metal door. The driver's pounding echoed down the dark street, waking the restaurant's staff. A popular poster hanging on the wall above the mossy fish tank showed a rose in a crystal vase beside a plateful of fried eggs, sausage, toast, and orange juice. I said I'd have that. *Méiyǒu*, the waitress replied, unsmiling. The driver chose an unlucky fish from the tank. The waitress raised it above her head and slammed it to the cement floor. It made a familiar sound.

The driver ordered a case of Five Star beer. He said that "Chinese are good, Americans are our friends." He placed the chili-stewed fish's head in my bowl to prove it. "For our friendship." I was already tiring of that line, but at least I understood it. The driver, the old man, and Franklin clinked my tall brown bottle and began extinguishing the day's adrenaline.

Looking back, I can see that this unlikely trio prevented me from catching the next flight out of China, and undoing the life that has followed. I, not the bus, was the one that plunged.

The men played a popular singsong drinking game called Guessing from Chaos. You cocked a fist and shouted a number while making puns. The loser chugged a glass of beer. I grasped the idea but not its execution. Exasperated, the driver placed a chopstick in my hand and said, "We'll play a very simple game instead. Even children can do it."

He banged his own stick on the rim of a bowl and chanted, "*Bàng Bàng Bàng Bàng.*" The word meant stick. This much I understood. The driver motioned for me to mimic him. Together we went, "*Bàng Bàng Bàng Bàng.*"

The driver shouted, "Tiger!"

I didn't shout anything. The table shook with laughter.

The driver scratched his head comically. "You speak when I speak. Say *stick, worm, chicken,* or *tiger.*"

"You can say *human,* too," Franklin added.

"What?" the driver demanded. "You can't say *human.*"

"You can! Worm eats stick, chicken eats worm, tiger eats chicken, and human beats tiger!"

"No! Tiger is the biggest. A human can't beat a tiger!" It was the most agitated I had seen the driver all day. "Who taught you this game?"

Franklin tensed and sat up straight. "My father taught me this game!"

"I understand now," I lied. "Let's play. Ready?"

The table fell silent and we leaned over our bowls. Rhythmically our chopsticks clinked against the rim.

"*Bàng Bàng Bàng Bàng.*"

The driver shouted "Stick!" as I screamed "Human!"

"Stick beats human," Franklin said with finality.

"Correct!" the driver said, filling my glass with Five Star to slam. Then he tossed his chopstick on the table and held his fist up to his ear. "No more kids' games! Guessing from Chaos! Ready? A one and a two and a . . ."

CHAPTER 2

ON THE STALL-FOR-TIME RIVER

P EACE CORPS STAFF listened to my retelling with bureaucratic dispassion. Why had I traveled alone? What compelled me to take that bus? Their job was to nurture U.S.-China friendship, not individual volunteers. The most helpful thing the director did was point me to an office computer, where I typed a statement to file with Chengdu's American consulate, recounting the incident in detail.

I printed a copy to post home to Minnesota, which my mother saved, along with all of my letters, which gave her a glimpse of a country she had never seen. My mom grew up in Detroit, the daughter of a Ford factory worker, and had raised my younger sister and me all but single-handedly, sometimes working two jobs—daytime secretary, nighttime cashier—before remarrying and working at a Minneapolis construction company she later owned.* "It was the worst of times," she recalled of our upbringing in her first letter to me, "but it was also the best of times. You kids were my life's work." From childhood, she was my most supportive reader. But she was also, always, my mom: "I didn't realize that after you raise your kids, they just drop off the face of the earth and you never see them again," she wrote. "Are you finished with trying to change the world yet? I'm sorry, that was cruel. I look up at the moon and realize you're looking at the same one. That always cuts the distance between us down to size."

---

*Later, when the television drama *Mad Men* aired to accolades, I would wager she was one of the few viewers who noticed that its set designer's attention to period detail extended to 1960s door locksets.

I wish that the intellectual depth of our correspondence matched the emotional honesty, but we were both new to China, weighing our expectations against my experience, learning the country from the ground up.

"Any indications of communism are nowhere to be found," I wrote myopically after landing.

> Private businesses thrive, from kiosk vendors to department stores. An education official said that China is now in a socialist phase and will someday pass on to capitalism. I have felt no culture shock. It reminds me being on the Texas-Mexico border. People seem happy, and are tremendously friendly. The food is amazing. Skies are almost always overcast, and the air is dirty. It leaves a bad taste in your mouth . . . The slogans say, "Modernize, but maintain stability." Talk about an oxymoron. But it's really a spectacle— China is 50 years behind the West, but seems to be trying to close that gap in five years. People here are surprised to see an American. Everyone seems to know the word "Hello." I love being here—it's a musty country being opened at last.

Move over, Marco Polo! Although I wince at the shallow (if accurate) observations, I am also reminded that a very young man wrote this letter. In the postscript, he asks his mother to mail him boxes of Stridex acne pads.

Her defense is that she came of age during the Cold War, when little news trickled out of "Red China."

"I'm surprised it's not what I imagined," my mom replied. "I find it hard to believe it's so modern, but I don't know why, it's a civilization that has been around for thousands (?) of years."

I laughed reflexively upon reading this; already after the first month, I was tired of hearing that China had *five thousand years* of history, as if civilization were a video game where the highest point total wins. On television she saw that New York businesspeople were paying fortunes to have their offices rearranged by feng shui masters. "It sounds like common sense to me, like put your desk facing the door so you can greet your clients." In her postscript she added that she was reading the books I had left behind, and especially enjoyed the Jane Bowles short story in which a scholar is attacked by nomads and turned into a babbling clown for their amusement. "Kind of what I imagine could happen to you."

My story has a happier ending. Three weeks after the attack, I wrote home, honestly, that I was "fine"—the preset Midwest emotion my parents would understand. (Chinese uses a similar shorthand: people insist they are *hǎo* or things are *kěyǐ*, even when they are not.) "Violence like this is rare in China," I continued, parroting what the Peace Corps had told me, but not mentioning how the police had extended the mayhem. Instead I wrote that the cops "are a foreigner's best friend. I was never searched or asked if I was a spy." In retrospect, that set the bar pretty low for friendship, but it was true. Moreover, moving forward without looking back was a very Chinese response to misfortune.

Still, there was protocol to follow. The Peace Corps scheduled a counselor to phone from D.C., a twelve-hour time difference away. I was excused from a training session in which volunteers unrolled condoms over unpeeled bananas. The counselor's voice broke through static and began the conversation asking why I preferred being called by my last name, not my first. It was a playground nickname that stuck; my school had a lot of Michaels, as did our extended Catholic family, including my dad. "So your father is also named Michael," she said, suddenly intense. "But you don't like that name." Right, I said, then raced to add that my dad and I were close; that wasn't why Peace Corps told her to call me.

She carried the conversation after that, and my mind wandered away from the bus to the violence my American high school students had experienced and written about in class, and their unwillingness, when I—trying to be helpful—urged them to talk to the school counselor. And how eager they were at "meds time," when I, as required by law, handed out Ritalin to the kids who had been prescribed it. Forty students in that class, clinging to the edge of six round tables like life rings. The first thing I did after walking through the door each morning was to erase the Gangster Disciples' Star of David emblem from the blackboard. The second was to walk around the room and give each student a handshake or high five, since rules on teacher-student contact were not enforced in that forgotten corner of the district. Then we got to work.

Leading that packed "learning environment" made transitioning to a similarly crowded classroom in China much easier, and I doubted I would have to hand out prescription drugs to the college students I'd be teaching. Still, I was warned, there would be obstacles. In the last week of training we studied a columned sheet of mimeographed paper titled "Confucian vs. Dewey Ideals of Teaching." Confucius, we were told, felt instruction should be "Teacher-centered," while the American education reformer John Dewey held it should be "Student-centered." The columns meant to contrast classical Chinese and modern Western pedagogy:

Confucian ideals	Dewey ideals
Teacher as all-knowing expert	Teacher as facilitator
Conform to tradition	Discover something new
Written word sacred	Multi-media learning
Test is ultimate measure	Test is tool for further learning

The Captain gruffly announced, "This is why one culture is in the toilet and the other one's great!"

Nobody asked which one.

My new class of students sat two to a table, three tables across, four rows deep. *Twenty-four*, I counted, standing on tiptoe to peek through the classroom window, set high on a wall painted seasick green. They were sophomores, twenty-year-olds, taking a three-hour class named, simply, Writing. Over time I would appreciate how Bureaucratic Chinese is more of a suggestion than a rule, but after being posted to Neijiang Teacher's College as half of its first pair of Peace Corps volunteers, I expected strict guidelines of what to teach—or, more likely, what not to. When I asked the department chair for guidance, he looked bemused. "It's a writing class," he stated. Mr. Wang stated everything in a detached monotone that suggested he was reading a clock instead of talking to a human—which, he later admitted with a laugh, is close to how he saw me and my site mate Kevin then: ticking time bombs that he was charged with defusing for the next two years.

Mr. Wang was a short, doughy Party member in his late thirties who smiled when he grew uncomfortable, a reflex that simultaneously made his eyelids descend. What should I teach students, specifically? A smile creased his smooth, pale face. With eyes closed, as if answering a great philosophical riddle, Mr. Wang finally said: "Teach them writing."

My other class, he informed me, was called Civilization. I asked which one. "Western," he replied, without missing a beat. (Sarcasm was an American export that would trickle in over time via films and television.) I was lucky: poor Kevin, a Chicago native who had never taught before, was assigned classes named Intensive Reading and Extensive Reading. Which came first?

Mr. Wang handed me a curriculum he had outlined on thin paper flecked with wood pulp. I read: "Ancient Rome, the Bible, the Renaissance, the Enlightenment, the Beatles, the Stock Market." Mr. Wang chuckled low. "I think the students should know these things. China is changing." I started hearing that sentence even more than *five thousand years of history*. It shut down conversation just as effectively, explaining nothing and everything at once.

The two-day weekend was made official that summer. Why now, Mr. Wang? "China is changing." A Kentucky Fried Chicken restaurant would soon open in Chengdu. Was this good or bad? "China is changing." The government just ended its restriction on imported films. (GOOD NEWS! read a hand-painted campus poster. MORE HIGH QUALITY AND ENTER-TAINING FOREIGN MOVIES WILL WIDEN THE EXPERIENCE OF MOVIE-GOERS.) So, Mr. Wang, did this mean Hollywood no longer exported "spiritual pollution," as the government used to say? "China is changing." Coming soon to campus: *Forrest Gump*, *The Lion King*, and *Judge Dredd*.

The teachers college loudspeakers usually roused students at 6:30 a.m. to assemble for morning exercises with the brassy blast of "The East Is Red." In my first week on campus, however, I awoke to the lilting flute of "Morning Mood" from *Peer Gynt*. The next day it was replaced by the crunching opening chords of Nirvana's "In Bloom" blasting through the old public address system in teeth-rattling treble. *China is changing*, I thought. The next day, "The East Is Red" returned as our reveille.

In his office, Mr. Wang asked, "Do you know what the most important word in China is right now?" I guessed *family*.

"'Money,'" he replied. "I should say 'family,' but it's money. That is our reality these days." Mr. Wang was a member of the Communist Party. I thought everyone in China was enrolled at birth, but only 6 percent of the population belonged to the organization that controlled the country. Top high school and college students were invited to join, or a person could be nominated by an existing member or apply on their own with the support of one. In their induction oath—the only time he had taken vows, Mr. Wang said (wedding ceremonies are civil affairs)—inductees promised to "fight for communism." In practice, however, the Party had spent more years dismantling a Marxist economy than building one; since Mao's death in 1976, reforms ushered in a market-oriented, state-supported hybrid the Party called "socialism with Chinese characteristics." Mr. Wang joined the Party because he was a patriot, and also, he readily admitted, because it was good for his career. Its 83 million members made up the world's largest private club, with access to powerful people and an inside track to government jobs, such as teaching, since the state ran the school system across all levels.

After a summer of being browbeaten in training about propriety, about "face," Mr. Wang's candidness surprised me. It shouldn't have: soon, over faculty dinners and on the basketball court and on the campus's lone, dirt street, I learned that people spoke without a filter, asking the sort of direct questions that, back in the States, would get a drink tossed in one's face or could only properly be answered after an exegesis of great books. How tall was I? What did I weigh? What was my blood type? How much did I earn? Did I believe in God? Who holds the map of our life's journey? Is wisdom more important than morality?

I was twenty-three, preparing to teach courses titled Writing and Civilization with textbooks, a box of chalk, and a cassette player. These made up the contents of the college's "Technology Closet." In this it resembled my former American high school. The chalk was the same length and the same color, and still smarted when I pressed it against the callus that had hardened from writing on the blackboard across the previous year.

I was a teacher, accustomed to classroom life. Acclimating to China as a journalist or businessperson or foreign service officer would have been a different introduction to the country, as would being posted to a large coastal metropolis instead of Neijiang, a city of two hundred thousand— small by Chinese standards—located between the former wartime capital, Chongqing (Chungking), and the provincial capital, Chengdu, four hours northwest by train. High-speed rail would later cut that journey to under an hour (and one million more people would move in), but in 1995, Neijiang was the boondocks. Pronounced "Leijiang" in local dialect, its name means Inner (*nèi*) River (*jiāng*). In English, the school's promotional brochure said that it was located "in the hinterland of the center of Sichuan with the Tuojiang River running by."

Only one bridge crossed the water, separating town from fields of rapeseed and the dirt road that ran two miles under a canopy of tall bamboo to campus. Downstream, a floating bridge made of planks lashed to oil drums was bookended by lean-to tollbooths whose attendants charged two jiao (one-tenth of a yuan, the equivalent of a nickel) to people, but twice that for each pig. Neijiang was a leading pork producer as well as sugarcane grower. The local propaganda bureau had branded it Sweet City, a nickname that to me seemed akin to calling Fargo the Winter Wonderland. There was, however, some truth in this advertising. In downtown Neijiang, spindly rows of hard purple stalks leaned against buildings, blocking sections of sidewalk. Vendors lopped off sections of sugarcane with large knives, charging five jiao for a length that customers gnawed like pandas chomping bamboo. It tasted like syrupy bark.

Upstream, a rusty flat-bottomed skiff ferried farmers to town. It charged twice as much as the bridge but allowed them to board with oxen. Its pilot worked the crossing in fifteen-minute intervals, unlike the lone bus that ran into town, which wouldn't turn its engine over until every seat and then stools set in the aisle were filled. I preferred the ferry. But aside from the bank and post office there was nothing for me in town except the stares of locals.

I grew up in and around lakes but am wary of rivers, which are more watery highways and dangerous borders than recreational. In Neijiang the Tuo ran brown and looked deceptively shallow and still. But when the ferry pilot aimed upstream, cut the engine, and floated at an angle into the rubber tires buffeting the landing, you could feel the current's pull. Sixty miles south, it emptied into the Yangtze.

The river's name not only sounded like the act of spitting, it actually was the Chinese word for it too: *tuò*. No, said Mr. Wang. The character was actually pronounced with a rising tone: *tuó*, but local dialect reversed it. With his index finger, he traced the river's name on his palm. I nodded, understanding nothing.

Later, when I flipped through my little red dictionary, I found characters for *tuo* that meant camel, ostrich, tearful, and the verb *stall for time*. I love the literal directness of Chinese—a toupee is "fake hair," pajamas are "sleep clothes," a giraffe is a "long-neck deer"—and again the language seemed spot-on: it did feel as if I had moved to the muddy banks of the Stall-for-Time-River.

Mr. Wang smiled when I told him this, reflexively closing his eyes as usual, giving him the appearance of a man about to savor a moment. In school and at Party meetings he had learned that foreigners looked down on China. They complained about its polluted cities and praised its underdeveloped countryside. Now he could correct this *pìhuà* (fart speech) and, as he put it in English, "combat sentimentalism." Our *tuo* (沱) was an antiquated noun not listed in my dictionary. It just meant "a branch of a river." (A slow-flowing branch that stalled for time before meeting the mighty Yangtze, I told myself, while nodding at Mr. Wang.)

Earlier that week, when I first arrived on campus, smoke from morning cooking fires shrouded the countryside's spindly firs. Everything looked new to me. A newcomer to a city like New York or London will recognize landmarks from a lifetime of movies and shows; a first-timer to the French or Dutch countryside might find the landscapes familiar from paintings. I had never seen even a snapshot of Sichuan, let alone its fields. I sounded as giddy as *The Tempest*'s Miranda ("O brave new world . . ."), drinking it in for the first time. I watched a blue-suited farmer with rolled-up pants trail a row of geese down a packed-earth path. But mostly the land was empty of people and full of terraced paddies silently filling with rice.

"It's beautiful," I observed to Mr. Wang.

He picked at the label sewn outside his sport coat's cuff in the popular style, so the brand was on display. "You are wrong," he said. "It's not as good as Chengdu. Chengdu is developed. This," he said, stabbing his pricey Red Pagoda Mountain brand cigarette at the landscape, "is very backward."

But not to a newcomer, or at least someone who could leave.

My first class was scheduled to begin after dinner, and I worried the students' energy would ebb across the next three hours. I opened the classroom door to Writing. The students stood and clapped. I introduced myself in Chinese, chalking "Teacher Plumblossom" on the board in characters: 梅老师. The students gasped—"He writes with his left hand!"—and cheered: "You must be really smart!" Most Chinese are forced as children to write right-handed; southpaws such as Bill Gates and President Clinton (and later, President Obama) evinced lefties' superior intelligence. But a Chinese character's strokes are written from left to right, as are sentences, so the side of my hand smeared the words as I wrote. My chalked name looked like it had been trapped in a wispy cloud. I saw no eraser—it turned out to be the threadbare rag steeping in a plastic water bucket—and so I moved down the board to write my name again. There, chalked in English in tight, cursive loops, I noticed that a student had written: "Lilies that fester smell far worse than weeds." It was a line from a Shakespeare sonnet; back in America, my students were chalking six-pointed Gangster Disciple tags. The Neijiang student who had copied it from a textbook said, "My English name is Rambo!"

I was relieved to hear that someone could speak English. "That's a lovely name for a young woman." All of the students, she said, had chosen their own English names, after Mr. Wang had told them to, so the foreigners could keep them straight. She handed me a seating chart she had carefully drawn with a ruler; each of the sharp-edged rectangles representing their table desks held two names. She asked what Shakespeare's line meant: Was it about corruption? Sure, I guessed.

"Thank you, sir! Do Americans favor an open China?" Some do, I said cautiously. "Do all Americans write with their left hand?" Finally, a question I could answer with certainty.

I asked if I was the first American they had met. Twenty-four heads nodded yes. After a few silent seconds, another hand went up. A boy who called himself Longfellow said, "Tell us about American girls!" His classmate Jefferson added, "Will an American woman mind if I guess her age older than she really is?"

Three women—Dinger, Chinatown, and Larry—leaned close, whispering, before finally Chinatown ventured, "If you commit a crime in one state, but run to another, can you still be punished?"

In the front row, grinning, sat, in order, friends who had named themselves John, Paul, George, and Ringo. I hoped they were also in the Civilization class for the unit that came between the Enlightenment and the Stock Market. Ringo asked, "Why do Americans love religion?"

"Why aren't the Indians allowed to leave their reservations?" inquired Zeus.

A girl named Sail: "Who was the sixth president of the U.S.?" I shrugged. "John Quincy Adams!" she said with a mischievous giggle. "I tricked you, because I know the answer!"

A serious-looking student who called himself Kane asked, "Why are you here?"

I turned to the blackboard to write "U.S.-China Friendship Volunteer" in English. At my back, I heard, whispered in Chinese, "Peace Corps." I wheeled around and grinned. The class exploded in laughter. Training had instilled in me an expectation of Confucian-Communist classroom piety. I imagined teaching to be as interactive and mirthless as a sermon. The students' sense of humor, so similar to my American kids' quickness to laugh, and often at themselves, was a happy surprise.

To gauge each student's writing level, I told the class to write a paragraph advocating their choice of a school mascot. Chinese universities didn't have mascots then; the gate of Neijiang Teacher's College was garlanded with a banner announcing: REFORM OF REAR SERVICE WITH A CENTER OF AN INDIVIDUAL CONTRACT AND ARRANGEMENT QUOTA.

Wiseman raised his hand and said that this mascot-making activity wasn't in the textbook, a primer as thin and pink as a copy of *Trout Fishing in America*. "The first lesson in there is on observation," I said. "So that's what we're doing. Imagine you could choose a symbol to represent the character of this school. What would it be?"

"A pig!"

"A motorcycle!"

"*Mona Lisa*!"

Three hours of class passed in a blur of exclamation points and question marks. When I pivoted from the pocked, black-painted cement slab that made the chalkboard, I stumbled off the concrete step that formed a narrow lecture stage. "Chinese teachers always stay on that!" the students howled. I walked between their rows, knelt beside desks, urged them to read their work aloud, then exchange papers for editing. It was all new to them, but standard fare in an American school. The difference, for me, was that this was teaching freed from the meetings and paperwork that had sucked the light from my schooldays.

Twilight turned to night. I argued that our college mascot should be the Sugarcanes. The class (except Ringo, holding firm on the Mona Lisas) instead voted for the self-deprecating Pigs, pronounced peegs. The homework was to revise their paragraph introducing the Neijiang Teacher's College Pigs and also practice pronouncing a short i.

"Such modern methods," Carnegie whispered.

I laughed. The class laughed louder. Just as we quieted down, the power went out. United in darkness, the students cheered.

From my apartment balcony, I heard barges puttering against the current. The other noise was agricultural: a rooster crowing at dawn, the lowing of the mud-colored ox tethered in the building's courtyard. Fields hugged the school on three sides, producing broad beans, peanuts, and the rapeseed used to make cooking oil. (Its Chinese name, yóucài, means "oil vegetable.") The short, spindly stalks bloomed bright yellow, carpeting the fields with sunglow. Because gray clouds often curtain Neijiang, the ripe rape flowers were the brightest thing in view.

My apartment, in a white-tiled box that gleamed like a polished bathroom fixture, didn't match these surroundings. But soon buildings would be all that grew here. Over the next twenty years, a high cement bridge would replace the ferry, and fields of gray apartment blocks would sprout in place of the golden rapeseed. On the other hand, the city would also clean the Tuo River, lining its banks with wetland marshes and winding, shaded bike paths, and rebuild this backwater vocational school into a modern college. On its paved main street you would be able to eat a bowl of noodles without kicking rats away from a table, teetering on an uneven dirt floor, or first dunking a chopstick-pinch of vegetables in vinegar to kill errant worms. (The painfully scouring folk cure: swallow the contents of a cigarette. I do not recommend it.) Most locals would not stare at you like an aquarium fish; disarmingly, they would ignore you. Rolling brownouts would not cut out lights and hot-water heaters, and a bus ride into town would not require passengers to help push the vehicle up a

cobblestoned hill slicked with pungent mud. A visitor could stay at Neijiang's tallest building, a twenty-eight-story international hotel named for
the city's most famous son, the painter Zhang Daqian. The hotel would
stand on the former bamboo-shaded footpath that once led to a fortune-
teller's cave, beside mossy steps that climbed to a Taoist temple and the
painter's former studio.

Zhang fled to Taiwan after the Communists took power, so his museum
displayed only copies of his work. In a way, this was fitting: Zhang was a
renowned master forger, and several American museums had unknowingly
purchased his painted copies of thousand-year-old scrolls, only to discover
the deception decades later.

Back in 1995, his hilltop studio provided Neijiang's highest vista. The
view showed a skyline of unpainted seven-story cement rectangles. The only
splash of architectural color was seen at the main post office, buttered in
a yellow tile that matched the mustard flowers blooming in the fields.

I rode the ferry there weekly, placing letters home on a handheld scale
weighted with the little lead clumps I used to crimp onto a fishing line as
a child. Sealing the envelope required brushes of fish glue kept in a pot,
affixed to stamps showing brown "roundhouses" or traffic overpasses; the
former was the type of traditional Chinese housing now being obliterated
by the latter.

"The college staff seem nervous around me and Kevin, like they are
almost too eager to please," I wrote home at the end of my first month on
campus.

> They also often neglect to tell us when things are happening that
> require our presence. At 7:20 last night, a student told me there
> would be a dance in our honor. "Oh," I said. "That's very kind.
> When is it?" "In ten minutes," she said. So we go and there are
> 200 people there, and they give us a microphone and ask us to
> perform. Onstage we sang a few verses of "The Times They Are
> A-Changin'" as the audience limpidly clapped along. So we
> switched to "Old MacDonald Had a Farm," which they loved.
> Then we ballroom danced with them, or at least, with the boys,
> since students aren't supposed to dance with the opposite sex.
> Campus signs list the fines students are assessed if caught: Littering

5 yuan (about 60 cents), Spitting 10 yuan ($1.25), and Holding
Hands/Showing Affection 50 yuan ($6.25). Most of their parents
are farmers who earn $12 a month.

Peace Corps volunteers were paid 950 yuan monthly (the equivalent of
about $120), but I had little to spend it on. The college provided housing,
and my usual breakfast of a steamer of pork buns cost a green-tinted two-
yuan (twenty-five-cent) note; my lunch of egg-fried rice topped with pickled
radishes cost a single pink yuan more. It cost only four yuan to post a
two-page letter stateside; a third page tipped the scale, adding another pink
yuan. A five-yuan note was shaded brown, tens were blue, and fifties were
actually chartreuse. Everyone paid in cash but also never seemed to have
any change. I hoarded the smallest denominations of money, officially
called *rénmínbì*, or people's currency. (A yuan is its unit, just as a British
pound is to sterling.) In the days of the planned economy, the money
showed tractors, bridges, factories, and farms, but in the nineties portraits
of different ethnicities adorned the paper money: Manchu, Korean, Miao,
Zhuang, Dong, Yao, Uighur, Yi, Tibetan, Hui, Mongolian, and Han. In the
future, coins and the same tight-lipped portrait of Mao would replace all
of them, but then the smiling faces of ordinary people livened up the lower
units of colorful currency.

Not living from paycheck to paycheck for the first time was a novelty,
as was, at times, being paid at all. When I went to the Neijiang branch
of the People's Bank of China to collect the salary the Peace Corps wired
there, the teller looked up from her knitting and said, "We don't have any
money."

I asked if this was the bank.

"Yes. That's why we're out of money."

Already I accepted that in Sichuan her logic was irrefutable.

When I visited a doctor to alleviate the cramping, runny results of a
Mr. Wang–ordered meal of coagulated pig blood (*Always be polite!*) and
hot pepper river snails (*Don't make others lose face!*), the physician instructed
me to stick out my tongue. He leaned close and studied its color and
texture. "Food poisoning," he determined, then handed me a prescription.
In Chinese doctorscribble it said: *Watermelon. Pepsi.* The pharmacy stocked
both.

I did feel better, at least until my shower handle zapped me with a bolt of electricity. I dropped it, but my body hummed like a tuning fork. The plugged-in water heater that teetered over the tap needed to be repaired, but Mr. Wang said the "technician"—a man I often saw sweeping around the ox tethered outside—said there was nothing he could do. I might get shocked from time to time, Mr. Wang said. "But don't worry," he dead-panned. "The authorities have assured me your shower will not physically kill you." This, from a man who believed that Neijiang's few taxi drivers were correct to keep their headlights switched off at night—"To save the battery"—and that forsaking the bathroom would amplify the intoxicating effects of the watery 3.2 percent local beer. "Tonight," he once said, grabbing my arm as I rose to use the hole behind the restaurant, "there will be no discharge of urine."

As the first semester progressed, I learned to say no, to push back, to not always be polite. This was not always wise. My college-assigned Chinese tutor was accustomed to reading from the podium, not sitting beside an inquisitive foreigner. When I interrupted him to ask a question, he looked startled and disappointed, as if I had just dropped a fresh bowl of spicy noodles. Impatiently shortsighted, I ended the lessons.

Kevin continued his studies, while I relied on my students and daily interactions to learn Chinese. He began playing soccer; I ended each day on the basketball court. Although we were the first Americans on campus, and the officials preferred to display us as a pair, we fell into our own routines. The campus confines cosseted us, allowing us to acclimate to China at our own pace. Dumpling stands enveloped the dirt street in puffs of steam clouds at breakfast time, giving the river-misted, nameless strip a timeless air. The dozen hand-painted signboards placed in front of single-story brick hovels advertised knife-shaved noodles, a laundry, a barber, a photographer, three sundries shops, a table of public phones—no sealed glass boxes for private conversations here—and a "small eats" stall whose name translated as No Big Deal. Mr. Qin, the proprietor, made the best wonton I've ever tasted: little wrapped packages of pork and scallions floating in a salty broth.

In the morning a wet market appeared, run by women selling hot peppers, soybeans, slabs of pork, red onions, and green-peeled Sichuan oranges. The produce brightened the lane, whose five hundred yards was often slicked with mud. Also adding color: bed-headed customers browsing in their silk pajamas and wearing furry, oversized slippers decorated to look like panting, googly-eyed puppy dogs. It always made me laugh to be singled out with a point and shouted "*Lǎowài!*" as if I were this street's spectacle. Of course, to a local's eye, I was.

There was no newsstand; the world, as far as we knew, was basically what we saw in front of us. It was a safe place to be naïve. A novice does not have to excel to adapt to a new place, only to try.

The Peace Corps attracts curious people who are comfortable being alone—one reason, perhaps, why it has incubated so many writers. They have taken a chance by coming, and all subsequent career moves, such as working independently, feel far less risky. Volunteers usually establish their own routines; Kevin and I saw each other when we wanted to, such as at dinner, because eating alone in a restaurant as a foreigner brought many stares, and a round of *érshì wèntí* (twenty questions). The tedious game began by my staring back at the inquisitor and confirming—with a mouthful of rice—that, yes, I could use chopsticks.

Peace Corps veterans often experience how the intensity of being in a new place, and speaking a new language with new people, sharpens one's senses, making one alert to every sound and scene. "In *The Doors of Perception*," I wrote home, "Huxley said that the brain is a reducing valve. It collects information, then streamlines it into a neat package of comprehensible input that we can handle. But here I walk and I'm electrified—colors, sounds and smells feel new. I'm hyper-aware, but also exhausted."

That was laying it on a little thick, and partly the result of being fat with time for the first time in my life, free to just observe. As a stranger, I arrived in Neijiang with no money and no status, which brought a sort of freedom. I also had no past or reputation beyond the fact that I was from a country most of my students thought was a rich promised land—even if all but one of them circled "True" for my quiz item: "The American Dream is what Mr. Meyer had while sleeping last night."

I had distance to sort my impressions, noticing and recording what locals took for granted. Because I didn't have a camera, I depicted scenes in copious notes scribbled after class and in long letters home. Writing it all down was a way to make sense of what I was seeing and to try and make a faraway reader glimpse it too.

China was new and all around; at the end of the day my mind would ache from intensely observing, from trying to communicate, from attempting to decipher a page of *pīnyīn* I had rapidly transcribed without tone marks as someone spoke Chinese. *Zhongguo meiyou renquan, womende renkou shi tai da* . . . "What's meaning?" I asked myself, echoing the question my students—constantly and ungrammatically—always wanted answered. I stared at the transcription like an epigrapher, until discerning that the person had said, as many did then, "China does not have human rights. Our population is too big."

Kevin felt the intensity too. Holding a Five Star beer bottle's top against the table's edge, he popped its cap by pounding his fist down hard. "My brain's full," he said, and took a long drink. By night's end, the sides of both our hands smarted from opening beers—an occupational hazard in a place without bottle openers. Locals often pulled the cap off with their molars.

In the few weeks I had to prepare before departure to China, I had asked a Madison campus librarian for books about the country. She led me to a red-spined shelf in the stacks. The titles drew a Malthusian line across the past century as the nation's population grew: *400 Million Customers*; *Land of the 500 Million*; *800,000,000: The Real China*; *The Gang and 900 Million*; *A Quarter of Mankind*; *One Billion*; *Half the World*.

I pulled out a dusty book from 1919. It had an eye-poke of a title: *With the Chinks.*

"How about Pearl Buck?" the librarian suggested.

Reading Buck as an introduction to contemporary China is as useful as reading Charles Dickens to understand modern London. But as the child of missionary parents, Buck had grown up in China and spoke the language fluently. Tucked amidst her novels' anachronisms (such as foot-binding) and biblical suffering (such as locusts) was an admonition to see the place as its own and people as they were—as individuals. Her lectures were more overt.

"If you are willing to lend yourself to China," Buck told a group of GIs shipping out during World War II, "making no comparisons with other countries, you will see a great deal of beauty in the Chinese streets. And after all, what is the use of going abroad if it is only to complain because things are not the same as they are at home?"

History does not record how the young grunts took this or if they wrote down the first sentence Buck told them they should learn in Chinese, which happened to be the first one I ever learned: Wǒ shì měiguó rén, "I am an American." But I copied her advice on a piece of paper and taped it on my mirror in Neijiang like an auspicious fortune cookie slip. *Be willing to lend yourself to China. You will see a great deal of beauty.*

Buck's books were not on sale at the state-run bookstore in town. Its English shelf held textbooks and dictionaries, a smattering of Dickens novels, and all of Shakespeare.

So I was more than surprised one day when the campus librarian, a woman with a quick laugh who practiced her English with me during the afternoon break (a siesta called *xiūxi*), tugged on a rope hanging behind her desk. The ladder that descended led to an attic whose shelves held classic English-language novels bound in plain covers with unbroken spines. I asked if they had been hidden during the Cultural Revolution, when books were burned, and "counterrevolutionary" English studies were forbidden. It wasn't that long ago: the librarian, now in her forties, belonged to the generation that missed a decade of education because most schools were closed. "I would never have imagined," she once told me, "that one day I would be practicing English with an American in Neijiang."

To a foreigner, Chinese politics could feel as present but uncommented on as the weather. To a local, however, policy could sweep into daily life as suddenly as a storm. Most often it wasn't a Beijing official pulling your strings directly, but your employer—your *dānwèi*, "work unit"—that steered your mind and mobility through "study meetings" and an assigned job. Women faced an additional scrutiny: the librarian said that female faculty and staff had to report their menses to the campus health office, to ensure they were not contravening the "one-child" policy then in effect.

When a person revealed a fact such as this, or spoke of the political campaigns she had lived through, it reminded me to consider current events from a local's perspective, including my sudden, puzzling presence. How long would this comparatively open era last?

The librarian said that the new, unread books had arrived in bulk the previous year. The college decided they were "too nice" for general circulation—a euphemism, surely—but I was free to check them out and to share them with my students, shifting onto my shoulders the responsibility of the corrupting wiles of Isak Dinesen's *Out of Africa*. Surprisingly, as my Chinese improved and my students worked hard and we laughed harder, I finally did wake with the rooster and stand on the loam-scented balcony with a cup of steaming jasmine tea and listen to the puttering barges cloaked in the morning mist, and for the first time actually thought, as Dinesen had: *Here I am, where I ought to be.*

CHAPTER 3

EVERY VILLAGE FACES THE SUN

I FEEL DISCOMBOBULATED AND homesick," I wrote home the next week.

I have no one to trust. People ask me about politics and bad-mouth Mao and "old China" (pre–Deng Xiaoping and reforms) and I just smile. As a government employee (unofficially, but still) I feel handcuffed and don't want people to know my opinions . . . Some of my colleagues were told by the "college leaders" not to socialize on weekends with Kevin and me, because we were too "busy." That's not true. My students said I have to teach them what's in the textbooks because they will be tested on it, beyond the exams I give them. We often hear that "Chinese students are so much more diligent in their studies and respectful of their teachers than Americans," but that's bullshit. Some are, but some also take classes because they're a requirement. In class this morning a student named "Jimy" lit his notebook on fire—not in protest, but because he was idly flicking his lighter in boredom and the thin paper went up in flames. He looked even more surprised than I did when it happened, and pounded it out on his desk with his loafer. He can't speak English and yet is required to take the course. I miss teaching little kids. You once told me that it takes a lot of courage to go to China but that it would take more courage to admit it if it wasn't where I wanted to be. Fuck, the power just went out again. P.S. Please send coffee. I am sick of drinking tea.

I never swore in front of my mother, but her swat could not reach me in Neijiang, where the honeymoon of settling in had ended after two months. Under normal circumstances a classroom fire would not have fazed me, but coming to realize that I understood very little about how things actually worked on campus sapped my motivation and made me feel power-less. So this was life in China.

The constant food poisoning didn't help; night soil fertilized the local crops, and I understood why Chinese chefs flash-fry ingredients in a sizzling-hot wok. No flames could kill whatever bacteria colonized my insides. "You're making more fertilizer," observed Kevin. "You're part of the circle of life!" Instead I waddled, clenching and cramped, to the circle of hell that was the campus toilet, a squatter's pit that did in fact empty into buckets to be spooned over the fields—my future dinner.

Being sick did allow me to substitute peanut milk for booze during the rounds of banquet toasts, pausing the pickling of my liver. It also excused me from the campus-wide lecture I was scheduled to deliver. Kevin took over, explaining the separation of church and state. A college teacher raised her hand to ask why Americans didn't demand that living conditions on Indian reservations be improved. Standing on an auditorium stage in front of two hundred people, Kevin cleared his throat and said, "You know, it's just not a pressing issue in everyday America. To the average American, sadly, it just isn't." The crowd murmured. Kevin added that perhaps the questioner regarded Tibet the same way. No, she said, because China liber-ated Tibet from feudalism.

Sitting in the front row, Mr. Wang shot a glance at the college leaders. Another professor stood to ask if it was true that American college students were free to have sex with each other. It was a deft, if surprising, way of derailing the other conversation, and soon the room considered the pros and cons of not fining students for holding hands. In 1995 this counted as controversial talk. Kevin was exhausted by the end of it, expecting a reprimand that never came, at least not transparently. Although, after his space heater broke, the college would not replace it, even as nighttime temperatures fell and we could see our clouded breath inside our apart-ments. Kevin took to sleeping in layers of clothes.

For the next lecture I decided to explain the history of the National Basketball Association. That wouldn't be a "sensitive" subject; one of its games was aired on Chinese television each Saturday, and China had a nascent league and a national team. My questioners' pressing queries included explaining the meaning of "Sonics" and "Knicks," and nicknames such as "the Mailman." The conversation still veered into sensitive territory. Why, a student wanted to know, had Beijing narrowly lost (to Sydney) its bid to host the 2000 Summer Olympics?

"The bribe was too small, apparently." Only Kevin laughed. I said that in the West the vote was seen as punishment for the crackdown at Tiananmen Square six years earlier.

Silence. Mr. Wang stared ahead blankly. Had I made a mistake, blurting out to a campus-wide crowd of strangers a sentiment I already had shared in class among people I knew? My students had been taught that while the army and armed police did open fire in Beijing, they aimed at looters or in self-defense, to restore order to the capital. Because the Party suppresses research of the event, casualty estimates vary widely: According to the government, 10 soldiers and 13 paramilitary police were killed by civilians, whose deaths numbered 218—including 36 students—while 5,000 soldiers and 2,000 civilians were wounded. Unofficial accounts put the death toll as much as five times higher.

I found myself standing alone before a quiet audience who had lowered their heads like ostriches. After what seemed like a very long time, a hand finally went up: one of my favorite students asked if I was happy that Michael Jordan came back from retirement to rejoin the Chicago Bulls. I sprung on the question as if it were a life preserver, animatedly pacing the stage and expounding on Qiáo Dān, as the Chinese called him.

At the post-lecture dinner, Mr. Wang assured me I could say whatever I wanted. Like him, many students regularly listened to the BBC World Service and Voice of America on shortwave radio. As a graduate student in China, Mr. Wang wrote his thesis on British Romantic poetry. Now he recited a Party line, with the usual dispassion: "Deng Xiaoping said, 'We have nothing to fear from the West.' He also said we must 'Seek truth from facts.'"

But which ones? Chinese rulers, dynastic or Communist, believed their legitimacy to rule was perpetuated by a meticulous accounting of their actions; the official version of history exalted them and was thus inviolable. Foreigners' facts and opinions could be dismissed by saying, simply, that the *lǎowài "bù liǎojiě zhōngguó,"* didn't understand China. And of course foreigners could speak more freely than Chinese, because foreigners could leave. I had another nineteen months here, however.

To his credit, Mr. Wang urged me to discuss any subject with the students. Even the demonstrations at Tiananmen Square were not off-limits; they already knew the "correct" version of events.

"And also," he reminded me, "please teach them the Beatles."

As I tried to pinch a bit of fried egg and tomatoes between my chopsticks, I asked when our telephones would be installed; the Peace Corps required each volunteer to have a landline in case of emergency. It would also be nice to receive phone calls instead of booming knocks on our metal doors, informing us of schedule changes or banquet meals that began ten minutes later. Mr. Wang said the phones would arrive *mǎshàng*, immediately, which by now I knew meant the opposite. Also, my shower was still zapping me. When could it be fixed?

"You know," Mr. Wang said, with a comradely pat on my flannel-shirted shoulder, "everyone gets shocked by their showers from time to time."

"Do you?"

Mr. Wang laughed the Chinese laugh that means *It is time to change the subject.* When I asked him what he thought about *liù sì* (June 4, as the violence that took place around Tiananmen is known), he made the sound again.

Even though Beijing was twelve hundred miles from this nameless dead-end dirt road, news from there came to me the long way, via Minnesota. "I've enclosed a couple of articles that ran over here about the Beijing women's conference," my mom wrote. "Did you hear about that?"

Earlier that autumn, Beijing had hosted its first large international forum, the United Nations Fourth World Conference on Women. A banner welcoming the thirty thousand delegates said, in English, "Expect everything will go as you wish." It did not. As China sought to soften its post-Tiananmen image, delegates threatened a boycott after their meetings were moved far outside of town and blanketed by police surveillance. On the evening news, my mom watched a series of reports on female infanticide and poor conditions at orphanages.

"I just can't get excited about you helping people who kill and neglect babies like it's nothing," she wrote.

For the record, the students and faculty of Neijiang Teacher's College were not doing these things, any more than they were personally detaining the labor rights activist Harry Wu, a story that received prominent coverage in the American news. Chinese media, meanwhile, reported that America had the world's highest rate of children living in poverty, homelessness, and gun violence.

College friends wrote to say that by accepting a posting in China I was "legitimizing an undemocratic regime" and "exporting capitalistic tendencies." Little did they suspect that, by then, Madison probably had more Marxists than Beijing did.

It certainly wasn't a coincidence that the Peace Corps, a development agency, happened to establish a toehold in China at the same time the rest of Washington, D.C., was trying to influence its political and economic evolution to favor American values—and business. At the end of training, the American consul general, a former Peace Corps volunteer in Thailand, said, tongue in cheek, that my mission was to "create more customers for Pepsi."

"Should Americans stay home instead?" I wrote my mom. "Cease all foreign aid, or send a faceless check to an opaque autocracy instead of working on the ground, face-to-face with people?"

During Peace Corps training I read for the first time *The Ugly American*. In the annals of misunderstood titles, a special place belongs to William J. Lederer and Eugene Burdick's novel. Today the phrase is shorthand for compatriots who wear tube tops to the Vatican or shout for Big Macs in Berlin. But the impolitic travelers in *The Ugly American* are the so-called educated elite of the diplomatic corps, whose insensitivity to local language and customs prompts observations such as this, from a Filipino minister to an American diplomat:

> The simple fact is, Mr. Ambassador, that average Americans, in their natural state, if you will excuse the phrase, are the best

ambassadors a country can have. They are not suspicious, they are
eager to share their skills, they are generous. But something happens
to most Americans when they go abroad. Many of them are not
average . . . they are second-raters.

Published in 1958, the book is often confused with another Cold War–
era novel set in Southeast Asia, Graham Greene's *The Quiet American*,
which appeared in 1955. Yet *The Ugly American*, which depicted the struggle
against insurgent Communism in the fictional nation of Sarkhan, was the
bigger success, spending seventy-six weeks on the bestseller list and selling
roughly five million copies. Writing in the *New York Times Book Review*,
the paper's veteran Asia correspondent Robert Trumbull called it a "devastating indictment of American policy" and a "source of insight into the
actual, day-by-day byplay of the present titanic political struggle for Asia."
As a novel, it's a clumsy mash-up of vignettes based on real-life characters. The story begins with Ambassador "Lucky" Lou Sears stewing in
his luxurious compound, incensed by an editorial cartoon showing him
leading a Sarkhanese on a leash to a billboard for Coca-Cola.
He fumes, too, over his Soviet counterpart's latest checkmate. "The
American ambassador is a jewel," the Soviet diplomat—who is fluent in
the local language, customs, and religion—cables Moscow. "He keeps his
people tied up with meetings, social events, and greeting and briefing
the scores of senators, congressmen, generals, admirals, under secretaries of
state and defense, and so on, who come pouring through here to 'look for
themselves.'" Sears undermines a Wisconsin dairyman's self-started project
to raise nutrition levels in the Sarkhan countryside, and thwarts a band
of anti-Communist irregulars formed by a militant Massachusetts priest.
The "ugly" American of the title is not one of these bunglers but the
book's hero, a wealthy retired engineer named Homer Atkins, whose
calloused and grease-blackened hands "always reminded him that he was
an ugly man." Homer is the very model of the enlightened ambassador
(in the unofficial sense) the authors thought America should send into the
world. He and his wife become a proto–Peace Corps couple, homesteading
in an earthen-floored hut and collaborating with villagers on inventions,
including a bicycle-powered irrigation pump. Homer's voice sounds

surprisingly contemporary, as if he's channeling contemporary polemics against global development practices. "Whenever you give a man something for nothing," Homer warns, "the first person he comes to dislike is you."

"Our aim is not to embarrass individuals," *The Ugly American's* authors declared in their introduction, "but to stimulate thought—and, we hope, action." One person it inspired was John F. Kennedy, who mailed a copy of the book to each of his Senate colleagues. Its epilogue argues for the creation of "a small force of well-trained, well-chosen, hard-working and dedicated professionals" fluent in the local language—an idea that became the Peace Corps, which Kennedy proposed in 1960.

Perhaps the book's more enduring legacy is its argument that "we spend billions on the wrong aid projects while overlooking the almost costless and far more helpful ones." America annually allocates more funds to its military marching bands than it does to the Peace Corps.

Early in my volunteer assignment, I realized that the Peace Corps was not a panacea. Its three goals—meet a need for trained workers; promote an understanding of Americans; teach Americans about "other peoples"— can seem maddeningly ambiguous. But when it comes to projecting America's values abroad, the Peace Corps' spirit comes closest to what the fictional Homer Atkins advocated, decades before the symbol of a different kind of ugly Americanism, Homer Simpson, told his children: "Kids, you tried your best and you failed miserably. The lesson is, never try."

In my mother's next letter, stories set in Chinese orphanages had faded from the news cycle. Instead, she responded to the snapshots—taken by the campus photographer—I had sent, and the conclusion of an American murder trial:

> This two-week time lag between our letters is really annoying. I loved the photos! It puts everything in perspective. I was picturing the worst, you know. You looked really good in your picture. Your skin looked great and you look really healthy. I could taste the air pollution there, however. The sky looks really heavy. Did you hear about the O. J. [Simpson] verdict? It was like we were all watching

the same thing and seeing two completely different things. The TV talk says everyone realized the thin veil of racial tolerance toward each other is very fragile. We all thought things were going along so well but we have a long way to go . . . On the other side of the coin, Colin Powell is favored to run for president. I guess you really aren't missing much all in all. Our pop culture just keeps going downhill to the trivial. I guess we are lucky that we are so blessed that we don't have to worry about survival. I just worry that we are being lulled into complacency and some evil anti-Christ will take over. No, it won't be Newt Gingrich. He decided not to run for president.

She was being sarcastic; our distance made our political differences amusing instead of contentious. Our airmail's jet lag also reminded me that the ups and downs of acclimatizing were temporary, like turbulence. Writing about the bumps in early November meant I would receive her reply in mid-December. By that time, I hoped, I would laugh, remembering how I had overreacted to slights, perceived or real. In her next letter she asked, "I thought China was going to be this superpower, but they can't even install a phone? Do you like your apartment? Do you like the town? Do you ever miss the U.S. and get really lonely? Are you busy all the time? Are you feeling better? Is teaching there challenging or do you just read the lessons from the book? Do you have any close Chinese friends? Have you mastered the money and language where you feel comfortable? Do you feel cut off from the world and feel like you are missing a lot?"

Yes, to all of the above.

For Thanksgiving dinner, Kevin and I rode a bus along the newly opened expressway that halved the journey to Chengdu to two hours. Sichuan province's first Kentucky Fried Chicken opened in a building topped by a billboard whose propaganda commanded CONSOLIDATE HEALTH CONSCIOUSNESS. Standing guard at the door was a mannequin of Colonel Sanders, who looked different: puffier, with narrow eyes, thick-framed glasses, and a high forehead. "He looks like a Chinese official," Kevin said. Perhaps the sculptor had previously churned out busts of Chairman Mao.

Inside, Chinese diners ate their french fries with toothpicks, slowly spearing each one. Chinese cuisine is not finger food. "This place won't last long," I said, stuffing ketchup packets into my pockets to bring back to Neijiang. After nearly half a year away, it was the only Western food I craved. I never found ketchup on sale in stores, even though it is said to have been invented in China. (In its southern dialects, a brined tomato sauce is pronounced with variations on *kechap*.) But after I brought the condiment back to Neijiang, I realized I had nothing to put it on except flash-fried cauliflower. The chef at the one-wok, three-table restaurant where I ate dinner every day improvised some french fries out of the stubby local tubers. I appreciated his effort but preferred the way he usually made potatoes, sliced thin and fried in sesame oil with chilies.

To generate a writing topic, in class I asked the students to make a list of things they liked about campus life. Their classmates, they responded, and school dances. They did not like the stones they bit into when eating the canteen's rice, and their lack of *guānxi*, the "connections" one needed to win academic honors or a scholarship.

I did the lesson alongside them. I knew what I didn't like about being here. But what was I enjoying?

The placid ox tethered in my building's courtyard that didn't moo *lǎowài*.

Practicing Chinese with my students.

The secret attic library.

The young couple making out against a wall whom I startled when walking home from dinner after curfew. Risking fines or worse, they were being human.

Living on the rural side of the river.

In an attempt to placate my complaints about my cold-water shower, or lack of a phone, or broken heaters—for now mine had also failed, and I began warming my fingers with a hair dryer as I corrected students' papers—Mr. Wang and two administrators took me fishing. On a cold, misty Saturday we stood next to a shallow cement pool tucked amidst a peanut field and waited for fat carp to decide to take a bite of a languid worm suspended in the murk. As we stared at our bamboo poles, I asked Mr. Wang what the slogan daubed on the redbrick farmhouse said. He squinted at the fading red paint. "Every village faces the sun."

I thought that was beautiful. Was it a classic saying? Does every Chinese village face the sun so it can absorb more sunlight?

"It's from the Cultural Revolution," Mr. Wang replied. "The 'sun' refers to Chairman Mao."

Sometimes I preferred not knowing the meaning of things, and the way life really worked. The carp was not biting, and so a farmer hurried things along by wading into the water and unsportingly scooping it into a net. "Lunch," announced Mr. Wang.

At the end of my first semester at Neijiang, I found in the attic library *Main Street*. As a Minnesota teenager, I had felt no connection to its author, a fellow Gopher from a small town a short drive from my own. I needed seven thousand miles of distance and a new perspective to appreciate Sinclair Lewis's caustic book, published in 1920. I dog-eared page after page to share with the Writing students, such as: "Doubtless all small towns, in all countries, in all ages, have a tendency to be not only dull but mean, bitter, infested with curiosity. In France or Tibet quite as much as in Wyoming or Indiana these timidities are inherent in isolation." My students said that Gopher Prairie sounded like their hamlet hometowns. They also brightened at Lewis's criticism of American cultural imperialism: "Sure of itself, it bullies other civilizations, as a traveling salesman in a brown derby conquers the wisdom of China and tacks advertisements of cigarettes over arches for centuries dedicated to the sayings of Confucius."

Indeed, as the bus pulled into Chengdu on my Thanksgiving trip to KFC, it passed under a new archway billboard that showed a lassoing cowboy and declared: MARLBORO COUNTRY.

I read, too, the non-*Gatsby* novels of F. Scott Fitzgerald. The Minnesota native wrote that "the test of a first-rate intelligence is the ability to hold two opposed ideas in the mind at the same time, and still retain the ability to function." My morning walk through our dirt road's wet market had me muttering: *China is progressive, China is backward, China is beautiful, China is brutal.* Was Neijiang making me a genius? Or should I have been concerned that Fitzgerald made this observation in his self-autopsy of nervous exhaustion, an essay he titled "The Crack-Up"?

In the library attic I also found, under a blanket of dust, a calculus text-book, whose brittle spine cracked upon opening. I had never taken calculus at school, and so began filling that mental gap slowly and ponderously each morning over steaming tea as the barges puttered unseen on the misted river and the campus public address system broadcast news of a new campus gymnasium, a new city water treatment plant, the new provincial expressway. "Calculus is the mathematical study of change," the textbook's introduction said. To my mother, I wrote, "Sichuan is the Chinese study of change." The calculus book was much easier to comprehend.

That letter took three weeks to cross over; the expectant walk to the small gatehouse where the mail was delivered became a daily ritual. A grumpy woman commanded the post, and she seemed to relish yelling "*Méiyŏu!*" when spotting my approach. Uniquely, perhaps, she had excellent eyesight; at a time when eyeglasses were seen as a demerit for Party membership or an unaffordable luxury, all the long stares a foreigner attracted merely could have been an attempt to focus. If there was mail, she sullenly pushed the envelope or aerogramme at me as if it were infected. Letters from home were a sensory thrill: receiving the envelope with two hands, carrying it with anticipation to a flat boulder overlooking the river, studying the stamps and postmark, tearing it open, unfolding the paper, tracing the pen strokes, hearing the voice, returning to it later.

I often read from my mother's letters to students to evince that, despite what they believed, American parents *did* love their children, even if they wanted them out of the house at age eighteen. The students remained dubious. Then they asked if they could have the letters' stamps.

My students had been tracked into their major due to the results of an entrance exam, and after graduation most did not see any other choice but to accept a government-assigned position at a village elementary school. We heard whispers of a student who had dropped out and taken off for coastal Shenzhen—located across the border from British-controlled Hong Kong—and was making a fortune working in a factory, assembling shoes or computers or skateboards or something. The product changed with each retelling, just as his salary rose. At minimum, we heard the guy made one thousand yuan a month, four times more than what they would make as teachers. His leap was daring, and his family had to pay our college to release him from a teaching post, since he had tested into the school and attended tuition-free. In class, only Ringo said his peer had been smart to take the risk. The other students admitted that while they dreamed of getting away, of seeing the larger world, of striking it rich, they would do as they were told and stick close to home, as teachers. There was no Chinese equivalent to the Peace Corps; once they started working, they would likely stay put their entire life.

We caught glimpses of the Other China via the Peace Corps–provided subscription to the large-circulation *Newsweek* magazine and an anonymous benefactor's gift subscription to the *Christian Science Monitor* newspaper. The two publications' China coverage seesawed between luridness and sobriety. Seeing China through *Newsweek*'s periscope made me aware of how a handful of writers shape our perception of foreign countries, and especially the developing world.

One of its editions showed a sultry, lipsticked mouth. The cover story began:

"SEX—Joining the Party"
Neither romantic love nor carnal lust had any place in Mao's utopian vision. Now the masses are rediscovering both—with revolutionary zeal.

"There's not a quilted suit in sight at NASA," the caption read, "a Beijing disco where the only 'little red books' are for addresses."

My students didn't get the wordplay, but this was the High Pun era, when headlines riffed on the Great Wall, slow boats, emperors, and dragons. Even Peace Corps volunteers did it: our newsletter—a chronicle of ups and downs—was named the *Sweet and Sour Times*.

Verbal elbows to the ribs aside, my students loved paging through *Newsweek*—after Mr. Wang flipped through it first, that is. He didn't censor any pages—not even a report that U.S.-China relations had reached their lowest point since 1989, after Tiananmen Square. Instead he suggested I "teach the ads." They were a window into what the United States was really like, he guessed—and proof that my country had propaganda and slogans too. He pointed at a full-page shot of a laughing woman—a "baby" who had "come a long way." Women drank and smoked, sports cars sailed along an empty freeway, Cindy Crawford—her mole in almost the same place as Chairman Mao's—modeled a wristwatch. A cartoon pirate pitched rum.

Chinese wanted this lifestyle, Mr. Wang said. There was no going back to the Marxist past. But still Uncle Karl's portrait hung on Mr. Wang's office wall. His bearded mug impassively watched us as we talked. Next to him were posters of Lenin, Stalin, and Mao. The lineup of stoic faces reminded me of old baseball cards: here was the real Murderer's Row. What statistics were listed on the posters' backs?

Mr. Wang had not swapped Mao for Mammon, however. He fretted about saving for his young daughter's college education, a decade away; Mr. Wang correctly guessed that soon free tuition would cease, just as a private housing and insurance market would take off. Yet his personal ambition was not to accrue a pile of money, or even a new apartment, but to go abroad, only not as a tourist. His dream, Mr. Wang admitted, was to attend Cambridge University to study modern British poetry.

My student Welles, who parted his frizzy black hair in the middle and wore a waistcoat and necktie to class, read aloud a *Newsweek* story to practice his pronunciation and test his peers' listening comprehension. He set the magazine carefully upon the podium; its staples always fell out after students passed it around throughout the week. I plugged in the boom box to complete the lesson, which required students to fill in the missing words of the lyrics I had chalked on the board. For example, I'd write, "With the lights out, it's less _____ / Here we are now, _____ us / I feel _____ and contagious," and the kids would sit stunned, writing nothing, because Nirvana's "Smells Like Teen Spirit" sounded like skinning rabbits when your favorite song was the Carpenters' "Yesterday Once More."

I assumed Mr. Wang's directive to "teach the Beatles" derived from his interest in British poetry, but it turned out he was giving me sound pedagogical advice. The Fab Four sang clearly, to a hummable melody, for about two minutes per song. One of the unexpected pleasures of being abroad is experiencing one's own culture anew. As my students smiled and bobbed their heads to tracks off the album *Please Please Me*, I suddenly realized why, when I was a child, my mother enjoyed watching me sing along to "Love Me Do," spinning on the vinyl LP she owned at that age.

On this day, I played a later-era Beatles song twice, and the class polled each other on the correct transcription. Welles recorded the results on the blackboard, chalking: "We all live in a yellow *summer rain*."

"Yellow Summer Rain" was a hit. A girl named Lucy said, "How poetic it is! I like to imagine I am living in the yellow summer rain."

The class didn't believe the actual lyrics were otherwise. A yellow *subma-rine*? Nobody lived on submarines. And who'd ever seen a yellow one?

"It's a Ringo song," I apologized. The class jeered the cowlick-haired young man who called himself that, smiling in the front row.

Sitting on my apartment floor, hunched over the manual typewriter the college provided, I started writing slices-of-life articles for my former employer, the *Wisconsin State Journal*, describing everyday interactions, such as that class. This was forbidden, but not by the Chinese. The Peace Corps did not allow volunteers to publish; the gag order was meant to protect the agency from charges from host countries that it was really a cover for investigative reporting or intelligence gathering. I realized I was serving two masters, navigating two sets of rules, and that the way to maintain a modicum of independence was to do as the Chinese lived. Asking for forgiveness after the fact, my students often said, was easier than asking for permission beforehand.

I doubted dispatches from the muddy banks of the Tuo River would cause an international incident. Instead, they brought rebuke. In letters to the editor, Madison-area readers—reacting to the same innocuous story of, say, my fishing outing—said I was either too critical of the developing country or that I was too compassionate. Only one reader sent praise. She was also the only respondent who had once lived in China: "I was in the first batch of Americans who went to teach in the PRC in 1979. I am delighted that foreign teachers are now found in places other than Beijing and Shanghai, and that you are getting a chance to live in what I think is the representative setting for understanding contemporary China."

Still, writing about China seemed to make one either a polemicist or a patsy. I looked for examples of a pragmatic, middle alternative.

Peace Corps volunteers passed around two dog-eared paperbacks. One, called *Coming Home Crazy*, was a series of personal essays by Bill Holm, a Minnesota English professor who had taught in China for a year. He made observations familiar to anyone who had spent time here, such as "This is what culture shock really means, either making your own peace, or leaving. Nothing is ever the same after you have gone 'crazy.'"

The second book was *China Wakes*, written by Nicholas Kristof and

Sheryl WuDunn, a husband-and-wife team of *New York Times* correspondents who had been based in Beijing. The authors' stated aim was "not really to portray daily life, for a *typical* slice of a *typical* peasant's life would be an uneventful morning wading barefoot in the muck of the rice paddy." That presumed a lot: more than half of the nation farmed, and surely some of these 600 million individuals had interior lives—families they loved, and things they dreamed and feared. They also raised myriad crops other than rice. But such were the pitfalls of making sweeping statements to "explain" China; to their credit, the authors of *China Wakes* warned readers that they reported the most striking stories, the ones assuredly not representative of quotidian life, and that "China is such a vast and confusing subject that it is difficult to be sure of either the facts or the conclusions."

In Writing, my students tried to emulate *Newsweek* articles' straw man template, which stated a fact and then turned on it with *but* or *yet*, as in: "President Jiang Zemin at last finds himself standing clear of the paramount leader's shadow. *But* the real power struggle has just begun . . ." or "Hundreds of millions of Chinese are now able to change jobs, get divorced, take vacations, complain vociferously on talk radio and vote out their village leaders. *Yet* about 3,000 are in prison for their political views" (emphasis added).

This was a standard journalistic hook, I told the class. *Your neighbor's kitten is cute. But what you don't know about that cat might be killing you.* In China, a "land of contradictions," it was also entirely logical. I couldn't make a statement like "The Chinese countryside is tranquil" without racing to append "but also harsh."

This compulsion was diagnosed decades before by a writer named Lin Yutang. I found an English paperback copy of *My Country and My People* moldering on a shelf at Neijiang's state-run bookstore, the only shop in town where I didn't feel self-conscious while browsing, because the Chinese customers stood with their noses in novels or sprawled in the aisles, poring over textbooks. In a city without a public library, the locals effectively turned the store into one.

My Country and My People was a purple-covered brick of a book tucked between slim volumes of Kafka and O. Henry. I had never heard of it, or its writer, but took it home after reading the first page.

"China is too big a country, and her national life has too many facets, for her not to be open to the most diverse and contradictory interpretations," Lin wrote. He lamented the trickle of news and firsthand accounts of everyday life, a dearth that made foreigners "either [China's] implacable critics, allowing nothing good for her, or else her ardent, romantic admirers."

Born in 1895, during the last days of China's last imperial dynasty, Lin Yutang earned a doctorate in linguistics in Leipzig, then returned to teach at Peking University, where he edited a satirical literary journal and coined the Chinese word for "humor": *yōumò*. He looked like a man quick to laugh: uniquely for portraits of Chinese intellectuals, his round face, topped by combed-back, oil-black hair, is often smiling, and his eyes flash behind round spectacles. Later, Lin wrote a Chinese-English dictionary of modern usage and invented the first Chinese typewriter. Published in 1936, Lin penned *My Country and My People* at the urging of his friend Pearl Buck. Two years later she would become the first American woman awarded the Nobel Prize in Literature, for her books set in China, including *The Good Earth.*

"Who will, then, be China's interpreters?" Lin wrote. "It is difficult to deny the Old China Hand the right to write books and articles about China, simply because he cannot read the Chinese newspapers. Nevertheless, such books and articles must remain on the level of the gossip along the world's longest bar." Often, Lin said, they spun the same tales once told by Western sailors who had landed in China, "minus the sailors' obscenity of language, but with essentially the same sailors' obscenity of mind."

Meanwhile, my students read aloud a *Newsweek* item that asked, "What Do Women Want? Sexy Underwear," and went on to note: "History does not record whether Confucius ever considered the WonderBra." My classroom echoed with questions such as "Thong panties, what's meaning?" and "Lingerie, how to spell?"

Understanding a foreign country, Lin said, "especially one so different from one's own as China's, is usually not for the mortal man. There must be a certain detachment, not from the country under examination, for that is always so, but from oneself and one's subconscious notions, and from the deeply imbedded notions of one's childhood and the equally tyrannous ideas of one's adult days."

I am a camera, I thought, recalling the beginning of my favorite of the attic library books, Christopher Isherwood's *Berlin Stories*. I should capture all that I saw, and print it later, after its meaning had become clear. Yet, in China, indelible impressions often formed viscerally, far from an intellectual remove.

As my first semester in Sichuan came to an end, I walked past the tethered ox and up the hill to the teaching building, only to find a notice on the classroom door saying class was canceled: students were to report to the soccer field. From the concrete bleachers we watched two flatbed trucks loop the running track. Standing in the back of each, with hands pinned by officers, were men whose age and features were indiscernible from a distance. All we could see clearly were shaved heads and the boards hanging from their necks, displaying their names crossed out by a black-brushed X.

"They murdered someone," my student named Welles explained. That was all he had been told, aside from the fact that the men would be executed with a shot to the back of the neck, and their family would be billed for the bullet. I was relieved that the trucks exited the track with the men still alive. "They're going to visit another school," guessed Welles. No one had cheered, or applauded, or hurled insults. It was the quietest school assembly I had ever attended.

In our next class I asked the students what we had seen. How did they feel sitting there? Was this an example of "scared straight" education? Did it happen often? Did the students support capital punishment? Would knowing the victim's name and the circumstances of his or her death change their opinion? My questions kept coming, faster and with annoyance, as the students pursed their lips tighter and bowed their heads lower. Within minutes, I stood facing not twenty-four faces but scalps.

"America has the death penalty too," I tried. "You often tell me how my country's justice system is unequal, and I answer all of your questions. We've been together five months now; I thought we could discuss this."

The room's silence pulsed in my ears. Were they embarrassed by the assembly, or that I had seen it? Had the college administrators told Welles, the class cadre, to inform the students the event was not open for discussion with the foreigner? I stood alone in front of the room, fuming. Nearly three hours of class remained, but I snapped "You're dismissed" and stormed out.

In America, my students would have cheered. But two hours after I passed the tethered ox and climbed the stairs through the shoe-printed stairwell (why were people always kicking the walls?), a knock resounded off my apartment's thin steel door. I opened it to air; looking down, a stack of papers waited on the broom-bristle welcome mat. Each of the twenty-four students from whom I had bolted had written what amounted to a "self-criticism," the Chinese act of penance. My anger subsided into regret; I had browbeaten them like an impudent official.

But then I sat on my orange pleather sofa with the papers and slowly filled with teacherly pride, seeing how their English had improved over our first semester:

"It's true, in the past I very hate Americans. Americans gave me a bad impression, but Mr. Meyer changed it. Meyer is tall and thin, he has brown hair and deep eyes, long long neck. His neck looks like a deer's neck. (Mr. Meyer don't be angry, it's my true thought!) But you know, Chinese are shy, traditional. They don't want to speak their minds in public, they'll be criticized. So at most time, we keep quiet. Please don't be angry. We like you very much. We have improved forward." Sail.

"Don't worry! You have helped us a lot. Your class is wonderful. These days, we might be stubborn as ever. A rolling stone breaks oak! We have accepted you completely. Don't lose your heart. Teaching here is very different. In our country, we always obey the customs. That is, the teacher teaches us something, and we all agree with what he teaches us. I think it is a stupid way. Your method is different from ours." Kane.

"China is not the best in the world, but we have enough food to eat now, so we want to know more about the world and the peoples in other countries. We still do our best to make a better life and we spend most times on it. In free times, we talk about anything, including the politics. When we face to you or stay with you, we think you come from other country, so it's a good chance to know about the world. We are not politic machines. We are people. We have feelings and loves, and we spend most times on them. Do you think it is strange? You are my teacher but I like to call you: my friend." Rambo.

"I must say I didn't like Americans before you came. In my idea, the American government always stretches its power as possible as it can. In some way it's bad. Why it always interferes in other nations' internal affairs? So I have some prejudice on American government and also on American people. Ideas are changing little by little after your coming. In fact, American people are very kind, helpful, just like our teacher, you, Mr. Meyer. I'm not praising you. I just speak out loud my opinion. What's more, there are a lot of evidence to show that. No matter how tired you are, you always express your idea to us, give us new information about America, hold a lot of lectures for us. Sometimes, I am afraid you will break down from your hard work someday. Can you sustain? I'd like you to have a rest. The vacation is coming, wish you have a good time." Wiseman.

"What you need to do have been done. That's only what you think when you feel tired and miss your hometown, your relatives very much. You should be proud. I remember in the first lesson, you asked us our name and if we had a brother or sister and our hobbies and our favorite writer, and if we had 1000 yuan what would we buy and the questions made us interested! It was very easy to shorten our distance. We trusted you. PS: You should speak faster than before." Ringo.

His postscript made me laugh. Tacking on some advice to an apology was very Chinese. Or was that too sweeping of a statement? It was very Neijiang; that was the only China I knew.

CHAPTER 4

SINKING IN

S CHOOL PAUSED FOR three weeks so students could head home to
celebrate Spring Festival—*chūnjié*, as the three-week New Year holiday
is called. I would be twenty-four in this, the year of my zodiac animal, the
rat. The lunar calendar turned to a different animal in a twelve-year cycle;
when your year came around, tradition held that you incurred the wrath
of Tai Sui, the god of age. The next twelve months were said to hold
nothing but bad luck. Wear red to ward it off, my students advised. Red
clothes, red socks, red underwear. I didn't have anything red, and nothing
sold in Neijiang's shops was big enough to fit me. A student tied a red
string around my wrist instead. "Don't take this off until next year," she
warned me.

Kevin and I were free to leave campus. His parents had sent him a
Lonely Planet guidebook, whose cover depicted an old man smoking
a pipe. On arrival in China, I would have described the man as "wizened"
or even "chill," but now I noticed his weathered face, callused hands, and
threadbare, sun-bleached shirt. He could have been the hard-farming father
of one of our students.

Kevin agreed, then flipped to an entry that made me fill a backpack:

> Dali is a perfect place to tune out for a while and forget about
> trains, planes and bone-jarring buses. The stunning mountain
> backdrop, Erhai Lake, the old city, cappuccini, pizzas, and the
> herbal alternative (you can pick it yourself) to cheap Chinese beer

make it one of the few places in China where you can well and truly forget about China.

We boarded the twenty-four-hour train south to Kunming city, from where we would continue on to Dali, tucked in southwestern Yunnan province, which borders Burma. Yunnan means "south of the clouds." As if on cue, the gray overcast sky lifted as the train chugged away from Sichuan. I realized I had not seen its cloudless blue in months. My spirit lifted, until I realized the red string had fallen from my wrist.

The train attendant paced the hard-seat carriage before spotting me. She handed me a red armband and said to follow her. In the dining car, talking too quickly for me to fully understand, she said that I and the Chinese passengers from other carriages had been deputized as monitors. Our job was to report rowdy behavior, gambling, and theft. We slid the armbands past our elbows and wordlessly returned to our posts.

My shift passed without incident, or at least any that I was aware of, since I spent most of the night underneath the seat, trying to sleep on pages of the *People's Daily* that other passengers shared while assuming the same position. They snored loudly while I flicked cockroaches out of my hair. When we pulled into the Technicolor dawn of Kunming, the attendant collected my armband. "You know I'm a foreigner, right?" I asked her.

"Of course I do!" she said with a laugh. "No one else in this carriage wanted to do this job, so I chose you. You didn't say no."

Kunming looked so different than Neijiang: wide streets lined with camellia bushes and palm-shaded parks. Unlike my town's nickname, "the Sweet City," Kunming lived up to its sobriquet: "Spring City." It also held what had to be southwest China's only coffee shop, located in a white-tiled stall that reminded me of a public toilet. The province grew coffee beans, a remnant of French plantations here and farther south, in neighboring Vietnam. The shop sold fresh-baked baguettes and served the coffee in white porcelain mugs to a clientele whose average age appeared to be eighty. They drank it Turkish-style; the grounds peppered my teeth, while the strong brew made me ask, with some urgency, where the actual public toilet was located. One of the customers showed me the way. He was a pastor, he said in English. His parents had been converted to Catholicism by French missionaries before the war. The coffee shop had been around for decades; his parents used to bring him. He was worried it would not last as its customers passed away. "Chinese people prefer tea, you know. Coffee tastes bitter, like herbal medicine. Which, in a sense, it is." He continued talking even as we squatted beside one another; in China, going to the bathroom was as communal an activity as taking the bus.

The twelve-hour bus ride to Dali paid off: the little town looked just like the guidebook had promised, a maze of cobblestone alleys and white-washed stone houses with gates topped by flying eaves. So not all Chinese architecture resembled the Stalinist sameness of Neijiang's boxy cement buildings. And China's landscape held more variety than a muddy river winding through muddier fields. Dali sat between a large blue lake and an eleven-thousand-foot-high line of pine-shrouded mountains. Also surprising: people did not stop what they were doing to stare at a foreigner. In Dali, the majority of the population are not Han Chinese but ethnically Bai. China's minority groups are exoticized by Han, who extol their folk songs and colorful native dress instead of their intellect and hard work. Later, in Beijing, I thought that the incorrect English road sign for the human zoo called the Ethnic Minorities Exhibition Center correctly directed visitors to "Racist Park."

In Neijiang, I was an aberration; in Dali, I was just another backpacker. Uniquely, I did not have to protest "Big nose, big price!" as I often did in Neijiang, arguing with a vendor or ticket seller who charged me the "foreigner tax." In Dali my interactions with people lasted only as long as they needed to, instead of across a semester, when my missteps steeped like tea leaves.

"I am not looking forward to returning to campus," I wrote home. "I feel so relaxed and happy and going back to work is going to be depressing. It's psychologically wearing, always being 'onstage' representing America while trying not to get my students or colleagues in trouble. Four volunteers in my group, working at other schools, are quitting."

But still Kevin and I would board the bus north, which would carry us back to campus via the mountain town of Lijiang, 120 miles away. The night before that trip, the ground shook in Dali; a 6.6-magnitude earthquake flattened most of Lijiang—an estimated 358,000 buildings, many of them single-story wooden homes built by the Naxi people in their vernacular architecture. Three hundred and twenty-two people died.

After that, I dared not complain about the thirty-six-hour trip to Neijiang, even after a thief picked my pocket while I transferred in Chengdu. A helpful policeman said he would round up the usual suspects; the cash would not be recovered, but the wallet probably could be retrieved. I agreed: the $15 folded inside it was nothing compared to my ID and family photos. A few hours later the cop handed back the wallet, emptied of cash but with its other contents intact. He asked if I wanted to file a report, but I declined. If I had learned anything from dealing with Chinese police, it was not to stick around until I was satisfied that justice had been achieved.

Before he headed back, Kevin lent me money for a later bus to Neijiang. The town welcomed me home with a gauntlet of "Helloooooo!" and a cabdriver who insisted I pay him double the standard price for a ride across the river to campus. Arguments such as this usually made me storm off and petulantly walk, a Pyrrhic victory, with a prize of sore feet. But I was exhausted and stretched thin; breaking the Peace Corps rule against riding motorcycles, I hopped on the back of a Honda that would take me for half the fare. The driver sped under the canopy of bamboo stalks, getting me home just in time to feel an aftershock that shook our campus's buildings. The college ordered students and faculty to evacuate their dorms and apartments and bunk down for the night en masse atop blankets that quilted the basketball courts.

I decided to take my chances in bed. The next morning, as I pottered around the apartment, swatting spiders and gingerly approaching the electrified showerhead, I found, there on the green indoor-outdoor carpeting that covered my living room floor, the red string I was supposed to be wearing to ward off the god of age's wrath. I tied it on again.

Later that week, in the lean-to named No Big Deal, I plucked two worn chopsticks from the tabletop basket and scraped them together rapidly, as if trying to spark a fire. The ritual had become reflexive; the Chinese said it killed germs. With the utensils I pinched a tangle of cold noodles and raised it to my mouth, when two students suddenly exchanged punches outside on the dirt street. One darted into the stall, grabbed a cleaver off the round slice of tree trunk that made a chopping block, and raised the weapon, screaming, before running toward the other man. The cook, Mr. Qin, pounced on him from behind, wrenched the cleaver away, told the boys to knock it off, walked back inside the lean-to, rinsed the knife under the cold-water tap, and said, "I don't like it when people take my things." He resumed chopping celery. The name No Big Deal took on a new meaning.

By March, I was back on solid ground. "Class rolls on," I wrote home. "I have gotten more involved in the social side of campus, practicing Chinese over chess, Ping-Pong, basketball, and mah-jongg." The Peace Corps said the administration could not account for the funds it was paid to improve and repair our apartments. Still without a phone, I continued to mail updates. "I realized that in America my students were afraid of their future, and its limited opportunities," I wrote to my mom. "Chinese are not nostalgic: my students don't talk about how great things used be; they only think about the future. It's exciting being around that energy."

As I mailed this letter, my mom sent one that ended, "You have been gone for nearly a year. It seems a lot longer. Sometimes it feels like you don't even exist anymore. You are accomplishing great things. You always adapt so easily."

I laughed out loud at that. The last two lines were a loving thought, but it felt like I had accomplished very little, and at a plodding pace. Babies preternaturally know to learn to crawl before learning to walk, but I had landed in China burning with the same missionary zeal with which I taught American teenagers in failing schools, a workday that, with grading and planning, could stretch to fourteen hours. In Neijiang, I taught ten hours weekly. I complained about this to Mr. Wang, demanding more work, wondering—internally—what had happened to the toughest job I'd ever love, as the Peace Corps slogan promised. Pre-departure, I had a vague notion that I would be delivering babies in the moonglow.

Luckily for U.S.-China friendship (and babies), I was instead handed a piece of chalk. And what seemed to me like "just another day on Planet Neijiang" looked, to a faraway reader, like hard work after all.

"I find some of your situations to be so bizarre that I am not able to conjure advice," my father wrote at the end of my first year in Neijiang. He paraphrased my recent letters back to me: "A student set his notebook on fire while a man was being paraded through town on his way to being executed while the earth violently shook (not to mention my stomach from the odd meat I ate last night), which was hard to differentiate from the noise of the crowd yelling 'Foreigner' at me when I tried to walk past the meat cleaver fight in the street to find the ox blocking the entrance to my apartment."

Once my energy dimmed—once I slowed down and stopped pushing my classes to shift their shape to one that I recognized—my life became easier, and more rewarding. "Don't throw eggs at a rock," as my students said, quoting a saying; you won't break the stone, only waste eggs. "And eggs taste good," they added, just in case I missed the moral.

Which isn't to say I surrendered. I just picked my battles. I could not make Mr. Wang assign me more work; he explained that while Kevin and I had arrived, more students did not; our classes took teaching hours away from the existing faculty who had previously taught English. This made me feel terrible; it was a sudden realization how my presence altered local lives. Teachers had relationships with their students before I came; work contributes to a feeling of self-worth and identity; you wake up and know your purpose that day and what role you play on the stage of a community.

"Actually," Mr. Wang admitted, "the teachers are happy you are here. Now they have time to earn extra money as English tutors for high school students studying for the college entrance exam."

I could, however, get Mr. Wang to agree that while locking Kevin and me inside our building at night may well "protect" us, it was also annoying to have to roust a watchman to let us in after midnight, in addition to trapping us inside if there was a fire. He insisted the lock had to stay, but gave us each our own key.

As my second semester ended, we worked through our list of complaints. No more "performances in our honor," please: it was us who always ended up performing, "for our friendship." Cut out the banquets and drinking sprees before a priest needs to be summoned to sanctify our condition. We would leave campus on weekends without first obtaining approval. We were tired of being told to wear the school pin on our shirts. Stop giving us new pins, Mr. Wang. If we caught students cheating on exams or plagia-rizing, we would assign them a failing grade; yes, we know we don't under-stand China and that colleges here often don't punish this behavior, but in our classroom students should follow our rules. We would find and hire our own language tutors, instead of having them vetted and assigned by the college. In fact, we were going away for the summer to enroll in university Chinese courses. Finally, fix my shower already. It's not funny anymore.

Reflexively lowering his eyelids as he smiled, Mr. Wang nodded and wrote all of this down. "I hope," he told me, "you will never be the ambas-sador to China. We would be at war in minutes. You're too honest." Still, he met every request. And we, in turn, cheerfully greeted the inspection team who arrived annually from some faraway Party office to pace thought-fully across the campus, examining the swept sidewalks, scrubbed chalk-boards, and dusted potted plant leaves. It was during these pantomimes that I felt sudden empathy for the drudgery of Mr. Wang's bureaucratic routine.

In my final lecture of the school year, about America's perspective on Taiwan, the first question from the audience did not assert that China considered it a renegade province, or that America sending an aircraft carrier to the Taiwan Strait that spring during the island's first presidential election was a belligerent act that could have led to war. By now I knew to begin a talk by acknowledging the Chinese position on a topic. This old rhetorical device disarmed critics by first making their argument for them. A foreigner who can mutter even a single word of Chinese will be fulsomely praised for how well he speaks the language, but, to convince a Chinese audience that I was worth listening to, I realized it helped to say something familiar, something they believed to be true. I could feel the audience relax; I was now on the "Understands China" side of the ledger, and could hold their attention as I presented an opposing view.

Instead of asking about Taiwan, however, one student wondered what compensation American universities gave their students for losing a week of classes in order to scrub the classrooms, bathrooms, and canteens so the school could pass inspection. Before I could answer, he added: "Because this year," he said, "the college only gave us a new metal rice bowl. We were disappointed." The audience murmured in agreement.

At dinner afterward, Mr. Wang suggested we take a break from campus-wide lectures.

After my first year of classes ended, I took the overnight train four hundred miles north to the central city of Xi'an to study intensive Chinese at a university program whose tuition the Peace Corps covered. Aside from a British woman named Bea who was wrapping up her gap year before starting at Oxford, my classmates were Korean and Japanese business students, building the foundation for a career. My goal was lower: learn to read rudimentary characters so I could be self-sufficient enough to decipher menus, train schedules, and road signs.

It felt like starting the language over: Imagine being able to comprehend this sentence upon hearing it but making no sense of the black marks that pattern this page. I felt a kinship with my students, whose English reading comprehension far exceeded their speaking ability. In the Xi'an classroom, I was the one haltingly sounding out the sentence a teacher chalked on the board. The Chinese characters said: 我 I . . . 是 am . . . 一个 a . . . 外国人 foreigner.

It was a hot and lazy and pleasant summer spent on a near-empty campus south of the city center, fueled by dà pán jī ("big plate chicken"), a dish of braised meat and stewed tomatoes served over hand-pulled wheat noodles. It tasted more Central Asian than Chinese, a reminder of Xi'an's ancient past as the start of the Silk Road, the trade route connecting China to the West.

Neijiang's river bluffs and dirt roads made walking the usual transport, but Xi'an was paved and pancake-flat, and for the first time in China I had a bicycle, and the urge to explore a city. Here, for a change, I could sense the illustrious past—a bit of that five thousand years of history—my students kept invoking in class. When Xi'an (Western Peace) was called Chang'an (Perpetual Peace), it had been capital of ten imperial dynasties, including China's first—the Qin (221–206 B.C.)—and one of its greatest, the Tang (A.D. 618–907), whose city of two million was the world's most populous, rivaling Rome in influence and development.

With Bea, I walked Xi'an's old perimeter wall, slurped noodles in the

intimate lanes around its historic, tree-shaded mosque, and visited the
fabled army of terra-cotta warriors (*bīng mǎ yǒng*, "soldier horse funerary
statues"). The eight thousand figures were buried to guard the tomb of
China's first emperor. They stood unperturbed under the arid loess soil for
over two millennia, until 1974, when farmers discovered them while digging
a well.

In 95-degree heat, I elbowed my way through tour groups—herded
behind the yellow flag held aloft by their bullhorn-bleating guide—and
stood at the rail overlooking an excavated pit of statues. Aunties waved
postcards depicting the same view in my face, and pushed miniature terra-
cotta warriors into my palms. I stiff-armed a man who shouted "*Lǎowài!*"
He limply batted his clutch purse at my back. So this was sightseeing in
China. *Never again*, I silently vowed. *No more mass tourist sites*.

As I threaded my way to the dusty parking lot I noticed a man sitting
alone at a small wooden table. A hand-lettered sign taped to its front said
he was one of the men who had unearthed the site twenty-two years before.
He no longer grew sweet potatoes; he sat and posed for pictures, retelling
the day he hit pay dirt. The farmer said that many superstitious villagers
had warned his well-digging group not to disturb a plot of land that, because
of the objects that had surfaced over the years, they suspected held a tomb.
The men dug anyway. After they uncovered the first group of relics, nothing
evil immediately befell them; the gossip had been wrong. But an elderly
villager, sizing up the man-sized statues, worried that the eerie objects
would spook the area's birds, causing them to attack the ancient figures.
How to keep them away? The old man fitted his straw hat atop one warrior,
creating a terra-cotta scarecrow.

China's oral history is often more interesting than the official, edited
one. But on this hot afternoon I was the farmer's only visitor.

After summer classes ended, I took the long way back to Neijiang via the
Yangtze River's Three Gorges, a natural wonder about to be flooded by
construction of the world's largest dam. SEE THEM BEFORE IT'S TOO
LATE! exulted the posters at a riverside travel agent in Wuhan city. GONE
IN 1997! Diagrams of the dam hung alongside photos of the beauty it
would soon submerge. SCHEDULED FOR COMPLETION IN 2009! one

poster cheered. THE DAM WILL BE 175 METERS HIGH, 2,335 METERS WIDE, AND RELOCATE ONE MILLION PEOPLE!

A ticket tout snapped, "Buy or not buy?"

I proceeded to an operator whose poster showed photos of a modern ship with a swimming pool. "Only three hundred," he offered, then laughed when I dug out yuan. "That's three hundred *dollars*. I take Visa."

That was nearly three months of my salary. I waited until nightfall at the state-run wharf. At 9:00, in a dingy ticket hall, a piece of wood slid away from a barred hole in the wall.

"To Chongqing. One please, for a two-bed cabin."

An unseen woman demanded the Chinese equivalent of $20.

"I'll see the gorges?"

The voice said sure.

"How many days to Chongqing?"

The voice said four. Maybe five. Could be six.

"And I'll see the gorges?"

The voice said "Next!" The word echoed in the vacant hall.

The rusted, single-deck boat limped to the dock. I was the only passenger without sacks of grain or luggage that didn't cluck. I feel no lost romance for this era of China travel. Once I settled in to my berth, I wrote, "So this is what a generation feels like."

My students came of age in years that would see Beijing's outward face swing from tanks in Tiananmen to fireworks exploding above it, opening the 2008 Olympics. As it upgraded roads and infrastructure, China was bound to experience catch-up growth: in the two decades after 1996, the country paved seventy-seven thousand miles of expressway, leapfrogging the United States' federal highway system, which started in 1956, and laid more high-speed railway track than the combined length of the entire world's. These state-backed, pump-priming projects employed millions, inflated the gross national product, and projected confidence. They also cast a shadow of unwanted suspense. Were these shiny skyscrapers and new schools safe? Who was mixing the cement for that bridge? Could you really, for the first time, ever, dam the entire Yangtze?

Chinese remember how a dam collapsed in 1975, killing 230,000 people.

Yet the Three Gorges Dam's turbines would generate one-fifth of China's electricity, equivalent to the output of eighteen nuclear power plants. The country felt it could engineer anything. Meanwhile, in my deck's bathroom, feces flopped like landed fish across the sopping floor.

At sunrise, I set a wooden stool at the front of the boat. All day I stared at the Yangtze. Schools of white Styrofoam instant noodle bowls floated into eddies of plastic water bottles. I bagged my trash and handed it to the deckhand. In one unbroken movement he received the sack and tossed it overboard. For a few seconds the plastic bag imitated a buoy before sinking. That afternoon, a Queen Princess liner rumbled past. Its decks showed tiers of Bermuda shorts, pale legs, and camcorders capturing the local color, such as our rust-mottled ship.

On the third morning, a bloated body rolled by the boat like a cork. Face, back, face, back. Some of the passengers stared silently from the rail. More turned their heads and moved starboard, cursing our—not the dead woman's—bad luck. In China, I learned, a corpse crossing one's path is common enough to be considered a sign of misfortune.

At lunchtime onboard, a male passenger chased another man down the hallway with a cleaver raised above his head. Forget the Three Gorges; one hadn't really seen China until witnessing a cleaver chase. On the boat, I stuck my head out the cabin door and into the empty passageway. From the galley I heard the cook's crunching cleaver strokes on his cutting board, which sounded the all-clear, just as it had at No Big Deal in Neijiang. My students often told me they were thankful that private gun ownership was forbidden in China, and I understood why.

At sundown the boat reached the Gezhouba Dam, then the Yangtze's largest. We rose and fell through a series of locks. My summer professor in Xi'an had told the legend of Da Yu, a man who for thirteen years worked to harness the Yellow River. His story ended: "He didn't even once visit his house when he walked past it." The moral, the teacher said, was an individual's duty to the nation. After a pause, he wondered, a bit too knowingly, if in fact the man was a henpecked husband living in a crummy house. As ever, his personal story was more interesting than a myth.

Where were the Three Gorges? Given their depiction on the back of the five-yuan bill, I expected a natural spectacle on par with the Grand Canyon. On the fourth day our captain roused passengers at midnight, saying, "We're here." A single spotlight stabbed at the darkness cloaking the boat. It was like seeing the Grand Canyon through a viewfinder, ten square feet at a time. At the channel's narrowest point, I could reach out and touch the river-smoothed rock face. The current roared. I couldn't discern a thing. My fingers ran along the stone until, a short minute later, it was gone.

CHAPTER 5

PARTING THE CLOUD OF COMPASSION

T HE BOAT DOCKED at Chongqing, a peninsula city of history and hills, or so I had heard. That I could live, for a year, oblivious of a metropolis of 15 million only a two-hour bus ride away from Neijiang was a measure of the Chinese countryside's insulating effect.

I was in no hurry to return to campus, and while crossing the Yangtze in the aerial tramway that ran on delicate-looking wires high above the river I saw a moss-spackled courtyard surrounded by a tiled rooftop's flying eaves. The architecture looked nothing like the rest of Chongqing's boxy buildings clad in white bathroom tile; it was hard to believe the same culture could create such extremes.

The Ciyun—Cloud of Compassion—Temple had once been the disembarkation point for male and female pilgrims to the holy mountains, such as Mount Emei, tucked inland from this upper reach of the Yangtze. Monks and nuns lived here together, the sign explained, making it the only such monastery in all of China.

In the temple's dining hall, I ate a vegetarian lunch with an elderly nun. She said it had been a long time since she had a visitor. I wondered if she thought I was someone else, someone she knew. My skin had tanned to the color of walnut; cataracts clouded her eyes. She asked, "Where in China are you from?"

"From Neijiang," I said, in dialect. *Leijiang*.

"Where's that? Is that on the other side of the river?"

"Yes, north of it."

"I've never been over there. I live here." She tapped her wooden cane on a paving stone. "I live here. I lived here yesterday, I live here today, I live here tomorrow. I want to live here forever."

When the Three Gorges Dam was finished, chopping the three-thousand-mile water snake of a river in two, the nun said that the temple would become either lakeshore property or an underwater relic. I felt for the first time that flash of anticipatory nostalgia, missing a place before it was gone. Soon the feeling would become routine. Later the water rose but did not drown the monastery. A new, elevated expressway cleaves the temple and its ancient Yangtze landing. The road runs at window height. Now the nuns gaze outside and contemplate traffic.

How long does it take to settle into a place? How long before it feels like home? Is it after you sleep through the night without rising at every strange sound, or break in the kitchen with a first cooked meal, or automatically reach for light switches without looking for them, or hang your own pictures, or finally receive mail?

An unexpected result of being away for the summer was that my colleagues and students looked at me differently after I returned. So I was staying long-term, they said, and not just passing through—as if my first year had equaled only a week on Planet Neijiang's calendar.

This was an important lesson I had stumbled upon: Settle in, figure out How to Get Things Done, and then, after a few months, leave. Return a short while later and notice how people react. The day I returned to Neijiang, as I ate my first bowl of fried rice at No Big Deal, a guy selling watermelons caught sight of me for the first time and began acting accordingly. The cook, Mr. Qin, told him to leave me alone; I had lived here a year already, longer than the watermelon vendor. "I'm crouched on a stool with my bowl in my hands in this hovel," I recounted in a letter to my mom, "with flies and fleas around me and I'm pouring sweat but I'm happy because I'm *home*. When I rose to pay, Mr. Qin said the meal was on him as a thank-you for teaching in the village, my 'Chinese hometown.' He called me his brother."

After that, I felt like I belonged, meaning I was no longer a novelty, and ignorable: *It's just the* lǎowài. *We know all about him.* Now I could set my own agenda.

Yet, although they knew me, my students still complimented my blue eyes (they are brown) and spoke of my white skin (it is olive and darker than theirs), and still gasped when I picked up the chalk and wrote with my left hand (they were all righties). I began our first exam of the year with what I thought was a gift: "True or False: *All Americans are left-handed.*" In a class of twenty-one students, seventeen answered "True." "Well, you're the only American we know," they explained. That class's new vocabulary word was *stereotype*.

For their midterm, I asked students how their thinking about America had changed since Kevin and I had arrived on campus.

"When I was a child," wrote Batty, "the grown-ups always told me: America is a bad country, very very bad. Now I see I am wrong. American government and American people are two different things. American people are as friendly as Chinese. They are all human beings. Maybe we are influenced by the government and think Americans are not kind. Before you came to China, maybe you had the same idea that the Chinese are hostile."

A woman named Cicily, who often submitted essays detailing her close-knit family and their farm, wrote, "I thought that money was the dearest thing that American people like, and it became their lover. Americans treat each other very cold. The husbands don't care about their wives. Parents don't look after their children. But Meyer's mother often writes him letters. Americans are not work machines. In fact, Americans spend more time playing than us."

I was happy to see her finally write my preferred name, instead of the Chinese for "Professor Plumblossom." I asked students if they wanted me to call them by their real names; by now I could memorize them without difficulty. But they refused to ditch their self-selected ones: English class was role-playing, a chance to pretend to be someone else, someone confident and able.

Newsweek's ads made Linda realize, "American women are socialized, just like Chinese. Many girls are influenced by fashion or advertising, and so they want to be tall and thin. It is the same in China." Her desk mate Sophie liked to read the magazine's political coverage, including First Lady Hillary Clinton's efforts to enact national health care. "In the past, I think the women in America has limited rights, they must take care of their husbands and their children like the Japanese women," Sophie wrote. "Women in our country has this similar situation, the husband is their sky. But after the women's liberation it is OK if a woman in America wants a career instead of a family. They can hanker after power as a man, or go beyond a man. Maybe in the future, America will vote a woman as a president. It's possible, who can deny?"

A short, wispy woman who chose the English name Tyson wrote, "I had thought homosexuality wasn't permitted in America. I thought American government must take effective measures to control it. To my astonishment, it's not a strange and serious thing. It's just a person's hobby. I know I am wrong again."

I made a note to explain the word *hobby* to the class.*

Rena, set to graduate in December, wrote that her parents had forbidden her from "falling into the net of love" with a boy from a poor pig-farming village far from hers. "I never thought that Americans have true love, when a boy and girl met, they fell in love with each other and married but in a short time, maybe in a month or in a year, they divorced. They treat their marriage like play game. I have thought that for a long time. One day, I saw an English videotape, *Love Story*. The hero and the heroine love each other soon, but the boy's family didn't accept this marriage because they are rich and the girl is poor. But the boy and girl love deeply. At last, the girl got a cancer and died. The boy fell into deep sorrow, he will miss her forever. I was moved. This is TRUE love, in America the true love has existed, but I didn't know it. I wiped off my prejudice."

I was surprised: until this point, Rena seemed most passionate about diagramming sentences—although, on the occasions she did laugh, she didn't cover her mouth demurely, hiding her crooked teeth, as her class-mates did. Her eyes sprung open as if a button had been pushed, and her waist-long ponytail swung as she eschewed a girlish giggle for an outright guffaw. The last time I saw this, the trigger had been a Three Stooges–esque fall, when a classmate missed his chair while sitting down and hit the floor like a sack of rice.

To her essay, Rena added a postscript that reminded me my students

---

*In 2001, five years later, China declassified being gay as a mental illness.

were more than mute receptacles, or "ducks to be stuffed," as traditional Chinese pedagogy put it, and that in China a foreigner often became a confessor. "I don't want to anger my family," Rena wrote me. "After all, they love me and I love them also. I don't want to be a rebel of my family. I don't want to break their hearts. They're older and older. They need to be taken care of. I can't leave them by themselves, because neither my sister nor my brother is in Neijiang. But on another hand, I can't leave my boyfriend either. That also will break his heart. What about your opinion? P.S. Please point out my mistakes in this paper."

Where to begin? *Run*, I wanted to say. But Rena had called off the relationship by the time we talked; her boyfriend said he expected her to adhere to the tradition that a wife moved to the husband's village.

After graduation, she would find that officials in her own village demanded payment in exchange for a teaching position, which her family could not afford. "Now I really know how complex the society is," she wrote to me. "It is more complicated than I imagine. I have no *guānxi*. I can't find an important man to help me. I am so helpless and lonely. I don't know what to do now. An official reminds me that I should give them some money and invite them to have a big dinner. The officials are very greedy. The smaller power they have, the greedier they are."

Eventually, her father called the last-ditch play: he contacted provincial authorities. They ordered the lower-ranking village cadres to employ Rena. But instead of teaching her major, English, she was assigned to teach the two subjects she hated most—math and politics—to 159 elementary-aged kids. "I'm very sorrowful and disappointed," she wrote. "I have to obey the decision of the government or I'll be out of work. This is life if you have no power and money."

Rena sent an update every few weeks. Her tone, if plotted on a graph, trended sharply downward. "I'm always worried about my students," she wrote after two months on the job. "The competition is so strong, but they don't realize this. I always tell them that they must work hard or they will lose their steps in keeping up with modern society. But they turn a deaf ear. They thought I was cheating them. These fools!"

Her letters also reminded me why Chinese college students often regarded their campus life as a sort of summer camp. When else would they enjoy such leisure? "I guess you are sitting in a small restaurant outside our school, eating, chatting and drinking," Rena wrote. "What a wonderful life you own! My guess makes me miss the life in our school, but that life is gone forever, never come back. I feel sad. Anyway, I'm a teacher."

As autumn turned to winter, my mother wrote: "Well, it's almost Christmas. Do the Chinese celebrate at all? You'd think they would, since they make all the decorations we use. More and more, everything that I pick up in the stores says 'Made in China.' It's beginning to worry me. We have quite a trade deficit with them. I don't think anything is made in America anymore. I hope the new year ('our' new year) finds you in good health. What year is it in China?"

A perpetual mist settled over campus. From my balcony, I heard the barges' disembodied *putt-putt*, somewhere beyond my frozen breath. While I was away over the summer, the college had installed in my apartment new green Astroturf for carpet, a landline phone, and a television. Like the rest of campus, however, my rooms lacked central heating.

I realized, after washing my disintegrating clothes, why my students wore the same outfit every day. Drying laundry on the line took three days, and even then it held the damp. I started wearing the same clothes, too: layers of T-shirts under a buttoned-up flannel pockmarked with hot pepper oil stains.

I wore this to bed as well. My students said eight people to a dorm helped during winter, as it generated enough heat to necessitate sleeping in their underwear. Yet they worked in unheated classrooms; chilblains rimmed their ears and dotted the backs of their hands. When correcting their lessons, my fingers went numb. To revive them, I steeped my left hand in a cup of steaming chrysanthemum tea.

The next batch of Peace Corps volunteers had trained over the summer, and two women, named Rebecca and Lisa, were assigned to Neijiang. Their arrival cut my weekly workload from ten to six hours. Mr. Wang assigned the newcomers the English conversation courses and gave me Western Civilization and also a class he called, simply: Movies. Show the students movies, he instructed. Preferably "ones with singing." All of the Beatles films would be just fine, he said.

Neijiang shops openly sold pirated Hollywood films on video discs, so creating a curriculum was easy. The students identified with the Cockney flower girl Eliza Doolittle as she attempted to speak the King's English in *My Fair Lady*. Every weeknight they sat in the required Mandarin Pronunciation class, reciting phrases aimed at smoothing their Sichuan accent. My students empathized, too, with the restless farmhand named Luke Skywalker. *Star Wars* featured characters—a droid, a Wookiee—whose English was worse than their own. "What are they saying? There are no subtitles when they talk." Yoda reminded them of a greener, shorter grandparent. The Ewoks rocked. Students called them the "Little Bears."

"These Little Bears are so wonderful, it seems they are jumping before me now!" Lucy bubbled in an essay. When, in the end, the Little Bears triumphed over the "Dark Raider," she gloated: "Meyer, you said they were foolish, but I told you they were good! Never underestimate the Little Bears."

As the semester passed Christmas, I observed—beaming like a proud parent—their teaching practicums in nearby elementary schools, worked my way down the shelves in the attic library, practiced Chinese, and played basketball every afternoon on the outdoor courts, perched next to the wide stone staircase that led down to the mail house and clumps of wild bamboo. You learned not to whip a careless pass toward that side of the court. Players' heads bounced along with the ball as it rolled down fifty steps, past the immobile mail house matron and out the school gate.

One evening I ate my usual dinner of spicy palace-style chicken and spicy pockmarked tofu at the campus restaurant that, when its front door was lowered shut, could have been mistaken for a single-car garage. As I cupped the rice bowl beneath my chin, a man nicknamed Emperor pulled up a stool and called for a round of Five Star beer. "Please," he said, "drink freely."

This meant no finger games, no round-robin toasts, and sipping instead of chugging. I liked Emperor.

"I watch you play basketball," he began. Emperor was a thin, sinewy, square-headed man—the friendliest two-by-four I had ever met. He ran the college's A/V department, overseeing the recording of ceremonies, performances, and speeches. The job exposed him to extremely high levels of tinny treble. Emperor tended to shout, even when sitting an arm's length away.

I found myself leaning back from his bellow as he explained: "There's a monthlong tournament between regional colleges called the Education Cup. I called the chairman. Since you are a member of our college staff, you are eligible to play. There is no rule about foreigners."

"Because nobody ever thought a foreigner would be on the staff of a Sichuan college."

"Ha-ha!" concurred Emperor.

Our team practiced for three hours a day, six days a week, at the new gymnasium. I had never been inside; it was the physical education department's domain. Although college life felt more akin to that at an American high school than university, the divide between majors was absolute. While English teachers hoarded chalk in a classroom whose old wiring often required the blackboard to be illuminated by candlelight, the PE professors worked on a cushioned, floodlit court. Many of them had—literally— majored in basketball.

Our point guard also taught *wǔshù*, martial arts, and was adept at leaping to pass while also "accidentally" kicking his defender's groin. In Chinese his nickname was Fear. Our shooting guard could sink three-pointers with a lit cigarette dangling from his mouth; if smoking had not explicitly been banned, he would have puffed during play. Alone among the players, he had chosen an English name: Archer.

Emperor made us run plays he had seen on the Saturday morning NBA broadcast: Utah Jazz pick-and-rolls; the frantic passing of the Seattle SuperSonics; a short-lived attempt to understand the Chicago Bulls' triangle. Since I was the tallest person, Emperor put me at center, a position I had never played before. No matter; I didn't have to do much, he said, except "look tall. Look really tall." Our uniform, a polyester knockoff of the New York Knicks', felt tight and revealing on my frame. I needed an extra-large; this was a medium. "It's good," Emperor said. "It makes you look even taller. Like a giant!"

Our first opponent, the Hydraulic Technology Institute, wore Bulls uniforms. I heard their bench wonder if I could dunk. During warm-ups, Emperor instructed me to grab the rim to strike fear into the opposing team. I was surprised when I clenched the hoop tightly, pulling it toward the ground. When I released it, the standard sprang back with a rocking thud. Never have I felt so tall: the baskets had been lowered six inches.

The scorer's table featured a clock, an electric scoreboard, and a gong, which was struck at halftime by a young woman wearing a red fur coat and matching lipstick. When I asked what kind of fur it was, she snapped "Fake!" while piercing the tournament chairman, seated beside her, with a look that said *Cheapskate* in every tongue. My teammates gulped hot tea during the intermission; our shooting guard smoked three Red Plum Blossoms. At the crash of the final gong, he smoked some more. We won by 30 points.

The Nursing Institute also wore Bulls uniforms. After a few roundhouse kicks while diving for loose balls, our martial arts–professing point guard finished fast break after fast break. The crashing gong sent the nurses back to their rounds.

The Railroad Engineering Institute was supposed to be our biggest challenge, but to me they looked just like the teams we had throttled. They wore Bulls uniforms too. Emperor warned me about the ref. "He doesn't like foreigners." The whistle blew when I touched the ball, didn't touch the ball, and—the longest, ringing *breet*—when I politely fetched a ball that had rolled out of bounds.

"You're staying in," Emperor said. "We need you on defense against their big man. Here's what I want you to do. Stay at the half-court line on offense."

"You want us to play four on five?"

"There's no shot clock," he said. Our martial arts expert dribbled for two minutes on the next possession, then three, before running out the clock by running figure eights around defenders until the gong clanged.

When the Statistics College team showed up, I began to suspect schools were sharing the same set of uniforms. These Bulls played more like bullies: their center's elbow to my temple resulted in what Emperor called a "panda eye." As the bruise darkened and my eye swelled shut, I launched a three-pointer that hit nothing but air. "*Yángwěi!*" the crowd yelled. The Chinese taunt of an air ball is the word that means impotent.

We played a succession of Bulls. Some refs called traveling; others allowed the Chinese variation of "three big steps," or *sān dà bù*. My black eye seemed to make me even more of a target, the way a bull grows confident before a wounded matador. I realized how hard it is to hide on a basketball court. After a month my stomped toenails matched the purple eye. Emperor had a cure for those; he straightened a paper clip, held an end under his cigarette lighter's flame, and bored a hole into the nails to release the blood.

We rolled through the brackets, clinching the Education Cup. Neijiang television broadcast the award ceremony, which Emperor replayed on the college channel for the following week. Never has Queen's "We Are the Champions" been played with such treble. At our victory dinner, he set the trophy next to a bubbling cauldron of bloodred oil. "Bring plates of pig brain," Emperor told the waitress. "And four orders of chicken throat." They were Sichuan hot pot delicacies; what would we have eaten had we lost? The team raised a toast to Neijiang Teacher's College. In small towns, little things can seem so big.

During the Spring Festival, or Chinese New Year, my co-volunteer and friend Rebecca and I headed south, to what I promised her was the back-packer paradise of Dali, where I had gone the previous year. We arrived to find that its secret was out: its four guesthouses had mushroomed to ten, and all were nearly full. Cafés had dotted only the main street; now they spilled into side lanes. The strenuous, two-hour path uphill to a Buddhist temple in the Cang Mountains now ran under the route of a chairlift.

Even worse, a freak snowfall made the town feel grayer and chillier than Neijiang. Not even cups of Coca-Cola boiled with sliced fresh ginger—a Chinese homeopathic cure—could alleviate our colds, nor did a two-day, twenty-four-mile hike through Tiger Leaping Gorge at the headwaters of the Yangtze. After slowly winding up its horse path to 8,800 feet, we trekked out the other side, crossing the jade-green water and catching a bus that slowly wound through mountains toward Burma, to the border town named Ruili.

Although we could walk its palm-shaded perimeter road in thirty minutes, Ruili buzzed with more activity than the far more populous Neijiang. Street-side karaoke machines filled the subtropical air with treacly love songs. Fresh-flower vendors also used blenders to make fresh papaya juice. The town's central bazaar filled with sarong-wearing traders who accepted renminbi or kyat. Shop signs displayed their names in Chinese characters and the Burmese alphabet. Judging by the bazaar, bilateral business was dominated by cashews and jade from Burma and clothing and household items made in China, but propaganda coating the town warned of the consequences of another trade. The posters showed the X'ed-out faces of people recently executed for drug trafficking. One faced a children's roller skating rink.

Before joining the Peace Corps, I spent two weeks working on the Texas-Mexico border, and now I was surprised to learn that border towns existed here too. Of course they did: China has the world's longest land border, stretching nearly fourteen thousand miles and touching fourteen countries, plus the "special administrative region" of Hong Kong, which adheres to its own laws. Yet my students and colleagues such as Mr. Wang only mentioned China's border in terms of the country's security.

Officially, China didn't have immigrants, or at least it had very few. The United States naturalizes around seven hundred thousand people each year; China's most recent national census counted 1,448 naturalized citizens in total.* The government made it difficult to legally settle in China, but far from Beijing undocumented workers (and brides) hid in plain sight. On each of my four mornings in Ruili, a Burmese man in the bazaar poured me a glass of Nescafé mixed with a little hot water and a lot of condensed milk. By the time I finished the coffee I was usually losing a game of Western chess with an English-speaking Burmese teenager who said he had crossed the border illegally for "freedom," a pretty subjective concept in Southeast Asia. "You mean money," I suggested.

No, he said firmly, it was freedom. Compared to Burma, China presented opportunities. Long before the Communist Party adopted it as a slogan, I heard the term "the Chinese Dream." This young Burmese man said he was pursuing it, just as immigrants chased the American Dream in my country.

Ruili, China's most southwestern city, made a cul-de-sac; the only way back to Neijiang was to retrace the overnight bus route, followed by a

---

* It also rarely grants asylum; aside from 300,000 ethnic Chinese who crossed over the border from Vietnam during the 1978–1979 war between the two countries, by 2016 a total of 583 refugees were in-country for processing. China had more billionaires.

twenty-hour sentence in a train's hard-seat class. Four people squeezed shoulder to shoulder on each bench, and more sprawled beneath us, on a bedding of newspapers. Suddenly the compartment's loudspeaker crackled on to deliver a special announcement. At 9:08 on the evening of February 19, 1997, Comrade Deng Xiaoping passed away in Beijing due to complications from Parkinson's. He was ninety-three years old.

No one wailed, as people did after Chairman Mao died; Deng had not infantilized the population that way. Instead, my fellow passengers said that Deng had lived a long time, that he was from Sichuan, that if not for Deng Xiaoping, China would never have modernized. Deng was only four feet eleven inches tall, a seatmate said. "But he carried himself like this"— and here he stood up with shoulders thrown back, as if striding through history itself. I wouldn't be here if not for Deng, he said. Maybe you, "my foreign friend," would not be here, either. "He went to meet Reagan in America."

"And put on a cowboy hat," another man added with a smile. He said "Seek truth from facts," to not follow whatever Mao theorized. He said it didn't matter what color the cat was, so long as it caught mice. He championed the Four Modernizations. He wasn't, as his name meant, "Little Peace" but its homophone, "Little Bottle," always bobbing to the surface just when his opponents thought he'd finally sunk. I heard a joke: Three guys are thrown into a reform-through-labor camp. The first guy asks the second, "What are you in here for?" Second guy says, "I criticized Deng Xiaoping." The first guy can't believe it. "I'm in here because I *praised* Deng Xiaoping." Then the third guy pipes up: "That's nothing! I *am* Deng Xiaoping."

Against the train window sat a middle-aged man in a suit, with black hair whose slicked-back sheen suggested he had dipped his comb in egg whites. From his breast pocket he produced a *dà gē dà*, as cell phones were called then, a play on the word "gangster"; in Hong Kong action films, they were the only ones who carried the expensive technology. The man told a young soldier wearing fatigues that he was welcome to call his mother.

The cadet phoned home. We passengers had a front-row seat to the transmission of historical news. "Yes, Mom, I got on the train just fine. HELLO? Can you hear me? I'm full, yes. I ate a lot. I ate what you packed. It was good. Thank you. Yes, I'll be back at camp in the morning. HELLO? Can you hear me? Yes, I'll watch my health, Ma. Have you heard about Deng

Xiaoping? He died. Tell Dad. HELLO? OK, I'm hanging up now. Hang up now! Yes, he died. I'm full. Don't worry. I ate! Hang up now."

On campus, a student named Connie, who professed to hating politics, and often submitted poems instead of essays in our writing class, wrote: "My mother told me that when Chairman Mao passed away, most people couldn't help crying loudly. Even if they didn't feel like crying, they did, because everyone else was. But I didn't cry when I learned that Deng Xiaoping passed away. I guess most Chinese didn't cry. We know we should look to the future, not think about the past. Though his death seems to be very far away from me. I feel it is very close to me. At least, most of my 21 years have been spent under his leadership. We know his theories better than Chairman Mao's, especially 'developing socialism with Chinese characteristics' and 'establishing a market economy.'"

I suspected they meant the same thing.

"He said 'to get rich is glorious,'" Connie continued, "and did a lot in order to make Chinese people grow richer. But there are still some people who are starved. So some people don't understand it. They complain about Deng's reform policy and say he betrayed Communism."

The Chinese press, of course, did not mention these criticisms. Nor did it address the fact that while many Chinese blamed the bloodshed at Tiananmen Square on the then premier, a man named Li Peng, he could not have declared martial law without either Deng's order or approval. Five days after the crackdown, Deng gave a speech praising the army's actions, and called the soldiers and military police who died that day "martyrs" and "defenders of the republic" against "counterrevolutionary riots." He said not a word about the civilians killed by their bullets and tank treads.

The *China Daily* and other state media predictably highlighted Deng's economic, not historical, legacy. I was interested in the other newspaper headlines that appeared after his death: "Experts Unite to Push Back Superstition; Asian Stock Markets Stay Calm, Rise; Improving Beijing Is Top Priority." That story promised that the capital's second subway line would be completed, that pollution would be curbed, and that taxi drivers would be required to take people where they demanded to go. (Twenty years later, one of these became true: the second subway line was completed, along with sixteen others.) The sports section reported that the Shandong

Flaming Bulls had "suffered a stunning defeat to struggling Beijing Ducks" and clung to third place in the Chinese Basketball Association standings.

Deng left behind a China where the death of a "dear leader" lowered flags to half-mast and canceled a few classes—but not basketball games. His passing only halted the nation for three minutes at 10:00 a.m. on Tuesday, February 25, when the whistles of factories, trains, and ships blew in remembrance. Then people went back to work.

With a month remaining in Neijiang, I sat on my apartment's green Astro-turf, hunched over the manual typewriter like Schroeder at his toy piano in *Peanuts* cartoons. An ad in the back of the Peace Corps newsletter announced that a bilingual Beijing school needed an English teacher. The job included housing and paid $15,000 a year. The number looked enormous; it was twelve times my current salary. I had no other leads, no urgency to return to the States, and—since my clothes had disintegrated over the past two years—almost no luggage. I also wanted to continue to study Chinese and see China. After two years adapting to the place and learning the language, it seemed that I had barely scratched its surface; it would be a tremendous waste of banked experience to just leave.

Balls of crinkled carbon paper rimmed off the trash basket as I attempted to peck out an error-free CV to mail to Beijing. I empathized with my writing students, whose final exam required them to compose and type a cover letter and résumé. Some of them mailed their papers to the area's new Pepsi distribution plant. Soon the soda's advertisements plastered the student canteen. I thought back to the American diplomat who, two years earlier, had said my real task was to create future customers for the soft drink. Mission accomplished!

I also typed my first travel article, recounting the Spring Festival trip to the border with Burma. A new Peace Corps volunteer from Missouri named Peter Hessler, posted to a Yangtze river town named Fuling, generously shared the addresses of newspaper travel sections. I mailed the story to the *Los Angeles Times*. "I want to find an editor who will challenge me a bit more," I wrote home, "instead of just printing pieces untouched without any questions or edits, which doesn't make me a better writer." The paper also paid $300 for a story and $50 for each photograph—a king's ransom compared to what I was earning. Surprisingly, the editor had replied: she returned my original pages, graffitied in red ink, with instructions to rewrite the story. I just hoped the envelope would get airborne; the dozen pages of typescript stuffed inside required extra tape to bind the edges, and enough postage—tall terra-cotta warriors and red Year of the Ox stamps—to nearly obscure the address. America felt very far away.

Sunlight woke me during my last week in Neijiang. This was a first; for two years I never pulled my curtains closed at bedtime, since the following day's sky would remain overcast, misty, or polluted. This morning looked so summery that I had a vestigial Midwestern urge to mow a lawn.

My letters home had slowed to a trickle since the installation of a telephone in my apartment. "The only downside to our calls," I wrote my mother, "is that it negates my motivation to write letters." However, in my final correspondence I recounted a delicious meal of fried eggplant, palace-style pork, *mápó* tofu, and fried rice with Kane, the student who, during my first class in Neijiang, asked, "Why are you here?" He wore steel-rimmed glasses and had spongy black hair that he often tugged straight upward when trying to think of a word in English. He was back in Neijiang to interview for a teaching job at a local middle school, a process that required him to give two lessons on two consecutive days, observed by two different sets of administrators acting as judges. Kane planned on doing something "radical" while teaching his assigned topic, "Writing a Letter in English."

"I'm going to hand out real envelopes," he said, "and have students seal their letter inside of it and write the address the Western way."

In Chinese, the postal code appeared in the top left, followed by the address and then the recipient's name, with the return address written in the lower right corner. I beamed while listening to him talk: he was indeed taking a risk, differentiating himself by extending the lesson beyond the textbook. However, wasn't Kane worried that the judges would penalize him?

Not if I walked to the interview with him, he suggested. That way, word would spread that Kane had been taught by a foreigner. If the judges liked his lesson, great; if they criticized him for going off-book, he could say he learned it from the *lǎowài*. In the end he didn't need a scapegoat; the judges were as enthusiastic as the students, and Kane won the job.

One more basketball game. One more walk out the back gate—*no mail!*—through the bamboo grove, along the footpath between cabbage and rapeseed fields, up to the shallows near the old stone bridge. One more hitched ride on a passing skiff back to campus. So long, Stall-for-Time River. One more pass by the ox tethered in my courtyard. One more tentative touch of the showerhead, which, like a pet python, I never wholly trusted. One more round of Five Star beers with Mr. Wang. One more meal prepared by Mr. Qin's cleaver at No Big Deal. One more strong-arm hug from Emperor. One more chat with the librarian, and no more books from the secret attic. One more walk past the campus's countdown calendar marking the days—thirty-two—until Hong Kong's July 1, 1997, handover from the United Kingdom, an event China termed the colony's "return to the embrace of the motherland."

One more round of pictures. The village photographer snapped farewell shots of my students. On the backs of our photos, presented to me in an album, they inked captions such as "Look, Meyer, in this picture I'm young forever! Wish you stay young forever!" and "How ruthless the time is! I'll unforget you all my life."

One of my favorite students, a bespectacled young woman named Lucy, wrote: "I feel more fluent to just call you Meyer. In fact, we are friends. Maybe I can call you Monkey, too. I wish you will realize all of your hopes: a happy family, lovely children, good job, and a whole happy life!"

A young man who called himself Freedom wrote, "You will leave us. Tell your friends and family about China. Please. I love my mother country. Let everybody know about China."

In the pictures we looked so similar, so young: I had just turned twenty-five; my students were twenty-two. Inside or outside the classroom, we were all of us just beginners.

CHAPTER 6

FAR AND AWAY IN TIBET

T HE BEIJING SCHOOL did not reply to my application, and so I
assumed I was about to be officially unemployed, have my work visa
canceled, and need to leave China. The three weeks remaining on my
residence permit took on a new urgency. If I had only one final place to
visit in China, where would I go? I thought about the Great Wall, and
strongly considered Wolong (Sleeping Dragon), Sichuan's panda preserve,
but a recent Peace Corps farewell trip to a national park named Jiuzhaigou
(Nine Stockades Gulley) had traveled the same mountainous road; even
in a four-wheel-drive jeep the route was treacherous—from landslides—and
numbingly slow—from driving around those landslides, by easing down the
riverbank and threading the vehicle through boulders in the shallows. I
couldn't imagine making the trip by public bus.

Instead, I decided to settle a debate. Of the films we watched in our
movie class, Neijiang students voted *Far and Away* as their favorite, and
not just because it starred Tom Cruise. The epic showed migrant homesteaders opening America's western frontier. I thought the class would
criticize the movie for its romantic view; there was no scene, for example,
of American Indians being forced off the land. Yet, although the action
took place a century and a continent away, my students loved *Far and
Away* for a reason that surprised me: they could relate to it—because of
Tibet.

The province, called Xizang—"Western Treasure Chest"—was being
Sinicized and developed at once. Although none of my students had been
there, its frontier was more alluring to them than east coast factories. As

part of its "Develop the West" campaign, the government paid professional-class Han Chinese subsidies and a higher salary to migrate to Tibet.

One of my best students was tempted by the offer. Wiseman was from a hamlet so remote, it had no road. Every other weekend the lean young man, wearing his usual outfit of a sport coat over a collared shirt with slacks and loafers, had walked a footpath from campus to check on his parents at home. For a writing assignment titled "The Two Most Important People in My Life," he composed a dialogue between two wheat stalks—his family's staple, and only source of income.

After he graduated the previous December, Wiseman accepted his appointed student teaching assignment near his home village. Shortly after he had started, he wrote me a letter that began:

"I'm a teacher, a formal worker of the state. I teach two classes. They work hard and we get along well. Sometimes I teach them Beatles songs. They like singing 'Yellow Summer Rain.' Every morning, I have to get up at 6:00, then I go to the students' dormitory to press them to get up and do morning exercise. Meyer, sometimes I feel that I am not a teacher, I'm still just a student. Only when I stand in front of the classroom do I feel that I'm a teacher. So I have to always remind myself: 'You are a teacher now, you must pay attention to your speech and your actions.' That's funny, isn't it?"

It was also entirely in character. Wiseman's lean features and buoyant personality made him appear younger than his twenty-two years. Two months passed until his next letter arrived.

"What I like best is America's attitude to achievement," he wrote. "They have a strong view of individualism. It's good. One should pursue his success. That's not selfish. That's doing good to himself as well as others. There is no inherited occupation to help others and hold the others back, so it's equal. If your father is a banker, maybe you are a farmer. But that's impossible in China. If your father is rich, you may be very rich in China. The poor must do much more to get success than the rich do, for they haven't a rich father. It's true. I hate it.

"Yesterday, I went home and my parents agreed with me to join the army. Please write to me and tell me your opinion, OK? In addition, one day, I met a word 'pollute.' Some books say its pronunciation is [pe'lu:t] but the dictionary says its pronunciation is [pe'lju:t]. I don't know which one is right. Meyer, could you tell me? Bye-bye. Yours truly, Wiseman."

After enlisting, Wiseman accepted the bonus money that came with being posted to Tibet. If he completed five years there, he would be released from service.

"Yes," he wrote, "maybe the life in Tibet will be very difficult and the condition there will be hard. But at least the salary will be very high. If I'm a teacher in a certain countryside middle school, the condition will be more terrible. That's true. One hand, it's difficult to find a suitable room, moreover, the salary is low. At the most, I can only get no more than 200 yuan [$25] a month. Sometimes, the teachers can't get it. As a teacher, if he can't get the poor money, then how can he live? How can he support himself? How can he support his family?"

Transferring his household registration (hùkǒu) from the village to Neijiang would cost 4,500 yuan, he said, equivalent to a year of his parents' earnings—and would still not guarantee he could find a teaching job.

"I'm a little puzzled because you said if I'm a soldier in Tibet you would be a little sad. I don't know why. Just because I should be a teacher but I will be a soldier? In fact, it's natural, because everyone wants to get a good job and get more money. At least he can support his own family. Now, many teachers in the countryside don't want to teach. Some of them go to find a new job to make more money. And many young people don't want to go to school. Because they think it's useless being educated. They think, even if they can go to college, after graduation it's very difficult to find a job. Especially as a teacher like me. It's really hard to find a school that wants you. So I make my choice."

In our movie class, Wiseman's former peers argued that he chose wisely—for himself and for his country. What was bad about developing Tibet? Just look at how America's frontier had turned out.

The term *devil's advocate* was not in our dictionaries, but I routinely asked students to argue both sides of a topic. On Tibet they abandoned me. The topic had no other side. The Chinese government had admitted "mistakes were made" in Tibet, the students chorused. But China hadn't colonized, invaded, or seized Tibet: it "liberated it from the slave-holding feudal system overseen by the emperor-god Dalai Lama."

Liberation was a loaded word in China, as sacrosanct as *independence* to Americans, just as "stability" was the ultimate Chinese prize, akin to America's "freedom."

I had learned that in China progress often looked like destruction, so one should never put off a trip to see an ancient city, such as Lhasa. In the waning era of two-tiered pricing, foreigners were charged twice what Chinese paid for plane tickets, so I spent a sizeable slice of my $4,800 Peace Corps "resettlement allowance" for a round-trip flight to Lhasa from Chengdu.

The in-flight magazine reported that the "extremely cold temperatures and altitude make the Chengdu–Lhasa flight one of the most dangerous in the world." Outside, the peaks of the Himalayas seemed to reach for our plane. The breakfast cart passed. Chinese passengers stuffed the meal, tray and all, into their carry-on luggage. I wondered if I had slept through an in-flight showing of *Alive*.

Deng Xiaoping welcomed me at Lhasa's city limit, declaring ECONOMIC REFORM AND SOCIAL OPENING! from a billboard. A dozen army trucks idled as a contingent of soldiers took position around an obelisk. I thought of Wiseman, back home, going through basic training.

"A bomb went off there a few days ago," the bus driver said, nodding toward the monument, which celebrated the Friendship Highway linking the city to Sichuan. "Tibetans have tried to knock it down four times since I moved here."

He had been in Lhasa nearly a year. Ethnically Han Chinese, he emigrated from Zigong, a city near Neijiang. He turned the bus onto Ethnicity Street, a wide, empty, flat concrete expanse lined with white-tile dumpling stalls run by Sichuan migrants. The driver waved at a statue of two yaks, standing in a traffic circle. "Those are from 1991, the fortieth anniversary of Tibet's liberation. No one ever tries to blow those up." Lhasa's police headquarters faced them across the street.

"Do I miss Sichuan? Are you joking?" the driver said. "Lhasa is better. The sky is clear, the air is clean. It's developing faster. Salaries are higher. No more *suāntián kǔlà*."

The driver had done his share of tasting life's "sour and sweet, bitter and hot." Now he wanted space, a steady job, the opportunity to save money for his daughter's education. He turned onto Dosengge Road, the first non-Chinese-sounding street we had traveled in the fifty-five miles from the airport. I smelled mossy incense. Just like that: one turn and a boundary crossed. The driver welcomed me to "Tibetan Lhasa."

Even when glimpsed through the incense smoke rising from story-high censers, the unmarked border was apparent: pilgrims circumambulated Jokhang Temple clockwise, twirling prayer wheels. Marching the opposite way, against their flow: Chinese soldiers shouldering rifles.

In the Barkhor, the bazaar ringing the temple, wizened faces—the toothless, lined sort that make the cover of guidebooks—offered to pose for cash. They removed their earrings and pressed them into my palm while naming a price. At the temple's front, pilgrims prostrated themselves on cobblestones smoothed by centuries of foreheads. A young bearded American with a knobby walking stick stepped around them, past the ticket window, and into the Jokhang, a site as paramount to Tibetan Buddhism as St. Peter's is to Catholicism. Yet a cross crowns St. Peter's, not a Vatican City State flag. The Jokhang was topped by a red banner of the People's Republic of China.

An hour later, on a café terrace, I sipped salty yak butter tea from a wooden bowl, letting the fat cover my chapped lips. In walked the bearded American. I asked why he didn't pay to enter the temple.

"The dude wanted thirty yuan [$3.70]. But I told him I'm a Buddhist, so I don't have to pay. The money goes to the government anyway."

When I asked how the temple funded its upkeep, the man made me disappear. From his chair, he willed me into nonexistence. It is a skill displayed in China by Westerners toward other Westerners who interrupt their road song.

A Tibetan seated at a neighboring table tugged at my arm hair. He gave a thumbs-up, rubbing his smooth forearm. Then he reached over and flicked my earring. Aside from little kids, who liked to paw my beard, no Han Chinese made curious contact like this. Men shook hands lightly, as if I were contagious. I grabbed the Tibetan's arm. Steel. He raised a fist. I recoiled. He laughed. I returned to my yak butter tea. As if we were back in a schoolyard, he playfully tugged my hair and left.

I overheard the bearded American telling a pretty blonde woman that he was a Buddhist. I rolled my eyes, as expatriates often do when coming across their kin. They make a mirror in which, as Jonathan Swift said about satire, we see every face but our own.

Dusk fell at 10:30 p.m.; Lhasa's clock ran on Beijing time, despite the capital being nearly as far away as Washington, D.C., is to Los Angeles. A soldier lowered the Chinese flag from the pole in front of Jokhang Temple. The five-starred national flag flying from its rooftop stayed aloft.

A throng of pilgrims and tourists walked shoulder to shoulder around the bazaar, trying to avoid the just-begun rain. A Tibetan teen wearing a blue coat with an arm patch that said PUBLIC SECURITY in Chinese pushed his bicycle through the crowd. From his sides, a pair of Tibetan men beat him down with their fists, crumpling his nose until blood splattered the paving stones. The attackers ran. The boy picked up his bike and continued walking, displaying no emotion.

"They called him a traitor," a woman explained in Chinese.

Through the rain, the same screeching Hindi hip-hop tune bounced from storefronts into my marrow. Everything spun clockwise—pilgrims, prayer wheels, my head. Lhasa was a terrible place to take a vacation.

As the clock struck midnight on July 1, 1997, fireworks bloomed above the Potala Palace. Banners announcing THE UNITY OF ALL ETHNICI-TIES ran down the steep, bleached ramparts. Video screens erected on Lhasa's new square showed a rainy night in Hong Kong as the territory reverted to Chinese rule. Around me, the crowd whooped as pyrotechnics popped like gunfire. They waved red plastic flags, one with five stars—China's—and one with a white bauhinia flower—Hong Kong's. Parents lined up to hoist their children into the cockpit of the decommissioned People's Liberation Army fighter jet parked on the square. "Fire!" one boy yelled. "Launch missile!" I followed his imagination's trajectory. The Potala was dead in his sights.

A middle-aged Tibetan man asked if I spoke his language, and I tried a line from the Tibetan phrase book on sale in Lhasa's bazaar. The man shook his head. "This is China. Speak Chinese."

In Lhasa, I felt like a double lǎowài: an American in China, and a Chinese speaker in Tibet.

Despite knowing better, I came expecting to see the mythical allure of the "Roof of the World." I pictured saturated opal skies over whitewashed Buddhist temples scented by smoldering incense and reverberating with chanting monks. But so had the British explorers who made it to Lhasa a century before, then glumly described the place as a fetid swamp of exposed sewage. I found the swamp replaced by a replica of Tiananmen Square. Take away the pilgrims, the temples, the open sky, and altitude sickness brought on by life at twelve thousand feet, and Lhasa's workaday routine bustled along just like any other Chinese provincial capital, with a modern grid traced from the same Communist stencil. The wide main boulevard, bisecting the palace and square, was even named Beijing Road.

I stood on its sidewalk as fireworks—*yānhuā*, "smoke flowers"—filled the night sky. A Tibetan man shook plastic flags in my face and said, in Mandarin, "Hong Kong has returned to the embrace of the motherland!"

I hoped, in vain, that it was the last time I heard that phrase.

Tiny yak butter candles illuminated the Jokhang Temple's cramped rooms, and the wooden staircases groaned with every step. The place was unlike most Chinese holy sites, where buildings that survived the Cultural Revolution have been bandaged with paint and sprinkled with tour guides—and closed-circuit surveillance cameras. The Jokhang was something else, echoing with chants, flickering flames, and the shuffling feet of sandaled pilgrims. Many walked months to reach here. As a tourist I felt entirely in their way.

From the rooftop, I watched the Barkhor traffic spin below. The azure enameled sky domed gold-garlanded rooftops, yellow awnings, chocolate-and-cream tapestries, and burgundy walls. Someday, surely soon, the Jokhang would be refurbished: electrified, scrubbed, painted, aired out.

A handyman repairing the roof invited me to share a thermos of butter tea. Like most Tibetans of preceding generations, he came from a family of nomads. They owned thirty-five yaks, selling at least one male a year and living off the money. A large yak brought in 2,000 yuan ($250), a small one six hundred ($75). The monk asked me how much I earned as a teacher. Nothing, I said: I was officially unemployed, although in the Peace Corps I had made $120 each month. He was the first person in two years to not shake his head in disbelief and declare the figure low. Teaching brought reliable pay, he said, adding, "Good land produces a lot, but when the government sees that, they say, 'We want it. Take your yak someplace else.'"

The man laughed, however, when I asked how vegetarian Buddhists reconciled themselves to eating yak meat. "It's necessary. I'd die. I can't only eat *tsampa*!" He had a point. The ball of barley flour dipped in butter tea reminded me of eating paste in kindergarten.

His mother had visited Lhasa one month before, to "clean her mind" and pray for a solution to their roaming dilemma. I asked him what changes bothered her most.

"She doesn't like to see all of the Chinese drunkards, the truck drivers. They want prostitutes, so now Lhasa has many Sichuanese prostitutes."

I had noticed that the western strip of Beijing Road glowed pink at night from karaoke hall signs. But the handyman said his biggest concern wasn't soldiers or vice. It was concrete.

"In traditional Tibetan architecture, we use timber, straw, and mud. It's all natural. It's healthy for the body, for the mind." He pointed up at the eaves shielding us from the sun. From below, I saw how their woven twigs held hay and dried earth. "But Chinese architecture is all concrete. Not natural. The buildings are so cold. They make us ill. I think, in the future, all the buildings in Lhasa will be concrete. All the Tibetans will be ill."

I asked where he saw himself in five years. He said the demand for traditional craftsmen was waning. From his sport coat's inner pocket, he fished out a thin paperback textbook titled *English for Tibetans*. "I'd like to be a tour guide," he said. "I could show Lhasa to Americans."

"I think there will be many more Chinese tourists in Lhasa."

"Maybe I'll be a teacher . . ."

"My Sichuan students are being recruited to come here and teach."

"I still have the yak . . ."

Lhasa's sister city is Boulder, Colorado, but Jerusalem could be its fraternal twin. On July 6, tradition called for flinging barley flour into the air to celebrate the Dalai Lama's birthday. Tibetans believed the current Dalai Lama, named Tenzin Gyatso, was fourteenth in a six-hundred-year lineage of men who were reincarnations of Avalokiteshvara, the Bodhisattva of Compassion, who served as a political and religious ruler of Tibet. The region had for centuries been yoked to imperial China with periods of de facto and declared independence, but in 1950 the Communists incorporated Tibet—three times the size of Montana, with vast minerals and strategic importance—into the People's Republic of China. Nine years later, during protests and street fighting, the then twenty-three-year-old Dalai Lama fled Lhasa and crossed the Himalayas on foot to a permanent life on the Indian side of the border.*

On the days before the Dalai Lama's sixty-second birthday, Lhasa police announced that anyone entering the city with flour, or even clothes stained by flour, would be detained.

At the Barkhor, a shopkeeper powdered my shoulders and hair. If everyone ignored the order, he said, the police could not arrest anyone. It snowed all afternoon. Tibetans flung handfuls of flour into the air even as lines of soldiers marched counterclockwise through the mist, dusting their olive green hats. I thought of Wiseman again and was thankful he chose to enter the army air force and not become a foot soldier.

The birthday celebration was a game of cat-and-mouse with an erratic, lethal cat. At one turn Lhasa seemed loose: the largest offerings at temples were to openly displayed photographs of the exiled Dalai Lama. A few days later the ban on images of the "splittist" was enforced, and monks tucked his picture inside their crimson robes. As elsewhere in China, anecdotes supplanted evidence, and word of mouth, not written code, ruled. When I went to the police station to apply for a permit to visit Samye, Tibet's first Buddhist monastery, the cops laughed. I had heard rumors of police there detaining and even deporting unlicensed visitors. The Lhasa police said it was news to them. They used the verb *tīngshuō*, "heard-said," as in "We heard-said no such thing."

My bus driver was amazed that the police indicated that I could go. "I don't think you're allowed. Better keep your head down until we pull out

---

*The Lhasa unrest of March 1959 is known as the Tibetan Uprising. On its fiftieth anniversary in 2009, the Chinese government declared a permanent provincial holiday on March 28, the date the Tibetan government was abolished in 1959. In Chinese it is called Bàiwàn Nóngnú Jiěfàng Jìniàn Rì: Serfs Emancipation Day.

of the station. Once I get on the highway, no worries. But if we see a police car, put your head down, or I'll get fined too."

After four hours and no cop stops, the driver dropped me in the Yarlung Valley, where I would have to find a ride to the ferry, eighteen miles away, that crossed the river to Samye. The valley was known as the cradle of Tibetan civilization. A green, fertile plain bearing apple and pear orchards stretched for forty-five miles between mountains bald but for their caps of snow. Legend held that the first Tibetan king descended here from heaven via rope, and that the first Buddhist scriptures landed on the roof of his castle.

The nearest town, Tsetang, looked imported from Sichuan. Strips of white-tile dumpling restaurants fronted its traffic circle. A restaurant owner parted the green plastic vines hanging from her doorway, inviting me inside. "Quickly!" She fastened the curtains.

"The officials told restaurants that we cannot serve foreigners, that you have to eat at the hotel, where the food is bad and more expensive." The woman's eight-year-old daughter looked up from her English homework and smiled at me. They had migrated from Leshan, a city in southern Sichuan.

I planned on walking out to the first Tibetan king's castle. Guidebook photos showed a dramatic, narrow fortress rising from the valley floor like an extended thumb. Built two thousand years ago, it was Tibet's oldest structure. The restaurant owner said not to waste my time. "The original was destroyed during the Cultural Revolution," she said. "The castle is a replica."

"How about the Monkey Cave?" And then I tried to say: "I heard a legend that it is the birthplace of the Tibetan race, where a bodhisattva, disguised as a monkey king, romanced an ogress." This was the most difficult sentence I had ever attempted in Chinese. I could not get it right. I finally punted and managed: "My ancestors were monkeys, too."

"Chinese come from dragons," the eight-year-old said.

I asked if I looked like a monkey.

"You *are* a monkey," she giggled, pointing at my beard.

I tried buying a bus ticket to the Samye monastery ferry crossing. At the station the Tibetan clerk looked uncertain. "You don't have a permit? I heard you can't go to Samye." The worst thing you can do in China is set a precedent. It is always safer to say no. But instead of just waving me away, the clerk said she was calling the police.

I walked quickly out the door, motioning downward with an open palm, Chinese for "I need a ride." A Liberation truck picked me up down the road. The Sichuanese driver said to keep low in the seat. He heard-said hitchhiking was illegal. Just like logging, he added, smiling slyly. His truck was piled with timber.

The monk at Samye did not ask to see my travel permit or passport when I arrived. Nor did he ask how I had managed to get there. The only information he wanted from me was a demonstration of my pop-up umbrella. He filled a thermos with yak butter tea and placed it beside my bed in the spartan, empty pilgrim's hostel.

With its yellow crown, whitewashed stones, and burgundy-dyed straw walls, Samye was once Tibet's monastic jewel. It represented the world as known to its builders in the year 775. The structure's first story represented Tibetan architecture, the second Chinese, and the third a Hindu temple. The monk pointed out the halls that had been converted to grain silos after Red Guards shuttered the complex during the Cultural Revolution. But first, he showed me, they used knives to gouge out the eyes of frescoed Buddhas and pockmarked their bodies with bullet holes.

Before 1950, when Tibet came under Communist rule, a quarter of its male population were monks; due to campaigns and crackdowns that jailed dissidents, the number fell precipitously, from 120,000 to 14,000 in the 1980s, before rebounding to three times that figure as the central government ceded the province a degree of self-rule promised in its official, administrative name: the Tibet Autonomous Region. Economic and not just political change diverted new clergy, however: Beijing heavily subsidized the province's budget, building infrastructure and modernizing social services. Increasingly, Tibetan families chose to place their sons not in the care of monasteries but in the public school system, where they learned Mandarin, a language that widened job and education opportunities in greater China.

The middle-aged monk guiding me around Samye said the provincial government was committed to restoring the complex to its original layout as a mandala, a geometric depiction of the universe. I stared at piles of gravel, muddy paths, crumbling walls, and the collapsed roof of the temple representing the sun. The universe had a long way to go.

Silently, the monk led me to a towering statue of Avalokiteshvara, the Bodhisattva of Compassion, with eleven heads and one thousand hands. A painted eye stared from each palm. "Look, isn't that beautiful?" He waved a candle, sending shimmering rays up the statue's hands. "It took a lot of people a long time to repair this," he said. "Look at it now."

I slept alone in the pilgrim's hostel, and woke before dawn from an ethereal sound: a monk blowing a guttural longhorn to summon his peers for prayer. I climbed the rickety stairs to the roof to find that the Milky Way had arrived too. The darkness pulsed from the brightest dome of stars I had ever seen—pinpricks of light so dense and close I felt I could run my fingers through them. "Hello!" a voice called in English. I leaned over the edge to see, filing into the cavernous prayer hall, Samye's resident monks. I counted three of them.

Food poisoning. That's what eating at unfinished temples got you. I fell ill on the return to Lhasa, where a doctor gave me a bottle of morphine tablets and advised I fly to Chengdu immediately.

China Southern Airlines' in-flight magazine quoted a tourism official who dismissed concerns about the propriety of vacationing in the Land of Snows. "The best way to understand Tibet is to travel there," he insisted. Though of course not quoted in this article, the Dalai Lama had made a similar statement, urging people to witness Tibet's culture and China's impact upon it.

Life in Lhasa spun around poles of tradition and development, religious and secular life, autonomy and subservience. In the rebuilt temples, monks often pointed at the closed-circuit surveillance cameras and whispered in English: "All I do is smile for tourists, never study my texts. We are like donkeys now."

In three weeks I didn't meet a single Chinese person who spoke Tibetan.

At Chengdu's Traffic Hotel I checked into a shared triple room, praying I'd have it to myself, so I could occupy the bathroom long enough to gather the strength to walk to a travel agent and buy the cheapest return ticket to America. The desk clerk transcribed my Chinese name from my little green residence permit booklet. "Mr. Plumblossom!" she said, suddenly. "We have a message for you!"

This was a first. Who knew I was here? Had someone died? The clerk showed me the number the caller had left; it began with 010, Beijing's area code. The job! I waddled carefully across the lobby and sat at the desk that held a push-button phone and a timer. Calling the capital cost 5 yuan (60 cents) a minute; the clock started ticking when the school's principal picked up. I nervously counted the fare as she spoke for fifteen minutes without pause, all without offering me the position. She said the school had hired another American but rescinded the offer after the secretary had heard the man had sexually harassed women at his previous Beijing school. From her desk drawer the principal had retrieved the résumé I had pecked out on my manual typewriter and mailed two months before.

The principal had called Neijiang Teacher's College, who said I had left, and then phoned the Peace Corps office, who said I went to Tibet. They told her to leave a message at the Traffic Hotel, Chengdu's cheapest lodging that took foreigners, where volunteers usually stayed. She had called just that morning, fearing she had missed me for good. Never have I been more thankful for food poisoning.

Until this moment, I had not thought about staying in China or what staying would mean. There was no careful consideration, no deliberation about how this opportunity fit my master plan. In populous Sichuan, I learned to act quickly and unconsciously. If you wanted that train ticket, that cut of pork, entry through that closed door, or that job, you pushed forward and grabbed it.

The principal said she needed an answer immediately. The school would provide a plane ticket. Also a bicycle, a coffeemaker, a computer, and an Internet connection. She asked why I was laughing.

"These will all be new things to me."

"This isn't the countryside," she promised. "This is Beijing!"

CHAPTER 7

Tomorrow Will Be Even Better (but Today Things Will Just Get Worse)

A FTER AGAIN HANDING the grim agent the tissue-thin paper that asked the capital's arrivals to self-identify for "mental confusion" and three types of psychosis (manic, paranoid, and hallucinatory), I collected the same duffel bag that I had carried to Neijiang two years before. Everything I owned fit inside, even the Compaq laptop and Rollerblades I had bought with what remained of my final Peace Corps payment.

"No other baggage?" asked a man holding a sign with my name. Behind his wire-rimmed glasses I noticed the familiar look that said, *Will this person cause trouble for me?*

The man was Chinese. I reacted accordingly and went through the routine I'd perfected in Sichuan, fawning over the introduction, saying I'd heard so much about him, how nice it was to meet at last, how hard he must work as the school's business manager, how sorry I was for troubling him to fetch me, and, oh, had he eaten?

His mouth became a bemused, tight-lipped bend. It was the look of a man fending off a hyperactive dog.

I kept barking. "What's your Chinese name? Don't worry, I'll be able to pronounce it. I've spent two years in Sichuan."

"Just call me Mac," he said. "As in Macintosh."

"Like the raincoat?" In Neijiang, my students' names often had unexpected origins. "Wellington" named himself after the boots, not the duke who defeated Napoleon.

Mac's eyebrow shot up quizzically. "Mac. Like the computer."

Departing the airport in his red Citroën hatchback, he honked around a swarm of Volkswagen Santana taxis and onto the airport expressway. I had never seen so many foreign cars in China; Sichuan cabbies usually drove flimsy domestic Xiali sedans. Now the road was lined with billboards for more overseas companies: Siemens, Ericsson, Nokia. Aside from the arrow-straight line of cottonwood trees bordering the road, and the faded-paint billboard announcing BEIJING WELCOMES YOU, nothing looked Chinese.

"Where's Tiananmen? Are we going past it?"

Mac waved out the windshield at the brown cloud. "We're going a different direction."

"I was told the school was near everything."

Mac laughed. "It's near many things. It's near the Summer Palace, the Old Summer Palace, Peking University." He saw my face fall from the realization that we were headed for the suburbs, and added, "The air is much better out there."

I stared out the window at people flying kites from the patches of grass between sprawling overpasses. In the sodium-vapor yellow light, next to open pits and bamboo scaffolding and swirling dust, the people looked small and disposable. Neon flashed from the side of the road: CHINA-JAPAN FRIENDSHIP HOSPITAL, ASIAN GAMES VILLAGE, MEAT PIE KING. A sign pointed to the Great Wall Expressway. *We're heading toward the Great Wall?* I said to myself. *I thought the school was downtown.* I did not know then that Beijing has no downtown; it has neighborhoods.

Mac steered around blue Liberation trucks. Their open beds were loaded down with sand, oil drums, and migrant laborers clutching shovels. "There are your *lǎoxiāng*," he teased. The word meant a "fellow townsman." In Sichuan—where daily I heard "our China" and lots of "*Lǎowài!*"—I believed that *us* meant "Chinese," and *them* meant "foreigners." But Mac's joke introduced me to the capital's divide. Beijingers blamed *wàidì rén* ("outsiders") for the city's ills, even if the migrants were the ones building the place.

I had landed on the drafting table that was Beijing. Here airport, here cropland, *here*—running graphite along the edge of a ruler—the highway into town, here the city itself, at the heart, the Forbidden City and Tiananmen. Around *that* the city wall. Don't want a wall? All right, let's erase it. There! An expressway in its place. The Second Ring Road. These X's mark the old gates. They'll be intersections! And *here*—the hollow hiss of sharp pencil on paper—a *Third* Ring Road. Why stop there? Let's make a Fourth. One day a Fifth! Now, we'll need some axis roads in between—the cutting echo of the pencil's point—we'll get rid of all this *old* stuff. Say, how about a subway?

We rolled through a stoplight—Neijiang had none—and turned onto a narrow road that ran a gauntlet of poplars. On the dirt shoulder, people sat around tables engulfed in steam. "Hot pot," Mac noted. "Very different than the kind you ate in Sichuan. You dip the food in sesame paste, not peppers." He said Beijing was cold-climate cuisine: wheat, potatoes, thick plum sauce.

I stared out into the flat darkness. "Everything here looks different from Sichuan."

"This isn't the countryside," Mac said.

It looked more desolate. There were no people. There were no stoplights. There were no vehicles. We approached a metal archway that said: WELCOME TO SHANGDI.

Translating the name, I asked: "*Shàngdì*? God's place? Heaven?"

"It's really not that." The name, Mac said, was a sales pitch to lure companies and residents north from the city center. "It's a 'high-tech industry development zone.'" He pointed at a field of satellite dishes, angled upward. "The government says the moon above Beijing shines brighter because of the signals beaming from here."

I leaned against the window and looked up. Darkness. I felt marooned, and more isolated than in Sichuan.

Mac turned into a complex of look-alike four-story white-walled apartments. In the stairwell he stomped his foot, activating the lights. My duffel scraped shoe-printed cement walls past windowless, triple-lock steel doors. This, at least, looked familiar; at night Chinese apartment entryways look as foreboding as the walk to Room 101 in George Orwell's *Nineteen Eighty-Four*.

"This is it," Mac said, depositing me in a ten-by-ten cement room.

"Good night." To open the window, I brushed a mound of sand off its sill. The grains spilled in an hourglass stream to an empty bookshelf, and then down to the bare concrete floor. I skritched between the three rooms, sand clinging to my bare feet. More fell when I cracked the fridge. Unlike my former campus, this neighborhood had no restaurants. My Mac-provided dinner would be pickled radishes from Sichuan, cans of Tsingtao beer, and a brick of silken tofu.

The only sign that the apartment had been previously occupied was a map of Beijing hanging on the door. My eyes began at the Forbidden City at its center, followed the blue ovals of its bordering lakes northward, then moved diagonally west to the broad patch of green and blue representing the old and new Summer Palaces. Shangdi, and my apartment, lay somewhere beyond them.

I was off the map, in this tiny concrete box. It was decidedly a step down from the Peace Corps. I emptied the fridge and ate with a plastic fork in bed atop humidity-damp sheets, regretting the decision to come.

Sunbeams tickled my eyelids at 5:00 a.m.; compared to Neijiang, farther west, Beijing's day broke early. Over the next hour I heard, in increasing volume, the *thunk-thunk-thunk* of sledgehammers, the tinking of chisels, the rumble of trucks. In Neijiang, I had woken to the squeals of pigs. I swept away the fresh-fallen sand from the sill and leaned out a patio window. Below, groups of grannies in loose sleeveless shirts sat gabbing on stoops, a child attempted to ride a training-wheeled bike, and a garbage collector in a white surgeon's mask pedaled a flat-bed tri-wheeler. I seldom saw bikes in Neijiang, a hilly river town, but Beijing was built on a basin, as low and flat as a griddle, where the North China Plain met two mountain ranges.

"*Bùtián, bùyào qián!*" an auntie called. *If it's not sweet, I don't want money!* Muddy oranges and apples piled atop her cart. She slipped on a Beijing fashion accessory, blue canvas sleeve protectors to keep the dirt off her shirt, and watered the fruit with a spray bottle, sluicing off the ever-falling sand.

On the corner, mirrored in the ice-blue windows of the vacant New Technology Center, a spry elderly man fluidly stabbed at his reflection with a sword, practicing the ancient martial art *tàijí*. Three teenage girls sat in his shadow, fumbling with their own Rollerblades. As I laced up and chatted with them, no one called me *lǎowài*, nobody shouted a three-octave *Hel-lo-o!* In the west, the afterthought of a full moon lingered over the line of mountains, showing three shades of green.

Before pushing off, I bought a *yóutiáo*—an "oil stick," or Chinese doughnut—from a stout jolly man whose white cropped hair matched his threadbare cotton tank top. This was another difference: in Sichuan, male cart vendors commonly went topless or rolled their shirts above their bellies. In Beijing, they wore the same stretched-out white singlet, even after the neck sagged to their stomach. "You like *dòuzhī*?" he asked. "What's *dòuzhī*?" It's what Beijing people drink! It's mung bean juice." He watched me write the word in the notebook I carried. "I'll get you a glass. Sichuan people don't have it."

I understood why. A steamed chicken foot tasted better than the sour, dreggy liquid. The man laughed at my contorted face and cursing. "You talk like a Sichuan person! That's really something: a foreigner who sounds like a farmer."

I had learned Chinese not in a classroom but by mimicking the people around me. To a Beijinger's ear, this sounded as doubly discordant as a Chinese person speaking Cockney English would to mine: the face didn't match the language, and the dialect was barely intelligible too. Until this morning, I wasn't aware that the Chinese I had spent two years mastering would make many Chinese people laugh. Thus began a process of over-writing my Sichuanese, mimicking Beijing's slurpy dialect, which appended a back-of-the-throat *r* to the end of many words. Saying that something "is fun"—*hǎo wán* in Mandarin—became *hǎo wáhrrrr*. I aped these sounds; within a few months Chinese people outside the capital would laugh at the foreigner who spoke *Běijìnghuà*.

"I studied English in middle school," the vendor continued. "That was forty years ago." He switched to a staccato voice: "Gah-ud morn-neen, tea-ah-che. Tea-ah-cher? Er, er, er." He flipped back to Chinese. "Beijing people always say *er*. Why can't I say it for teacher? Maybe my teacher was from Sichuan. Sichuan people can't talk."

In perfect Sichuan dialect, I spat: "Fuck you looking at, moron?"

The man's belly rippled from laughter. "Very good!"

I wouldn't have attempted the joke down south without bracing for a punch. But in Beijing, I would learn that any target was fair game. Beijingers have thick skin, and routinely mocked themselves and their city. A popular Beijing pastime was complaining about life in Beijing. Propaganda around town promised TOMORROW WILL BE EVEN BETTER. Listening to locals, you heard the city's shadow slogan: BUT TODAY THINGS WILL JUST GET WORSE.

As I skated in slow loops, the vendor pointed me toward Tiananmen Square, fourteen miles away. All I had to do was follow the traffic south and aim for the smudge in the distance. On the road, I weaved in between idling yellow *miàndi*, taxis named for their bread box shape. It would have been easier to climb atop one and skate from roof to roof.

When the traffic hugged the curb, I moved to the paving-stone sidewalks, skirting the orange fiberglass pods that hooded pay phones. A person using one looked like she was being swallowed by a malevolent ladybug. Next I caromed off a sack of empty plastic water bottles being lugged by an elderly picker and ducked underneath shuttlecocks flying between rackets in a round of morning exercise. They were the least of my worries; drivers fed up with clogged lanes steered over the curb and lumbered along the side-walk, sending the badminton players scattering like startled pigeons.

I grew up skating in Minnesota, and felt as comfortable on blades or wheels as in shoes. I had never been seriously hurt in hockey and had never fallen, not even once, on Rollerblades. In my first hour skating in Beijing, I'd stumbled through a pile of donkey manure, over a crate of smashed beer bottles, and off a bumper of a swerving *miàndi*. Then I fell, windmilling onto a grass median. I looked back to see what got me. I'd never seen roadkill in Sichuan, because there wasn't anything left to run over. Yet there it was, an unfortunate buttermilk snake, stretched flat in the morning light. I looked closer. An unrolled condom.

At the Jishuitan subway stop, I turned east and then south at Deshengmen, one of two remaining watchtowers of the imperial city wall, built in the fifteenth century but pulled down beginning in the 1950s to make way for the first subway, then the Second Ring Road. I imagined archers concealed behind the four-story tower's gray bricks, taking aim through slits at the traffic jam below. It was 6:15 in the morning.

Now I was within the Second Ring; there exists no First, although older locals remember the trolley that looped the Forbidden City palace, whose route was dubbed the "Ring Road." The Second Ring Road's beltway marks the border of "Old Beijing," an area of twenty-five square miles, equal in size to Manhattan, with a population to match. But while a walk through New York's core can be a neck-craning, shoulder-bumping scrum, crossing into Beijing's center felt like veering from the city's brisk current into a languid channel.

London and New York grew organically from ports, and their waterfronts still hum with beehive energy. Landlocked Beijing began with a planned design of walls and streets surrounding the Forbidden City's throne room, and even now, a century after the last emperor abdicated, the city's inner core exudes a courtly pace. Partly this is due to the string of five man-made, willow-shaded lakes at its center, which the imperial designers called "seas" (*hǎi*), to represent the emperor's far-reaching dominion. They had survived the Mao-led industrialization era, but so did the feeling that the city was made to be a garrison. In addition to the 165 foreign embassies, plus the municipal, district, and neighborhood government offices, all of the country's national ministries and Communist Party branches were headquartered here, along with the largest of China's seven military regions: an estimated three hundred thousand soldiers charged with defending the capital, as well as the nation's border with Mongolia and Russia. A stroll through Beijing's leafiest neighborhoods revealed a series of ENTRY FORBIDDEN signs, and guards manning closed gates.

But what really set Beijing apart from other Chinese metropolises were its *hútòng*, the narrow lanes that lattice its heart the way canals crisscross Venice. Lined by contiguous gray exterior walls of courtyard homes, the *hútòng* were built at a 1:1 ratio, as wide as their single-story houses are tall. Beijing's inner city hugged residents close, shielding them from the chaos outside.

For two miles I glided down tranquil lanes past red-painted wooden doors, until reaching the Forbidden City, whose glazed yellow roof tiles glowed from the morning sun. The air changed to heavy and wet. The clock atop the old Telegraph Building chimed seven times. Then it played the lilting melody of "The East is Red." I recognized the song from Neijiang's campus call to morning exercises.

After skating past Mao's portrait, I clunked downstairs under Chang'an Jie—the Avenue of Eternal Peace—and back up the other side. Tiananmen Square, WHICH ALL PEOPLE OF NATIONALITIES OF CHINA YEARN FOR, the sign announced. It didn't finish the sentence. Instead, it warned, in Chinese and English, that the square must be kept "solemn, silent, clean and in good order." To these ends, a few activities were prohibited: "parade, assembly, speech, writing, distributing, posting, hanging and spreading of words and propaganda materials."

Skating had yet to be forbidden, although a newly posted sign added, quizzically, NO WALKING. I pushed off, excited to race across the world's largest plaza, over eight football fields long and five across. My wheels barely got going before hitting the space between paving stones. I lifted up and tried again. Nothing. The divots were wide and deep. I skate-walked to the spot where I had read you could still see marks left by the army vehicles that violently cleared the square of protesters eight years earlier, on the morning of June 4, 1989. But the only evidence, set amidst the dust-colored flagstones, was patches of new ones, looking as smooth and white as bone.

At the square's center, rusty bolts the size of dinosaur vertebrae rested against lengths of scaffolding, to be erected to display red placards declaring CELEBRATE THE CHINESE COMMUNIST PARTY'S FIFTEENTH NATIONAL CONGRESS and CELEBRATE THE FORTY-EIGHTH ANNIVERSARY OF THE PEOPLE'S REPUBLIC OF CHINA.

I pulled out a notebook. An old man renting kites watched me writing and said, in Chinese, "You are writing."

"I am writing," I replied.

In Sichuan, whose history included several famines, a stranger would ask if I had eaten; in the sparsely populated rural Northeast, I would be greeted by "To whose family do you belong?" In know-it-all Beijing, people opened a conversation by stating the obvious. *It's hot. It's Friday. You are leaving your house.*

A shadow fell across my notebook. The man leaned over the page.

"What are you writing?"

"I am writing words."

"You are writing words," he echoed. "Not Chinese characters. Foreign words."

"English words."

"English words," he repeated. "See them?" The man pointed to a group of young men sidling toward stationary tourists. "*Biànyī*. Be a little careful." He tugged at his shirt.

I had never heard the word, and was never good at charades. What did the tug mean? Chinese is a logical language, however, and I broke *biànyī* in two. *Biàn* meant plain. *Yī* meant clothing. Plain. Clothes. The man's shirt tug. Plainclothes police! After *dòuzhī*, the vile bean drink, *plainclothes* was the second Chinese word I learned in the capital. Both were Beijing specialties.

I tucked the notebook away. The plainclothes officers looked exactly alike. Each had a crew cut, a nondescript face, a short-sleeved white collared shirt tucked into tan slacks, and thick-soled black shoes. Each carried a rolled-up newspaper. Every now and then one would talk into it, hold it up to his ear, then speak into it again. A man who looked exactly like him would approach, point to someone, then walk away. The men would have been less conspicuous in starched blue police uniforms.

On the ten-story cenotaph at the square's heart, Chairman Mao's calligraphy read, "Eternal glory to the people's heroes!" In English only, the sign at the monument's steps warned: NO URINATION.

By 9:00 a.m., it was too hot to remain in the square. I clacked down the steps and skated through the tunnel under Chang'an Jie, clacking back up steps to emerge before the rostrum that displayed the twenty-foot-tall portrait of a purse-lipped Chairman Mao. Just beyond his gaze, people stretched out on the stone benches lining the sidewalk that bordered the Forbidden City's southern wall. I went to sit on one when a man fussed, "Wait, wait, wait!" He unrolled a *People's Daily* and draped a page over the stone. "Sit on that, it's cleaner."

The man stood beside a homemade cart of two bicycle tires, a platform, and a rusty oil drum that spilled a sweet aroma. "*Hóngshǔ*," he announced. I shook my head. I didn't understand. He fished with tongs and pulled out a burnt brown lump, wrapping it in a torn square of *People's Daily*. He mimed peeling back the skin and taking a bite. My third Beijing word: *sweet potato*.

How much did I owe? He weighed the potato on a hand-held bamboo scale, just as Neijiang's mailman used to determine postage. Two yuan, 25 cents. (Other things that two yuan bought in 1997: a twenty-ounce bottle of Yanjing beer, a subway ticket, two local newspapers, and four domestic stamps.) I paid for another yam and bought a cob of roasted corn from another vendor. In a few years freelance sellers like these would be harassed off Beijing's streets by officials—appointed from faraway provinces, and so migrant workers themselves—who felt they harmed the city's image in the eyes of foreigners. Who, of course, traveled here to see exactly this sort of cultural heritage, enlivening the dead, museumed kind, such as the Forbidden City.

I leaned against its wall, which rusted my white Replacements concert T-shirt with vermillion dust. Traffic hummed behind the cottonwoods that shielded us from the Avenue of Eternal Peace. Another man, walking in relief against the red wall, pitched ices. "*Yī kuài yī gè'r, yī kuài yī gè'r!*" One for a yuan. Then, barely audibly, he finished, "*Kuàngquánshuǐ'r liǎng kuài.*" Mineral water, two yuan. His sales pitch reminded me of sitting in the bleachers, watching a baseball game. Beijing's street scenes then looked just as enthralling. The man called out loud and quick, his Beijing r's as thick and chewy as my sweet potato. I rolled its steaming, sweet pulp from one side of my mouth to the other, trying not to burn my tongue.

Around me, indifferent men and women sprawled on the benches atop *People's Daily*, smearing yesterday's events with today's sweat. An auntie walked past selling hand puppets that squeaked. I breathed in the sweet smell of yams and corn, the water seller's lilting call, the shrill punctuating cry of puppets; the wet air and still trees and traffic and lines of tourists running their hands along the red fortress wall; the clatter of construction. A drowsy male voice asked for the time.

"Ten minutes to ten."

Twelve hundred miles south, in Neijiang, the campus vegetable market was packing up. A boat or two moved lazily upstream. The dough sticks and soymilk got tossed in the slop bucket for the pigs, and dollops of pork were being wrapped into lunchtime dumplings. Building Socialism, the morning's first class, was being dismissed. A pinched voice crackled from the loudspeaker, reading the day's headlines from "our nation's glorious capital, Beijing."

Now I lived here, where the news was made.

CHAPTER 8

THOUGHT LIBERATION

THREE DAYS LATER, on a bright Monday morning, I followed directions and walked past the rebar-sprouting foundations of unbuilt high-rises, turning into a dirt lane that wound through a right-angled maze of redbrick lean-tos occupied by migrant workers. A few farmers held on in this far corner of the city: I angled right at the soybean fields, then dodged tractors and horse-drawn carts to an open-air produce market. This was Beijing? Save for the mountains brightening in the rising sun, it looked like a dustier version of Neijiang. Where was the school?

I heard the sound of electric guitars, and noticed that the only men around me not wearing blue serge "Mao suit" jackets instead sported black jeans, blacker T-shirts, and long black hair. A sign on a rust-flecked gate said MIDI SCHOOL. Later, I would learn that it was China's first conservatory for modern music, including jazz, blues, and rock. It would merge, like this neighborhood, into the Beijing mainstream, but in this moment I saw only the incongruous sight of chain-smoking headbangers loitering in front of a decrepit building covered in the ubiquitous white bathroom tiles, grimed by the Beijing dust.

The music school occupied the first story; the New School of Collaborative Learning perched on the two floors about it, absorbing every cymbal crash and bass line. My feet pulsed as I walked up the stairs.

The woman who had found me at Chengdu's Traffic Hotel turned out to be a middle-aged American speaking in rapid, comma-free, stream-of-consciousness sentences. After introductions, Stephanie said: "You'll teach grade six and seven and eight and nine and ten too."

Five grades, I noted mentally. I had been hired as the language arts teacher, which meant five different curricula and five books going at once. Not noticing, or ignoring, my surprise, Stephanie continued: "You'll teach social studies: Chinese history, American history, Chinese economics, American economics, Western civilization, and ancient civilization." I waited to hear, "And the Beatles." Instead, Stephanie said I would also oversee the yearbook and Model United Nations.

"You were in Peace Corps!" she said with a jaunty, can-do nudge. "This won't be nearly as hard as that must have been."

Stephanie opened the door to my classroom, a large space with a wall of windows that looked south toward the Summer Palace. "The other desk is your team teacher's. She's Chinese. You speak Chinese."

I spread sheets of paper on the floor and sat in the middle with a pen, plotting topics and objectives for each class. At noon, Mac came by to take me to lunch. I said I was going home for *xiūxi.*

"*Xiūxi?*" He fought back a laugh.

"In Sichuan, we take a break from noon until three."

Mac shook his head. "In Beijing, we take a half-hour lunch and go back to work."

At the restaurant, I complained about the bland, oily fare. The sweet-and-sour pork tasted candied, the palace-style chicken had more fried peanuts than peppercorns; my lips did not go numb. No one drank beer. No one smoked or spat or hollered *xiǎojie* (miss, as in waitress) when they wanted another dish.

Adjusting was even more difficult than when I had first arrived from the U.S. I thought I had acclimated to China. Now Mac said, "Sichuan is not China." But in my eyes, Beijing was the outlier.

That night the phone rang, resounding off my apartment's concrete walls. In Chinese, the voice asked for "Dān Dān." I said he had the wrong number. "I'm an American. I don't know that person. This is my house." The man said the woman's English name, Frances, and then added, "You're a foreigner? I thought you were from Sichuan."

The school only had eight teachers, balanced between Chinese and Americans. Will, one of the other Americans, was also new, having just finished a Peace Corps tour in Jamaica working in special education. He looked like the agency's poster boy: a fleece-wearing Vermonter with wire-rimmed glasses, wispy blond hair, and hiking boots, the kind of person grandmothers were moved to feed. He had applied to the same classified ad in the Peace Corps newsletter as me, and he had spent a semester in China in 1991, six years earlier. But he felt as out of place as I did, struggling to match what he saw with what he thought he knew.

Will was the "upstairs teacher," meaning he was in charge of kindergarten and first grade. I envied him. To prepare for class, I spent my time poring over history texts and novels. Will hung paper-cuts and made sure the paste pots were full. His co-teacher wasn't back yet, and so he didn't want to plan without her. As we walked to play basketball, he mentioned that she was traveling alone, down in Yunnan province. Her name was Frances. He wondered what she was like.

"Someone keeps calling my house asking for her." Now I wondered what she was like too.

At week's end I arrived for the staff meeting to find everyone around a table. Will sat next to a woman whose shoulder-length black hair framed her tan oval face and brown eyes, which lit up when she smiled. Unlike most women I knew in Sichuan, her hand didn't reflexively cover her mouth when she laughed.

As if in church, the assembled teachers did as they were told and together recited the school's creed: "To create a learning community in which students begin to grow into thoughtful, innovative members of the global community through an energetic pursuit of knowledge that is grounded in fundamentals, self-awareness, and an appreciation and respect for the world over."

Stephanie welcomed everyone back. "Turning all poison into medicine is the key!" she began. "Being able to see our good sides as well as our bad sides enables us and our students to develop wisdom and strength."

The woman beside Will interrupted. "What's your point?"

"Aha! My point, Frances, is that we help the students create value in their lives. Students want their education to be meaningful, right? When it's not, they don't care about it. So choose instructional techniques that enable them to take charge of their own education. Right?"

Frances nodded. We all nodded. Stephanie inhaled and plunged back in. Everybody nodded. The meeting was over. It all sounded like bromides to me then, but Stephanie's vision was clear: my students would go on to graduate from Stanford, Princeton, Wellesley, Northwestern, Berkeley, Michigan, and other top schools, becoming doctors, diplomats, designers, and academics. I went back to my classroom to write ten unit plans. Before I left, at around eleven that night, I walked upstairs to find Will and Frances at work.

"I think a man has been calling for you at my apartment."

"My big brother. I forgot to tell him I moved. Thank you."

I walked back downstairs. Her face filled my mind. This was a first: in two years in Sichuan, I never looked up the Chinese words for *attraction*, for *going on a date*. There was simply no need.

Frances stopped by my room after school. She laughed at my Chinese name and said her own wasn't much better, because Dān (from "peony") sounded lovely in Chinese but like a boy's name in English. She chose Frances after the saint from Assisi.

She asked for a book to borrow for the weekend. Recently she had read the new Chinese translation of Milan Kundera's *The Unbearable Lightness of Being*, and another bestseller, from the bookstore's burgeoning self-help section. "I asked the clerk for a book about the meaning of life." He handed her *How to Find Eternal Happiness*. "Controversial!" promised the cover. It said the author had been exiled from India and now lived in London. The jacket photo showed an aged man with a long white beard. "So he must know the answer," Frances had reasoned.

The first page, she told me, announced that depression came from denial of desire and pleasure. The author's solution, she said with a laugh, was simple: "Have as much sex as possible." She turned to page two. The remainder of the book explained, in throbbing detail, how three to five minutes of intense orgasm would result in three to five days of inner peace. That was how, the author averred, he had found eternal happiness. Frances wanted her money back.

I looked at the tower of required reading piled on my desk and pulled out Jack London's *Call of the Wild*. She asked why, and I launched into lecture mode. She listened but couldn't get in a question. Finally, exasperated, she said, "You talk too much! You never let anyone else say anything."

My students in Sichuan would have let me finish, giggled "Thank you my dear sir," and shuffled out the door.

She noticed my photographs of Tibet taped to the blackboard.

"Why did you go to Tibet? It looks depressing. This summer I hiked Tiger Leaping Gorge, in Yunnan. I went by myself. It was a lot different than I thought it would be. Very developed. All those stupid yellow arrows painted on the rocks, telling you what guesthouse to go to."

I was silently amazed. My students in Neijiang hardly went across the river downtown by themselves, let alone the length of the nation for a monthlong trip. And on my own hike through the gorge I had also hated those painted arrows defacing the trail.

That afternoon Frances joined Will and me to play basketball after school at the nearby Language and Culture University. Afterward, Will went home and Frances and I walked to McDonald's for a milk shake. To her the restaurant was old hat, but I was excited by its novelty, since none had existed in Sichuan. Our conversation continued over dinner, where we ate hot pot—thin slices of mutton boiled in water and dipped in sesame paste—at an outside table, beneath the stars. I never saw stars in Neijiang for the blanket of clouds and fog; Tiger Autumn in Beijing brought warm winds and clear, sharp skies that burnished the plane trees and turned the asphalt lustrous. Chinese cities look better at night, when people, not brutal buildings, dominate the view. The darkness shrunk Beijing's imperial grandeur and Socialist superblocks into lamp-lit, intimate neighborhoods, dimly beautiful. Life spilled onto the sidewalks and streets. Around us sang televisions, radios, and card games, kept in time by the syncopated thumps of drums that accompanied aunties fanning through the yānggē'r, the "Rice-Sprout Song." The folk dance was a popular nighttime exercise for middle-aged women. Frances watched it with a frown. "When I was in middle school we had to do the 'Rice-Planting Dance.' Big, fake smiles and joyful movements. But I lived on my grandparents' farm in the Northeast when I was a little girl. Planting rice is hard work."

Frances said that she learned a lot of songs in school. "Downplay American Imperialism" began "Socialism is good! Socialism is good!" I followed her bouncing head as she sang, before stopping from laughter. At dinner her mother used to tell her seriously to finish what was on her plate, because there were starving people in America.

Her dad had been a People's Liberation Army medic, posted to a midsize Northeastern town an overnight train ride from Beijing. Her oldest brother, the man who had phoned my apartment, had graduated from the provincial university with a degree in computer science and decided to *xiàhǎi*, or "jump into the sea," as the bold—and then rare—leap from a guaranteed "iron rice bowl" job was known. He bought a train ticket far south to Shenzhen, a new city Deng Xiaoping decreed a "special economic zone." Shenzhen could emulate the capitalism of colonial Hong Kong at its border. In 1991 he found computer work at a trading firm, which trained him to be among China's first generation of stockbrokers working the floor of the Shenzhen exchange that opened that year.

Frances's second brother finished high school and followed him south. Her sister married a local man who turned out to be an abusive adulterer; divorced, she moved to Beijing to attend the fashion design academy, where she fell in love with a Japanese classmate. After all of this, Frances's parents did not flinch when their teenage daughter told them she wanted to be an artist. Was that all? She could study with a tutor after her high school day ended.

Two classmates joined her to split the cost. They copied figures from art books—ruddy-faced miners seen through the lens of socialist realism. Their bleakness mirrored the dark Lu Xun stories they read at school. Like many Chinese teenagers, her favorite books were Jin Yong's martial arts serials, where the bad guys were punished by heaven, and the heroes Mistake Yang and Little Dragon Lady stood up for the bullied.

The drawing tutor had graduated from a Beijing art school, and returned home to look after his parents. He said it was really a simple thing, this jumping into the sea. The hardest part was making the decision to leap.

An idea grew inside Frances. She had already finished her core classes. What if? Her sister was in Beijing, and she could share her dorm bed. What if she went? Other art classmates had gone to the capital to study. What if she went to Beijing? She was now sixteen. That wasn't so young: her tutor went when he was sixteen, and her father had joined the army—leaving Yibin, Sichuan—when he was that age.

He. He, he, he. But she was a she. There were two rules a girl got drilled into her. One, don't leave home. Two, if you must leave home, don't leave your hometown.

Frances asked her older cousin, a man who had traveled and now held a steady job, to raise the idea with her father. The cousin came over and cooked the family dinner. She sat between them at the table, as anonymous as the net on a Ping-Pong table, over which their words flew.

She has talent and is smart, her cousin volleyed. *You left Sichuan when you were sixteen.* Her dad backhanded that one. *Beijing is a big place. It's not safe.*

The match dragged on. Frances lost track of the score. Finally, she told her dad: *I want to go, it's important to me that I go, and I would prefer it if you supported me.*

It felt strange to talk about moving to Beijing in such a resolute manner. The capital was more than a big city: it was the magnetic center of government, culture, education, and history. Just to visit the city for a weekend was a thrill of a lifetime most Chinese then would never know. To move there, study there, maybe even work there? Frances wondered if years of reading Hong Kong martial arts fantasies had poisoned her mind with happy endings.

Her father asked, *Will you take care of yourself, value and respect yourself, and not let anyone take advantage of you?*

Frances nodded.

She graduated high school early and moved to Beijing, eventually enrolling at a university known for teaching Chinese foreign languages, and foreigners Chinese. The campus itself was small, but shaded by pine and poplars. At its center, students mixed at the basketball courts, volleyball pits, Ping-Pong tables, and badminton nets. English books and newspapers filled the large library. On three sides of campus, under a canopy of branches and the shade of trees, rows of booksellers, music stores, money changers, and restaurants competed for students' yuan. For the first time Frances tasted sushi, Korean cold noodles, American hamburgers, English fish and chips, and Indian curry.

Her English proficiency also rose; never underestimate the impact of a teacher. A Boston native named Kathy did not make her students recite vocabulary words and phrases; she made them have actual conversations. One day outside class Kathy asked Frances, "What do you want to do with your life?"

She felt a jolt. No one had ever asked her. She stayed quiet until they sat on the concrete bleachers that overlooked the scrubby grass soccer field. Africans kicked balls across the pitch to their Chinese classmates.

"I don't want to just make money." Frances hesitated, then decided to say it. "I want to do something useful. Development work, like start a nonprofit organization for Chinese girls, to give them the opportunity to leave their village and go to school."

Kathy nodded. "Sure, you can do that. You can do anything you want to."

Americans didn't understand anything about China.

One night over a pre-graduation dinner of hot pot with a circle that included her sister and her friends, Frances heard about a potential job opening at a new school founded by the wife of an American diplomat. Instead of sending their two kids to a traditional international school, the woman created one where they could learn Mandarin and Chinese culture in tandem with an American curriculum.

The next day Frances was nervous to cold-call the school. She had no pedagogical training. But the thought of her only offer—working as a secretary for her older brother's friend—depressed her, and high heels hurt. She walked along the crowded sidewalk of Xueyuan Road past small shops advertising PUBLIC USE TELEPHONE. At the fifth one she stopped, bought a warm bottle of Yanjing, took a gulp, picked up the receiver, and dialed.

Stephanie, the school's founder, answered. She had hired a Montessori teacher from New Zealand, but needed a Chinese teacher to work alongside her. Had Frances worked with children?

Americans amazed her. So direct but so welcoming at once. They scheduled an interview for later that afternoon.

The *miàndi* wouldn't take her north to Shangdi, since no one would flag them down for a ride back. Shangdi was strictly a one-way fare. Frances waited for the one bus that ran out there—she had it to herself—got off, and stood in an isolated patch of the capital where soybean plants outnumbered people. She heard "Purple Haze" blaring from an electric guitar and followed the notes into the battered building, past the Midi School of Music, and up the stairs to her interview.

A Chinese woman wearing an expensive, silky dress passed her on the steps. "Excuse me," Frances asked, "where is the New School of Collaborative Learning?"

"Oh! I just came from an interview there," the woman said, eying Frances's T-shirt and sandals. "I think I got the job. I have a master's in educational psychology. How about you?"

Frances felt the urge to leave. But she continued upward, meeting Stephanie, who looked delighted to meet her. They entered a large carpeted classroom. Pillows, colorful stuffed toys, and puzzles filled the floor. A door opened to a rooftop patio that faced the Fragrant Hills.

Frances arrived empty-handed. She didn't have a résumé. She didn't even have a purse. Stephanie did most of the talking. Americans always did most of the talking. Frances nodded and smiled.

She told Stephanie her preferred English name; Stephanie spoke little Chinese but was learning alongside her teenage son and daughter. She talked about them, about purposeful living, about Confucius, about John Dewey, about values, about—and here she lost Frances—the Israeli-Palestinian peace process. At last Stephanie asked, "Where are you from?"

"*Dōngběi*," the Northeast, the region formerly known as Manchuria.

"Oh! I used to live in Japan."

Frances was unsure what to say to that. As a child she had played near "Ten Thousand Person Pit," a mass grave from the Japanese occupation.

Stephanie talked about possessing a sense of self, about knowing who one was and where she stood. Could Frances imagine where she'd be in five years, what she'd like to accomplish? Could she feel the earth turning beneath her feet?

Frances blinked and said nothing. Then she realized that Stephanie was serious. This was the interview. What did she have to lose? She said that she wanted to work in development, in education, not as a secretary. But she did not have a master's in education.

"Which is why I want to hire you," Stephanie enthused. "I need real people working here. I need heart and a willingness to learn. I don't want trained robots citing research instead of doing the right thing. This is a new school. That's why I called it that. I need new thinking. I can tell you are a real human being. Not fake!"

They went downstairs to the school office, where Frances signed a two-year contract at $200 a month, much less than the secretary job paid. But she was elated. Two years guaranteed in Beijing, a chance to use and improve her English, and a new career. All of this in the span of a day.

Sitting outside in the cool autumn night, a steaming hot pot cauldron bubbling between us, Frances thought *my* Beijing arrival story was the remarkable one. "Stephanie found you at the hotel, after you got sick in Tibet. And you spent two years in Sichuan because Peace Corps called your American classroom and asked if you wanted to go?"

She had been to Sichuan only once, as a girl, visiting relatives on her father's side. He raised her on its spicy cuisine, which tasted especially warming when it was thirty degrees below zero in her native Northeast. That reminded me of my Los Angeles–native father making me spicy burritos through Minnesota's winters.

"I know a good place to hike at the Great Wall, without a ticket gate or chairlift or any tourists," Frances said. "Do you want to go?"

I wanted to go anywhere with her, immediately. In two years I'd had scores of students and hundreds of acquaintances. But sitting with her I, for the first time, didn't feel like a *lǎowài*. Perhaps it was because I didn't see her that way. She appeared to me as an intelligent woman, a co-teacher who cared for her students, a friend with a sharp sense of humor. Chinese, yes, but the border was shifting.

She was more cautious; she had never dated a foreigner. Foreigners could leave at any time.

At her insistence, we split the check. Then we said good night.

When I got home, my apartment felt unusually empty.

Frances told her roommate she made a new friend.

Neither of us could sleep.

On National Day, October 1, crowds milled around Tiananmen Square's red-and-gold flower displays, a red-trimmed Great Wall replica, and red banners whose characters, Frances explained, hailed "thought liberation." People wore red shirts and waved red flags; against this background, the white-shirted plainclothes policemen were even more conspicuous than usual.

Frances wanted to show me where three hundred years of what seemed to be the impenetrable power of the great Ming dynasty ended one day in 1644. Rebel armies from the south and Manchu forces from the Northeast converged on Beijing. The emperor called for his servants and none had answered. He killed members of his household with a sword, exited the Forbidden City, walked up Jingshan (Prospect Hill), knotted a silk rope, tossed it over a locust tree branch, and hanged himself.

We walked to the spot through champagne-bright autumn air that smelled like roasted chestnuts and sweet potatoes. Locust branches shaded the stone path; the trees' leafy crowns formed a canopy over inner Beijing's narrow streets. Later I learned that the locust is also known as a scholar tree, and a pagoda tree, but because my little red dictionary translated 槐 (huái) as "locust," the word lodged in my mind. Unlearning is harder than learning—or, as Stephanie often told my puzzled teenaged students, it's easier to make an omelet from eggs than eggs from an omelet.

Locals called Beijing's center "a sea of green." It had only looked gray to me, the color of the hútòng courtyard walls, until I saw it from above. Jingshan was only fifteen stories high, made from the earth excavated for the Forbidden City's moat. But Beijing is so flat that from the hilltop you could see the entire palace, the lake of neighboring Beihai Park, the walls of the Zhongnanhai central leadership compound, and crane after crane after crane. Construction didn't stop on holidays. In the hútòng, the painted character 拆 (chāi, destroy) shone deathly white on gray courtyards.

Groups of tourists tromped up to the hanging tree for the obligatory snapshot. No sign noted that this was a replanted replica; during the Cultural Revolution, Red Guards were said to have chopped down the original, which the conquering Manchu had renamed the Guilty Locust, as if the tree, not their invasion, had caused the emperor's death.

Frances asked a man to take our picture. "Is he your boyfriend?" he asked in Chinese. She said it was none of his business. In Chinese, I said, "We're colleagues." The man said my Chinese was excellent. "Thanks," I replied. The man asked how long I had been in China, followed by the usual questions about homeland, height, and chopsticks.

No one in Sichuan had ever asked me, as Frances did, how often I had this pointless conversation each day. Too many times to count. She suggested that when a person praised my language proficiency, I should not say thanks, which sounded immodest, but reply, Nǐ gěi wǒ gǔlì, "You give me encouragement." After all, Frances said, the person probably wasn't really blown away by my Mandarin, but was just being polite. In Sichuan, no one had really corrected my speech or my manners. Soon we fell into the habit of bilingual conversations, speaking the other's mother tongue.

In Chinese, I asked her: "What do Chinese people think when they see us?"

In English, she replied: "Probably that I'm a slut. Or that I'm using you to get to America. What do the Westerners think?"

"That I'm a lucky bastard," I laughed. "Actually, they probably think as Chinese do."

"Or maybe they don't care; it's just interesting to see two different people together. Maybe we're having a good time, and they're on a miserable tour, so it's nice to look at us."

"Thought liberation! Do the stares bother you?"

"Not really. It doesn't bother you?"

After being called lǎowài every day for two years, an envious glance was a decided improvement.

In Beijing, people may have looked at us, but seldom made snide remarks. It was just those looks, those ever-watchful looks. It was exhausting, always being sized up and judged in a single glance. In some ways, however, we had it easy. Our co-teacher Will's wife was Japanese-American and just beginning to study Chinese. "Everywhere I go," she said, "people assume I'm Chinese, and can speak, and then curse me when I can't, and then call me other names if I say my family came from Japan. And then they look at pale Will, and back at me, and their eyes start on the other thing."

My two dozen students whoo'ed suggestively when they noticed us eating lunch together. After school we played basketball, or walked to the Summer Palace, or took the bus to Beijing Sammies, a café run by a young Canadian. It was the capital's second coffee shop and turned into a hangout for students, as there were no other places in town to gather around tables for hours.

American fast-food restaurants were as popular for their environment as their product; Chinese restaurants didn't let you sit as long as you wanted, didn't grant you the privacy of anonymity, and didn't have reliably toasty heat and frigid air-conditioning in a smoke-free setting.

Two cinemas operated in the university district, playing the same "official release" on the same schedule. The first movie Frances took me to was Zhang Yimou's *Yǒuhuà Hǎohǎo Shuō—Keep Cool*. An usher escorted us to our seats, the lights fell, and an announcement asked the audience to stand for the national anthem. Everyone remained seated.

Keep Cool opened with shots of Beijing's streets. *Miàndi*, destruction, construction, trebly rock music—it looked like it had been filmed the week before. Chinese movies I'd seen, and especially those by Zhang Yimou, such as *Raise the Red Lantern*, were set either in imperial times, the 1920s warlord era, during the Japanese occupation, or amidst the Cultural Revolution. These were safe harbors in which a story wouldn't sink from official, critical bombardment. *Keep Cool* started with a joke about the capital's migrant workers evading police, showed a new, dreadful high-rise apartment compound instead of a picturesque *hútòng*, and had a woman undressing to shame the ex-boyfriend who followed her home. A trend continued: my mental folder of things "Chinese"—in this instance, cinema—reorganized itself around the new entry.

The boyfriend, played by Jiang Wen—who later played an assassin in *Rogue One: A Star Wars Story*—is a likable lug of a bookseller who, in a street argument with an obnoxious businessman, accidentally smashes a passerby's notebook computer. The passerby demands compensation—but in a society without law, he's reduced to pleading with Jiang Wen, who's more concerned with regaining face from the businessman.

The audience laughed. I couldn't keep up with the dialogue. Frances whispered the translation in my ear. I understood the final act, however: Jiang Wen decides the solution is to attack the businessman with a cleaver. The cook emerges to take it back, but for once is unsuccessful. There was no happy ending; this was a Beijing story.

We walked home. The harvest moon shone bright in a cloudless sky, and as we passed the Physical Education Institute we noticed its wall had been dented with a toehold, a secret entrance for students returning after curfew. We climbed over and lay flat on our backs at the center of the cold, dead soccer field and looked up at the sky.

"It's funny," Frances said, breaking the silence, "stars look so close to each other, but actually they're thousands of years apart. The distance doesn't seem to be there."

She wasn't talking about the stars. But we kissed anyway. After a while we rose, dizzily, to get off the field before a security guard caught us. In the darkness, we retraced our steps and faced the flush wall. There were no toeholds here, only smooth, solid brick. We had followed a one-way route made for sneaking in, not for getting out. Trapped. Another Beijing ending. We cursed the indifferent wall, and kissed some more.

An estimated two hundred thousand workers died while building the Great Wall over centuries; in some sections their ground-up bones mortared the bricks. Two weeks after we managed to clamber over the P. E. Institute's wall, our bus wound through a valley bright with autumn colors. Frances told me the story that gave Huanghuacheng, the section of wall slithering along the hills above us, its name.

It literally meant "Yellow Flower Wall," after the woman whose boyfriend was press-ganged to the building site, where he worked to his death. Yellow Flower, taken by the emperor as a concubine, escaped the palace to claim her lover's body, only to learn that it had been entombed within the bricks. Grief-stricken, she wept tears bountiful enough to create a stream that swelled to a river, washing away part of the wall, revealing her man's remains.

Frances and I hiked uphill through thorny bushes to a crumbling section mortared more with sunlight than cement. The break allowed us to scale the wall's ten-foot bulwark. I was enthralled, mostly because this portion still remained. A stiff breeze buzzed saplings and brush sprouting from its sides. Patches of stonework had been removed, probably by neighboring farmers to fortify their homes. Tiny stairs pitched at acute angles. The wall doubled back upon itself, frequently twisting and turning down to a reservoir and back up the neighboring peaks. I couldn't tell which side was In and which was Out.

This section of the wall had not prevented the Manchu invasion that put foreigners on the Chinese throne in 1644, when the last Han Chinese emperor hanged himself from the Guilty Locust tree. Their armies had simply bribed sentries, or had a gate opened by a traitorous general. Border walls were a waste of resources and always failed; nature, history, and trade shoved people closer and closer together. That was what our generation thought: as teenagers—via television reports whose tone could not have been more divergent—Frances and I watched the Berlin Wall fall in 1989.

But where I saw the Great Wall as a forlorn relic, Frances saw a cultural marker. The wall's purpose went beyond keeping foreigners out, she said. It comprised multiple sections that marked territory between rival tribes and warring kings. In Chinese, the barrier is known as the Wànlǐ Cháng-chéng (the Ten-Thousand-Lǐ-Long Wall), a lǐ being a unit of distance equal to one-third of a mile. In fact, the line built during the Ming dynasty (1368–1644) stretched 5,500 miles, equal in length to America's border with Canada. As a child Frances had also thought it could be seen by orbiting astronauts. Like Yellow Flower's tears, that was just a legend: from above, the structure's tan bricks are camouflaged by the surrounding landscape.

Frances thought of the wall as a paranoid, protective fence to keep Han Chinese in—to set a boundary that said, *Everything within this is Chinese*, and thus under the emperor's dominion. She had grown up "beyond the pale," as land outside the wall was called, in the "great northern wasteland" where Han Chinese homesteaders opened its prairie as the last dynasty fell. Northeasterners still call China's south, including Beijing, *guānnèi*— "inside the barrier."

There had been no polished reconstruction at Huanghuacheng, as at other sections. The snaking wall shed rubble, looking simultaneously what it was—grand—and what it would be—dust. It was just us, alone on the wall with the mountains behind; no vendors peddled I'VE STOOD ON THE GREAT WALL T-shirts, a by-product of Mao Zedong's proclamation that one was "not a man" until one had stood on the thing. (He already had.) Nothing disturbed our hiking but the cold, late-October wind. It was a stunning backdrop for our first overnight date.

We slept in the village at the wall's base. The one restaurant didn't have much food; the owner set out a plate of freshly picked chestnuts, and made dumplings stuffed with fennel and pork—but mostly fennel. We followed the farmer home to spend the night spaced separately on his *kàng*, a platform bed heated underneath by smoldering dried corncobs. As a little girl, Frances had slept on one in her grandparents' Northeastern village; they burned rice chaff. After a while atop a toasty *kàng*, you started to smell like baking bread.

From the farmhouse windows the wall's outline was faintly visible. We grabbed a flashlight and climbed back up in the silent, starlit night. I had always thought of the wall as a cruel political mistake, or dismissed it as a prettified tourist site, but Frances was right: perched atop it, I felt entirely in China, a speck standing on its long brick time line. We came down out of the cold and went inside to simmer on the hard, hot bed.

CHAPTER 9

BEIJING SPRING

M Y APARTMENT BECAME a cement icebox at the first snowfall, on Halloween. I called Frances to ask how to turn on the radiator.

She laughed. "You can't. Beijing turns it on for you. The entire city is connected to the same steam system. The heat goes on November 15 and goes off in March."

I set out for school, crossing the snow-slick street without looking; on Shangdi's wide, straight roads you could spot a vehicle in the far distance, like a ship on the open sea. I turned into the warren of farmhouses. Several were not there. A parked dump truck accepted red bricks being tossed by workers. One of them had an inverted plastic bag on his head, fastened by wrapping the handle holes around each ear. The bag's corners stuck out like bunny ears—my favorite Chinese "native costume," to use the cloying term my sixth-grade students were studying in a unit about the country's fifty-six ethnicities. I asked the man what he was doing.

With his sledgehammer, he motioned to an exposed wall, marked with a white 拆.

"How much are you going to knock down?"

The man swung his hammer into a home's entry gate. The bricks went *oof*. A chunk of them cracked loose. The man picked up a chisel and hacked at their mortar. He set the unbroken pieces aside in a growing pile.

"Everything," he said. "This will all be developed into new apartments. We'll sell the bricks, though. They still have use."

My classroom windows overlooked the rubble. That morning, the eighth graders read aloud from the 1932 novel *Cat Country*, by the Beijing writer

Lao She. I had never heard of him until Stephanie assigned me to teach a semester-long unit of Chinese literature. The reading list included classic novels such as Wu Cheng'en's *Journey to the West*, starring the Monkey King, and Cao Xueqin's *Dream of the Red Chamber*, a courtly tale set in Beijing whose events paralleled the demise of the Qing, China's last dynasty. The books provided context for the changes we were witnessing; what felt wholly new to us was only a present-day manifestation of a history that cycled like the seasons.

Not every reading rang true, however. I began the course with Rudyard Kipling's poem "The Ballad of East and West." After reading its first line ("Oh, East is East and West is West . . .") fourteen-year-old Chris, from Korea, looked at his classmates—a girl from Queens, a boy from Beijing, another from Tokyo—and shook his head. "Man, the twain has *met*."

In their lives it was true. They were trilingual, well traveled, and unburdened by the past. They thought the Cold War was some battle during some winter. The Soviet Union was to them what Prussia had been to me at their age: a pink blotch on a map that no longer existed. The MX what? Sandiwhostas? For my students it was all as hard to imagine as using a rotary phone.

As they read from *Cat Country*, the muted sounds of toppled walls filtered through the windows. Lao She's voice reminded me of Mark Twain's, circa *The Innocents Abroad*. He thought his dystopian satire a failure, a story too cruel for his humorist heart. Now it read like a prophetic portrait of twentieth-century Beijing's turmoil. The book's narrator arrives in Cat City, capital of a land with twenty thousand years of history. Its citizens eat reverie leaves throughout the day, ogle foreigners in the capital's crowded streets (that is, when the foreigners leave their enclaves), believe in "Everybody Shareskyism," and worship Uncle Karl the Great. In an eerie premonition of the Cultural Revolution, Lao She wrote that Cat City's neighbors accuse each other of being "counterrevolutionary." Students tie up their teachers, taunt them, and threaten them with knives. Some children even murder their own parents. A Cat City survivor explains:

> You saw that teacher being slaughtered. That's nothing astonishing . . . When the teacher has no character, the students will have no character. And they do not simply lack character;

they are actually pushed back several thousand years, returning to the cannibalism of ancient times. Advancement of mankind is very slow, but regression is very fast. With the loss of character, men immediately revert to barbarism . . . When education can make men turn into wild beasts, you can't say it has accomplished nothing. Ha ha!

Lao She died three decades after writing those words, in the opening days of the Cultural Revolution. In August 1966, Red Guards belt-whipped the sixty-seven-year-old in the yard of Beijing's Confucian Temple. The writer's shirt was shredded from their blows; his blood splattered the placard they strung from his neck, branding him an "Unrepentant Counterrevolutionary." The next day Lao She's body was pulled from his favorite lake, nestled against the old city wall. His death was officially ruled a suicide. The wall is gone. The lake was filled in to build a subway station.

"Did they punish the Red Guards?" my student from Japan asked.

"Yes, the Gang of Four was responsible," answered his Chinese classmate.

It upset Ms. Zhang, my Chinese co-teacher, this pinning the responsibility on four jailed officials, including Chairman Mao's wife, arrested after Mao died in 1976. Ms. Zhang was a Beijing schoolgirl then. "A lot of bad things in China today come from the Cultural Revolution," she told the class. "Bullying. Looking out only for yourself. That anything old or traditional has no value and should be destroyed."

I looked out the window at the neighborhood being taken apart by hand. Maybe Beijing kept tearing itself down to bury its unexamined past. Memories didn't stick to the sleek sides of skyscrapers. Make the sofas thick, the music loud, the televisions large, the cars fast. Blur and round and smooth the past until it becomes as rumored as this disappearing *hútòng*. Older people will say it was there, they saw it. Their younger listeners will nod politely, unable to imagine something they'd never seen.

Ms. Zhang looked taciturn and tall, with waist-length black hair and oversized gold-rimmed glasses. She had played volleyball in college and taught with a coach's demeanor. We shared a classroom walled with south-facing windows and bookended by blackboards and cabinets holding English and Chinese texts. My desk faced the room from one side, Ms. Zhang's from the other. East and West met in the center, at the round table where we sat with students during lessons.

The New School of Collaborative Learning was bilingual and bicultural. Students—mostly expats whose parents were academics or businesspeople with longstanding ties to China—learned history in two languages, from two perspectives. In English, the Roman Empire spawned laudable engineering, literature, and art. In Chinese, the Roman Empire was the playground of landed men who conquered weaker nations and added to their treasure on the backs of slaves.

Class discussion was never boring.

But whereas our Western history studies spotlighted individuals, whose words we could read, whose actions we could debate, the Chinese history lessons felt as immutable as arithmetic. Numbers, not people, dominated discussion: the One Hundred Years of Turmoil (foreign colonization and mercantilism), the Twenty-One Demands (from militant Japan), the One Hundred Flowers Movement (a 1950s Party purge), the Three Difficult Years (the man-made Great Famine), the Ten Years of Chaos (the Cultural Revolution). But then the Gang of Four was sentenced to jail, and the Party pronounced that Mao's overall leadership score was 70 percent correct, 30 percent wrong. *That's a C–,* my grade-conscious students said, adding that their parents would disown them if they earned such a low mark.

Regardless, Ms. Zhang often stubbornly insisted, the number was the correct answer to an epoch's complicated calculus. She thought in blocks of cause and effect: because this period happened, this next one naturally followed. The eras were bracketed by years; the dash between the dates drew a line through the messy details. *When was the Cultural Revolution? From 1966 to 1976. Correct! Next!*

Yet Ms. Zhang also asked students to think about the period in which they lived. The events around Tiananmen Square had ended eight years earlier; had the demonstrators, in fact, won? Economic reforms had accelerated, travel and purchasing restrictions had been eased, and foreign exchanges had increased: Beijing looked more and more like an international city. Deng Xiaoping's death the previous year did not end this trend;

in fact, China was preparing its application to enter the World Trade Organization. Membership would require the country to adhere to rules it did not make. The United States supported its application during a time when politicians saw the country as a vast new market for American goods.*

Ms. Zhang, our students, my colleagues, and I were not aware we were living at the start of a stratospheric boom, one that in the next twenty years would make China the world's largest economy. Otherwise we would have handed our meager salaries over to Frances's stockbroker brother to invest in Chinese manufacturers. In the 1967 film *The Graduate*, the main character is advised that "there is a great future in plastics." In 1997 Beijing, I wished someone had pulled me aside and said, "I want to say one word to you. Just one word. Are you listening? Cement."

Still, the outward signs of growth were apparent, at least in Beijing. In 1989 you had to dial the city's one taxi company to order a cab. The 1991 movie *Woman-Taxi-Woman* shows a driver whizzing around the capital's empty streets, with little competition and even fewer fares: Who had disposable income for a cab, or even a place to go? Six years later, Beijing had two taxi companies—but seventy-five thousand cabs. Regardless, Ms. Zhang was thinking about buying a car; she was tired of waiting for the bus, tired of arguing with irascible cabbies over the best route to avoid traffic, tired of enduring the rolling fire that was a *miàndi*, whose interior filled with smoke from the driver's cigarette and the engine. The government encouraged private ownership to spur its domestic auto industry. Only 250,000 people owned cars in all of China then; in twenty years Beijing alone would have nearly six million vehicles—and those 75,000 cabs— gridlocking its streets.

One *miàndi* driver told me Beijing was becoming just like *mànhādùn*. I didn't understand. The cabby gestured up and down with both arms rapidly, leaving the wheel untouched. "This used to be trees. Both sides of the

---

*In fact, trade flowed primarily in the opposite direction: in 1996, China exported $51 billion worth of goods to the United States, versus $12 billion in imports, a trade surplus of $39 billion. In 2016 the surplus had increased eightfold, to $319 billion. Still, China is America's third-largest export market; the U.S. also has a growing surplus with China in services trade: $30 billion in 2015.

street. They were tall and covered the road with their branches. Now . . ." The *miàndi* fell into a pothole and climbed out the other side. "Computer companies! This is all Computer Street, Zhongguancun. Compaq, IBM, Founder, Legend, Sony, Apple."

In the first three months I had lived in Beijing, the just-finished road had been torn up and widened again. The latest generation of saplings took root, growing in a line as straight as the high-rises. The *miàndi* listed right, and I eyed the nearing sidewalk as he declared, "*Mànhādùn!*" The driver slapped the wheel left and lit another butt. "Lots of tall buildings, just like New York."

Manhattan. But not yet: as the driver sputtered along the tree-divided lane that passed the Old Summer Palace, he asked me, "Do you like honey?" He slowed and drove over the curb and onto the brown crabgrass. A Mao-suited old man stood beside the honeycombs he tended. The driver bought two mineral water bottles filled with golden syrup and handed one to me as a gift.

When he dropped me at home, I gave him a bill that he squinted at, crumpled, tugged, crinkled, and flicked. In Beijing, the crisp, hollow rap of money being slapped was as much a part of transactions as arguing over the price. The government had warned people to be vigilant of counterfeit cash. I had just changed my salary, paid in dollars, at a black market money changer's stall near the Language and Culture University; while the official exchange rate was eight yuan to one dollar, domestic limits on foreign currency deposits meant Chinese heading abroad had to sell yuan on the street. Some days the rate went as high as nine to one. The cabdriver handed me back the bill and declared it to be *jiǎde*. Fake. Take it to the bank to be sure, he advised, as I handed him a different note.

I brought the money into a local branch, where a clerk wearing a necktie sat tabulating deposit slips with an abacus. In Neijiang, I usually interrupted the teller's knitting.

"I think this is fake." I slid the bill under the glass.

The teller examined it under a blue light. "Correct." He pounded it with a red CANCELLED stamp. Without looking at me, he dropped the note into a drawer and turned back to his counting. I blinked, feeling had. In Neijiang the People's Bank had run out of money; in Beijing, it took money from you.

*

Our school only had one written rule: Be a *jūnzī*, a gentleman, in the Confucian sense. This meant taking responsibility for your own actions, demonstrating courtesy and respect, and doing unto others as you would have them do unto you.

The curriculum called for hands-on work. Unlike in Neijiang, where I was forbidden from taking my students outside, Ms. Zhang and I were free to plan field trips. We led our history class on an overnight train 350 miles south to Qufu, Confucius's hometown in coastal Shandong province. This was where the Master, who lived from 551 to 479 B.C., developed his rules for social order and happiness. The emperor ignored his teachings; Confucius was denied the status-raising government post he so desired. Yet, for two thousand years, the moral code of his *Analects* formed the moral underpinning of Chinese society. After 1949 the Communist Party demanded total fealty. The Cultural Revolution gutted Confucian temples, such as Beijing's, where the author Lao She was beaten. Red Guards also attacked Qufu, ransacking its temple and adjoining cemetery that held Confucius's tomb, ringed by the graves of seventy-seven generations of descendants.

Our class arrived to find, on banners strung above the Confucius hotel, over the Confucius bowling alley, in front of the Confucius karaoke hall, and on the door of the Confucius wine shop, the Master's saying: IT IS WONDERFUL TO HAVE FRIENDS FROM AFAR! Also: WE ACCEPT VISA.

Qufu's Confucian Temple isn't a single building but a maze of large halls, bell towers, dragon-carved columns, and rickety cypress trees. I spent the day hectoring my students to get off the backs of the oversized stone-carved turtles sunning themselves in the courtyards.

To my chagrin, my pocket book of Confucian sayings didn't have any sayings about protecting heritage (or turtles). Instead, I silenced the students' complaints with: "'In the presence of Goodness, one need not avoid competing with his teacher.'" Teenagers, however, usually get the last word. In a monotone that suggested she had rehearsed and pocketed the line for just this moment, a sixteen-year-old Chinese-American girl replied: "'Real knowledge is to know the extent of one's ignorance.'" She theatrically bowed to her classmates' applause, and asked me for extra credit. (Given.)

We rented bikes and rode under a canopy of crooked cypresses on a packed-earth trail that wound through the Confucian Forest. Headstones and grave mounds hugged the path. Eventually, we reached Confucius's grave, a simple hill of raised earth fronted by a slab carved with the characters for "Sacred Father."

An incense burner smoldered in front of the mound. Beside it crouched a man painting cherry blossoms onto rice paper. *Lovely*, I thought. And it was, even after he tried to sell me the work. "I paint these all day," he said, pointing to a rolled-up stack tucked behind a cypress. "Tourists love them."

In the coming years, the Communist Party would market itself through Confucius. By 2016 nearly five hundred Beijing-funded Chinese-language teaching centers named Confucius Institutes opened on college campuses around the world. A Party boss called them "an important part of China's overseas propaganda setup," or soft-power push. Chinese public schools, meanwhile, pulled down old Marxist slogans and replaced them with Confucius's exhortations of filial morality and adherence to order.

Reviving the legacy of a man who died 2,500 years before was easier, and easier to control, than bringing up the bodies of the recent past. The demonstrations centered at Tiananmen Square were, officially, a "counter-revolutionary uprising." Members of Tiananmen Mothers, a support group for victims' families founded by a philosophy professor and Party member whose seventeen-year-old son was killed, lived under de facto house arrest.

Beijing had museums dedicated to archaeology, art, aviation, geology, money, police, revolution, science, war, and dinosaurs—but not one for the Cultural Revolution. Instead, a restaurant commemorated it.

The themed eatery, Ms. Zhang said, was near our school and within walking distance of Peking University, where students turned Red Guards kicked off the decade of destruction. I imagined a décor making use of the big-character posters plastered on walls during the Cultural Revolution, exhorting upheaval. Only now they would announce the day's specials. I recognized the restaurant's name—Village Facing the Sun—from the faded propaganda on a Neijiang farmhouse, and Mr. Wang's explanation that the sun was Chairman Mao.

"I don't like this place," Ms. Zhang told me before we stepped inside.

To her, the notion of eating under reminders of suffering sounded about as appealing as picnicking at a concentration camp. A waitress led our group down a narrow corridor lit only by uncovered forty-watt bulbs. Painted propaganda images of lantern-jawed peasants, bumper harvests, and smoking factories lined the walk. Students gasped entering our clammy dining "cell," wallpapered with yellowed newsprint. The datelines read 1966, 1968, 1972—all front pages from *People's Daily* during the maelstrom.

A 1966 editorial proclaimed, "Long Live Mao Zedong!" The chairman launched the "Great Proletarian Cultural Revolution" to solidify his control of the party, and China. Schools shuttered, urban students found themselves "sent down" to the countryside to labor on collective farms, and workplaces purged their "class enemies," with the accused imprisoned or murdered. In Beijing, the first month of the campaign was now known, simply, as "Bloody August."

Articles from two years later depicted hordes of pig-tailed, Little Red Book–waving teenage girls on Tiananmen Square. One front page, plastered on the ceiling, dripped venomous commentary attacking the writer Lao She. A student from Beijing stood on a chair, craned his neck, and read the article aloud for the class. Lao She was an "enemy of the people" whose words were "poison to the masses."

I asked the boy if he knew that Lao She died not long after that article appeared. He nodded and said with a smile, "People were crazy at that time."

Ms. Zhang scolded him. "Not 'people.' We! Beijing people, Chinese people, were crazy at that time. We're all responsible for what happened. If the Japanese had done this to our country, you would be told to memorize the dates of every attack, number of victims, and damage to cultural heritage."

The student, age fifteen, blinked at her in disbelief. Ms. Zhang asked what his parents had told him about that era. "Nothing," he admitted. Was their silence born from willful blindness, or from shame? Ms. Zhang said that most people focused only on the future, especially earning money, which bought personal freedoms.

The restaurant itself exemplified this: its owner said she chose its theme for reasons other than politics. She told us her small, state-provided apartment had been cluttered by her husband's Cultural Revolution memorabilia collection. She wanted her space back, and her husband wanted to make money. They struck upon the idea of the restaurant. He combed antique markets for even more old newspapers, Chairman Mao badges, and pictures, while she chose an old standby for the menu.

"The most popular cuisine in Beijing is home-style—*jiācháng*—cooking," she said. That meant familiar, comfort food.

To my teenaged students, there was nothing familiar or comforting about the steaming platters being placed before them on rough wooden tables. "Back then, we never had meat," Ms. Zhang explained. The students' frowns sank deeper as waitresses presented rolled-up grass balls, flash-fried wild roots, and pasty corn cakes. "This is what suffering means to them."

The students yelped at the arrival of Steaming Ant Soup.

But then, being hungry teenagers, they warmed to the fare, challenging one another to sample the crispy pigskin, battered willow leaves, and fried crickets. Ms. Zhang stuck to rice.

The scorpions came last. Tossed alive into salted boiling water, the creatures were then fried in chili oil. They tasted like a chopstick-pinch of crispy ash, which evaporated on the tongue, leaving a faint aftertaste of wasted money.

Watching the students taunt one another with scorpions, Ms. Zhang wondered if they weren't actually learning the mad behavior of the Cultural Revolution after all.

In December, I mailed what was essentially my last stamped piece of correspondence from China. After more than two years of writing and sending letters home, I now kept in touch via e-mail, thanks to my apartment's NetChina dial-up Internet connection. "Amazing," I wrote my mother. "Transmission is instantaneous. I press a button and it goes right to you." Still, my application to graduate school had to be sent via the post. No one in my family had gone to graduate school, and my application was a spur-of-the-moment decision, made a few days before the deadline. Being around international teachers for the first time made me realize that people with masters' degrees earned more.

Frances, on the other hand, rightfully wondered why the foreign teachers were provided housing, vacation bonuses, and salaries multiples higher than her own. Why did her Chinese colleagues keep their heads down and tolerate it? When she asked her countryman Mac why, at a school with *collaborative* in its name, she was paid less than the Americans, he replied: "You are Chinese! We treat you like one."

She seethed as he pointed out that she made far more than she would at a Chinese school. Plenty of teachers would love to take her place. Also, the school was a nonprofit and was barely getting by. His MBA classmates were off making their fortunes, but he stayed to oversee the school's finances because this was a cause first, a job second. One stayed loyal at any cost.

Frances fumed. The wealthy and educated loved to lecture those below them about sacrifice. She wanted to continue her education, too, to study art in France. But the weak yuan and its inconvertibility at banks meant her salary equated to even less when she changed it on the black market.

We watched the postal clerk weigh and use a meter—no more colorful, fish-glued stamps—to process my oversized envelope to the University of California at Berkeley. The woman looked at us and blurted, "You two will have a beautiful child."

I asked how she knew. "Because mixed children are always good-looking." Chinese people often said that. I meant how did she know we were a couple?

We didn't advertise our relationship, but we didn't hide it, either. The school knew, our friends knew, my neighbors knew: an auntie called our principal to report that she saw us laughing together on the sidewalk. In China, I knew to be wary of an unhappy person with a grudge. Frances, on the other hand, told me to introduce myself to the woman the next time I saw her. It worked; before long, she was promising me that the two of us would have beautiful children.

After classes ended and our students went home, Frances and I planned lessons together, had dinner, and often went to hear new Beijing bands such as New Pants and Brain Failure at a club called the Busy Bee. Other nights we shopped near the south gate of Peking University, where pirated movies could be purchased in storefront back rooms. The suspense while riffling through the cardboard boxes of films, hoping to find one you wanted, was exceeded only by the occasional yell and then dead-bolting of the door as the room fell silent until the police had passed and the all-clear sounded.

Frances had formerly shared my apartment with the school's secretary before they moved farther away. Now she reclaimed it, a few nights at a time.

Once the winter cold settled in, our date repertoire expanded to ice skating. Groundskeepers at nearby Tsinghua University cleared snow from its island-centered pond, and flooded it daily. They hung lights and rolled in carts selling roasted chestnuts. A perfect rink. For a Minnesotan, this was winter bliss. A small but noticeable subset of Beijingers loved to skate. It made me realize how many lakes dotted the city, man-made remnants of imperial parks and palace moats. The capital looked prettier during wintertime; the snow dusted the piles of gray *hútòng* rubble and construction site dirt. People bundled themselves in colorful scarves and forearm padding. Kunming Lake in the Summer Palace became a wide sheet of ice, and it was open to skaters for free, as was the Forbidden City moat. We rotated our destinations, often meeting students there. I liked watching Frances, and them, and the rest of the city. Life in the capital was crowded and competitive, but on the ice the anxiety melted away. Beijingers looked as at ease on skates as they did on bicycles. It was a rare moment of being truly alone, and in control. In a city where you couldn't even turn on your own home's heat, it made a novel impression.

One January night at Tsinghua University, I sat on the pond's edge, lacing up. It was below freezing and only a half dozen skaters were out. The floodlight wasn't working, so the ice was a pale mirror of luminous moonglow. People flowed in the same direction, pushing and grinning and steaming. Then gliding and laughing, then turning. My eyes followed Frances, going around and around and around. The man selling chestnuts asked what I was so happy about. Only then did I realize that my face was frozen in a love-struck grin.

As the calendar turned to 1998, indecision became the third person in our relationship, an anachronism in new, go-for-it Beijing, like the aging Lada sedan you occasionally saw stalled on the Second Ring Road, snarling traffic. Frances pressed pause, not wanting to entwine herself with a person who would leave China, if not soon, then eventually. Over dinner, I asked if she would consider applying to university in the United States. It was an innocent and sincere question: in a rapidly changing country where nothing was guaranteed, she, like many Chinese, looked ahead and planned for contingencies.

When I had accompanied her to the local police bureau to renew her Beijing residence permit, I complained that the bureaucracy, in place to restrict the number of migrant workers, was a controlling nuisance. Was it really necessary to present to the cops a manila envelope stuffed with a letter from the school confirming employment, her household registration card from her hometown, her marriage status card, and a letter from her landlord confirming a fixed abode?

"I think of it more as insurance," she said, "to protect myself. I understand they need to control the quantity of people here, or everyone would want to move to Beijing. Nobody's ever asked me to show the permit, but it's good to have it just in case."

Frances operated on "just in case." One never knew what would be needed and when—so cover all bases, just in case. The previous month, she wrote to a family friend who had studied in Hawaii, asking how he found the experience. "The main difficulty in studying in the U.S.A. is to get a visa," he replied. "I believe that your goal will be reached as long as you keep trying, don't give up. The road to abroad is a long way, and sometimes is rough. You should be patient. Many of my friends took years to come out."

I was excited. I thought it was encouraging. Frances said the man misread her letter; she wasn't asking for advice. Enrolling in an American university was just a thought, like when you pick up a guidebook to a faraway place and flip through the pages, thinking, *Perhaps one day . . .*

Yet, at my apartment's dinner table, she shook her head when I wondered if she would apply to go to the States. "I would never get a visa," she said. "I'm single, and can't prove that I have any ties to China that would make me come back."

"Would you?" I asked innocently.

"Of course!" Her face flushed with anger. My apartment stifled as the nonadjustable radiators hissed malevolently. Frances opened the bedroom windows wide to the January air. "You shouldn't say things like that. You sound ridiculous, thinking Chinese people need to saved and brought to America so they can be 'free.' I'm perfectly free here. I don't want to go to America. I don't want your charity. I don't need your help. I'm not comfortable with this anymore."

"With my cooking?" I asked, trying to cool things down.

"With all of it!" She was livid. "We don't owe each other anything. I want to end this; it's over."

"Are we breaking up?"

"Yes! Speak Chinese! Why am I yelling in English? Speak Chinese!" She switched tongues. No language is as cutting as Angry Chinese.

After she left, I sat stupefied at the table, heartbroken but understanding.

I flew to my grandmother's house on Monterey Bay over winter break for a family gathering. China stayed close to mind: I couldn't casually flip through the *Santa Cruz Sentinel*; I nervously scanned for articles datelined China. Was the country still there? When I walked back through the doors at Beijing's airport, I was surprised to see a clamorous crowd. People cheered, some wept. Frances stood there, too, and ran to give me a rib-crushing hug.

The Air China flight was seven hours late: on the runway in San Francisco, the pilot announced it was raining, so we could not take off. The Chinese passengers mumbled "*Méibànfǎ*" (Nothing can be done) and sat back down. The Americans rolled their eyes and sighed, "*China.*" Through the plane's little windows we watched jets taxi and go. Later, for an unexplained reason, we descended and deplaned in Shanghai before continuing on to Beijing.

"Your plane was supposed to land last night," Frances said. "They didn't tell us where it was. We all waited overnight, gossiping about the worst. We thought maybe the plane crashed and they didn't want to tell us until they knew for certain."

The unnecessary drama, so typical in China, nonetheless revived our flatlining coupledom. We agreed to keep planning on multiple tracks while inwardly knowing that the chances of staying together were slim. We had reached the resigned state of *méibànfǎ*.

In February, at the Chinese New Year, Frances took me to my first temple fair, a traditional winter carnival of costumed dancers, acrobats, magicians, face painting, a snake lady, a haunted house, and fried food served on sticks. It reminded me of the Minnesota State Fair, to a point. The carnies running the shooting gallery games ushered in the Year of the Tiger by encouraging marksmen to take aim at pictures of tigers. You scored highest for blasting the animal in the heart and head. Top guns won stuffed tigers.

Nearly subsumed by the din of exploding caps was a man announcing it was "Save the Tiger Year." He solicited money for anti-poaching programs in China's Northeast, where the few Siberian tigers clung to their habitat. People—kids, mostly—stuffed bills into the man's donation box, an empty water cooler bottle. Then they moved on to target practice. Did one hand know what the other was doing?

"Don't take everything so seriously," Frances said. "It's good that they're raising money to protect tigers. I've never seen that sort of charity before. Maybe every year they'll protect the zodiac's animal."

"America could have used a Year of the Bison," I allowed.

An unseen hand flicked off Beijing's steam heat in mid-March, when the unseasonably warm weather was matched by an unusually tepid cultural climate. Western media began reporting on "Beijing spring."

The first Chinese production of *Waiting for Godot* debuted in the capital. In its review, the city's daily evening newspaper noted that the play "captured the dilemmas of market socialism." One of my students said the play's name should have been changed to the Chinese for *Waiting for the Bus*. Now there was an existential dilemma to which Beijingers could relate. Would it come? Would there be room? Did it even exist? My students noted that *Godot*'s "Nothing to be done" perfectly translated as "*Méibànfǎ.*"

On the political stage, China's newly appointed premier, Zhu Rongji, gave frank press conferences—uncharacteristic for a high-ranking official— that recalled the no-nonsense mien of 1980s Deng Xiaoping and his coterie of reformers. A former Shanghai mayor fluent in English, Zhu introduced popular policies to spur private enterprise and home ownership. Less popular, not least among the 40 million laid-off workers, was his command to close unprofitable state-owned enterprises. Rumors actually circulated in Beijing that armies of hammer-wielding unemployed men would descend on the capital, attacking civilians. I thought people were confusing real life with the popular Qing dynasty sword-and-cavalry soap operas that aired each evening on Beijing television, but then I realized that the middle-aged people spreading this rumor had lived through, or had been, Red Guards. Suddenly the story didn't seem so far-fetched.

An artist named Zhang Dali admitted to being responsible for the spray-painted heads on the ruins of Beijing's *hútòng*. His name was everywhere in the city media, though not on the police blotter. A graduate from Beijing's Central Academy of Fine Arts, the nation's top painting school, Zhang left China for Italy after Tiananmen. In the three years since returning to Beijing, he'd spray-painted two thousand heads around town. He titled the citywide exhibit "Dialogue," as in a conversation between Beijing and himself. Officially, Beijing did not respond, although art dealers began cutting out entire walls holding his work and selling them at auction. (Another word I wish someone had told me then: "Art." If only we had had the money and foresight to buy our peers' paintings, as Gertrude Stein advised Ernest Hemingway in 1920s Paris.)

The *hútòng* neighborhood between my apartment and school became a flat, open swath of dirt. While walking to class I noticed three pits ringed with clay-mottled soil. Two were rectangular; one was shaped like a key. No ropes cordoned off the scene. The *miàndi* and buses breezing down Shangdi Road didn't stop to stare. I ambled over the lip of a pit to find several carefully carved layers that ran ten feet deep. The floor was made of interlocking bricks. Bulldozers rumbled across the lot. Frances imagined the holes were cold storage cellars for the farmers' homes that formerly filled the land.

We continued toward school, weaving between the numerous other pits. One had brick designs of a table and chairs. Another showed patterns on its sides. A man surveyed the scene.

The Chinese archaeologist, as thin as a whip, wore a yellow mesh baseball cap that said, in characters, CULTURAL RELICS BUREAU. He smoked patiently as a crew of four cloth-shoed women scraped away at the soil. "I don't have much time." He motioned to the earthmovers parked nearby. "These will all be buried next week. *Méibànfǎ*."

Shangdi's "high-tech industry development zone" was being built atop what two thousand years ago had been a developed settlement that possessed technology. All told, the bureau had gathered more than a thousand artifacts, including pottery and tools.

My history class heard *tomb*, and the students' collectively gasped "Cool!"

hung in the classroom air as they abandoned their textbooks, stampeded downstairs, and ran to the site. One after another they rushed up to me holding stones, swearing they'd found a tooth or a spearhead stained with blood.

"Um," I said, peering carefully at a dusty shape, "that's a Marlboro butt."

The archaeologist lit another and let the kids explore. His team had already cleared the open tombs. Their only tools were a core sampler and four shovels. They had taken a *miàndi* to the worksite. The driver had run out of receipts, so the archaeologist would not have the fare reimbursed. "*Méibànfǎ.*"

I said that in America the site would delay, if not cancel, the proposed development. The archaeologist stabbed at the tan soil with the core sampler. "Your America is two hundred years old. I could drop a shovel anywhere in Beijing and find something older than that."

He said the magic number: China had *five thousand years of history*. A ground filled with toppled cities, and innumerous graves.

My students swarmed in the pits, letting scoops of loam fall from their hands as in an hourglass. Magpies squawked in the warm sky above them.

"I used to think living in China was boring, but, man, was I wrong!" exclaimed a student from Korea. We returned to school and resumed our history class, whose textbook seemed even drier than before. I began taking the students on walks instead; Beijing was the best lesson, even as it pulled itself down.

In March, Frances and I went to Haidian Book City in search of better teaching materials. College students squatted in the aisles, paging through programming manuals, a translation of Samuel P. Huntington's *The Clash of Civilizations and the Remaking of the World Order*, and biographies of Bill Gates and Leonardo DiCaprio, star of China's months-long box office champion, *Titanic*. "The poor passengers suffer at the hands of the rich," reported the *Beijing Evening News*, "and love between a rich girl and poor boy is forbidden." Its reviewer identified "class struggle" as the story's main conflict. He did not mention the one between Iceberg and Ship.

I was shocked to see a book on sale about Neijiang, *The Battle Between Virtue and Vice in the Kingdom of Heaven*. It chronicled the smashing of a crime syndicate that ran drugs and prostitutes during my time there in the Peace Corps. I flipped to its insert of mug shots to see if I recognized them: perhaps Mr. Wang was really a notorious thug! In focusing on the workaday routine, had I myopically missed all the signs, and the bigger story? But, no, my former English department chair was not the Sweet City warlord known as "Dragon Head."

Among Book City's bestsellers that spring was *Huǒ Yǔ Bīng* (*Fire and Ice*), a collection of critical essays on Chinese culture and politics. Its publication, and Book City's success, suggested that more than the capital's lakes were thawing.* Peking University hosted a conference on the translation of Friedrich Hayek's *The Constitution of Liberty*, a polemic against socialism that previously had been banned as apostasy.

A Hong Kong paper reported a rumor that the frigid relations between the Chinese government and Dalai Lama had surprisingly warmed. A planned meeting was rumored at Wutai Shan—Mount Wutai, or Five-Plateau Mountain—one of China's four sacred Buddhist peaks. Located in a remote area two hundred miles southwest of Beijing, the mountain's forty-two monasteries had largely survived the Cultural Revolution. Among them was one of China's most venerable wooden structures, the 1,200-year-old Foguang (Buddha's Light) Temple.

The meeting with the Dalai Lama would be scuttled, and my previous experiences at Chinese holy mountains—namely Mount Emei, the terminus of my violent bus ride—had been anything but enlightening. But our school's spring break was starting, and the days were warm and bright. I wanted to keep researching travel articles; that spring I received in the mail a copy of the *Los Angeles Times* travel section that ran, on two full pages, my article about the trip I had taken a year earlier, to Tiger Leaping Gorge and the Burmese border. It paid more than I had earned in a full year of the Peace Corps. Soon I was flipping through the *Writer's Market*, a phone book–sized tome that listed addresses of publications that accepted unsolicited submissions. Travel in China was cheap; I realized that I could write my way out of impending graduate school debt. I could also improve

---

*Though not for long: its author, Yu Jie, was later arrested and allegedly tortured for pro-democracy activism; he and his family emigrated to the United States in 2012.

my Chinese by interviewing people, reading local histories in the language, and spend more time with Frances, on the road.

We took an overnight train to the provincial capital of Taiyuan, and then caught a bus that seemed—to me—to contemplate a plunge as it edged over the ten-thousand-foot range to Mount Wutai.

The sign over the monastery gate advised: STUPID CONFUSED NAÏVE. It was, a monk explained, how pilgrims should orient themselves before they embarked on contemplation. I copied it to hang above my classroom door. It could also be posted in the International Arrivals hall at China's airports as fair warning.

A packed-earth trail over a frozen waterfall took us down the hill and set us on the road to Dragon Spring Temple. Crows flapped into the courtyard's eaves as we ducked inside a hall. A monk worked quietly at his calligraphy, dipping a horsehair brush into an inkpot and touching it to rice paper in vertical columns. I said it was beautiful work.

"This? You can have it." He placed the paper in my grateful hands. It said: *Hong Kong returns to the embrace of the motherland.*

In the village, the crisp mountain air filled with incense as monks made preparations for morning prayer. A shopkeeper handed me the only map of the area on sale on its hundred-yard-long main street. The map was printed on a handkerchief, and the monk demonstrated how to use it by holding it to his nose. A few doors down, the village's largest store flew a cotton banner proclaiming MONK'S FASHION DESIGN FACTORY. Its mannequins showed a man draped in a brown robe, and a woman draped in an identical brown robe. A hostel checked us in without a second glance and showed us to our room without demanding to see a marriage certificate. The bathroom was a shared hole out in the courtyard, and there wasn't a shower. There were probably some negative aspects, too, but to us it was perfect. We were together, away from Beijing. The future became irrelevant, the past an overnight train away. That left us firmly in the present, in a secluded monastic mountain town.

At noon, a high-pitched wailing reverberated from Illustrious Breakthrough Temple. A packed house of three hundred farmers sat rapt in its courtyard. Cymbals crashed and sticks clicked as an evil duke in a white mask galloped onto the stage. The crowd hissed. Kids sitting on the lip of the platform dared the duke to come near. When the performer did an impromptu grimace in their direction, they shrieked and leapt from the stage. After the opera finished, the performers, still in flowing blue-and-yellow costumes with faces painted red, white, and black, mingled in the audience. The fifty-five-year-old man who played the villain had been studying this local form of opera since age fourteen. "We tour the province and provide these shows for free," he said. It was an attempt, albeit a losing one, to preserve traditional Chinese culture in an age of satellite dishes. Just being here for a day reminded me how quickly Beijing made one forget about rural Chinese life. "You're lucky to catch us. But to really see something, come back tonight. We're doing an opera that's eight hundred years old."

The evening performance outdid that afternoon's in spectacle. The audience was all groundlings: Mao-suited men squatting on haunches and shawl-layered women sitting on stools carried from home. Candles illuminated the courtyard and its shrines. A slide projector scrolled the lyrics on banners of silk hanging beside the stage, prompting the audience to sing along. Not even a village-wide power outage or surprise snowfall could stop the performance. In the darkness, through the drifting flakes, the show carried on.

The next morning, as our minibus wound up and down peaks toward Buddha's Light Temple, snow floated around the trimmed birch trees lined up in the fields to make telephone poles. How lovely, we thought, a light dusting. The guidebook said our journey was only ten or so miles. We had plenty of time to make it from our guesthouse to the 1,200-year-old temple and back.

The guidebook was off by a lot. Had its researcher even come here? This is what happens when you listen to a foreigner, Frances said. Three hours later the bus stumbled, backfiring, into a one-road village, shuttered by the snowstorm. It was too late to turn back; there was nothing to do except see the ancient temple. As we stood in a foot of fresh powder, a lone teenage monk said the wooden prayer hall was built in A.D. 857, making it one of China's oldest extant buildings. (In Europe at that time, Vikings pillaged and an Old English poem recounted Beowulf battling Grendel.) We stepped gingerly in the monk's snow-denting footprints, trying to keep our running shoes dry. He led us under towering pine trees and inside an unlit prayer hall holding statues of three seated Buddhas ensconced under a ceiling one hundred feet high. The monk sidled into an alcove, leaving us alone.

Sequestered on this peak in the falling flakes, I heard the loudest sound in China: silence.

From the tall doorway, the snow-filtered sunlight barely lit the cavernous hall. The view outside showed only a blur of white streaks. The monk, meanwhile, never returned. Frances said we should go.

Our minibus sat empty on the village road; the driver had vanished too. At the lone gas pump, I asked a man fueling his Jeep if he would take us back to our guesthouse in Wutai village, located on the other side of the whited-out peak. "No problem," he said with a smile, thumping the hood. "This can make it over the mountain!" And if it couldn't? "You can walk!" We laughed and piled in as the flakes showered down.

Two hours later, after we left the stranded vehicle stuck in the snow and trudged uphill to the mountain's summit, we pounded on the Golden Loft Temple's door.

The old monk opened it a sliver to see who could be knocking on a day like this. From our side, the crack showed a pair of black eyes narrowed against the blowing snow. "Please," we begged in Chinese. "We need help."

"Come in, come in!" The holy man's smile flashed white from the tangle of brown robes that shrouded his head. Frances and I smiled back. Melting snow dripped from our red, chapped cheeks. The monk reached for our arms, pulling us inside.

He pointed to a stool and offered cigarettes, a worn metal cup, a thermos of hot water, and two pinches of dried jasmine flowers for tea. Although secluded at ten thousand feet, he followed the government-penned script and asked for our identification to register our arrival: even mountaintops were not beyond Beijing's controlling reach. He studied my passport and Frances's identity card, which said she was ethnically Han, from Jilin province. The black-and-white photo showed a slender face framed by black hair, wearing a smirk. The monk noticed that; most Chinese ID photos resembled mug shots. "That's a good picture," he said.

We huddled in front of the temple's lone steam radiator, noisily slurping down cup after cup of steaming tea. In the courtyard outside, snowflakes gently erased our footprints. No one but the monk knew we were there.

The room was so still that talking felt profane. Instead, we smiled at each other and exhaled calming sighs of relief. Making it to shelter chased away the boy-did-we-screw-up panic that comes from impetuously challenging nature. I thought back to the only other people we had seen on the mountain after the Jeep had broken down and its owner had walked in the opposite direction: four farmers holding open black umbrellas, balanced on a riding lawn mower that slowly puttered past us. The driving flakes had rubbed out their faces; they were simply four statues ascending to the holy summit. Where did they go? The monk said they hadn't stopped there. Perhaps I had imagined them; hallucinations could be a symptom of hypothermia.

The wind whipped against the windows, and the monk's slow movements pressed on the pine floor from behind the curtain that separated the rooms. No sounds but the wind and his cloth slipper soles falling on the wood boards. The calves of my jeans defrosted, and sensation returned to Frances's feet. The monk floated back into the room, smiling and explaining that, since we were not married, Frances and I would have to sleep separately— she alone in the foyer and me sharing a bed with the abbot. A framed picture of the old man stared icily from the wall. He looked gassy. I asked Frances if she wouldn't mind switching places, but she glared at me.

"What if the monk understands English?" she blurted.

"I can't," he answered in Chinese.

"Sleeping with the abbot would be fine," I lied.

Did the monk think the snow would stop in the next few days? It was possible, he replied. Would the road snaking down to the village get plowed? Eventually. Could we use a phone? There was no phone. The monastery's thin pine roof sagged under the snowfall. I looked at the brown robes hanging loosely on the monk's coat-hanger body. Did the monastery have enough food?

A thump at the door cut the monk's reply. We froze, and I realized why he had taken so long to answer our own knocks earlier: in the stillness of the snowstorm, the sound was startling. The monk unbolted the portal and stuck his head out. A curtain of flakes billowed inside. Muffled Chinese words passed between the warm interior and the cold outside, and steam filled the open doorway. The monk turned, waited a beat, and said: "It's for you."

A jacket with legs stepped into the room. Fumbling with the space that should have held a head, it unzipped itself, revealing a man. He announced that he was a taxi driver and that his front-wheel-drive Volkswagen Santana was parked out front. The driver's breath suggested that *báijiǔ*—104-proof booze—had fueled his ascent. "There are about twenty cars stuck at the base of the mountain. People said a foreigner and a Chinese woman tried walking up." We stared. "Well, do you want to go or not?" he asked, motioning down the cliff toward our village guesthouse.

I repeated pleas to the Goddess of Mercy as the VW fishtailed through the first turns, past bits of guardrail that divided road and whited-out abyss. *Here comes the plunge.* Steering with one hand, the driver leaned out to see past the iced windshield. A popular breathless ballad bleated from the stereo. "*Wǒde xīn tài ruǎn, xīn tài ruǎn.*" (My heart's too soft, my heart's too soft.)

Frances sat wedged in the backseat with three other passengers the driver had picked up before us. They laughed loudly, talking about money and how much they had. The driver leaned down, found his half-empty bottle of booze, and took a long pull. "*Wǒde xīn tài ruǎn, xīn tài ruǎn.*" I turned around and parried the backseaters' questions about height, age, and chopsticks. Frances laughed, then dodged a man's usual query about how much money she made, and a woman's unusually blunt question asking if the *lǎowài* was good in bed. "*Wǒde xīn tài ruǎn, xīn tài ruǎn.*" I leaned out the window for a last glimpse of the Golden Loft Temple's towering wooden gate and ancient prayer hall. But the storm blew hard in my face, revealing only an icy sheet.

"Hey," the driver elbowed me, his pink face smeared with streaks of melting snow. "Wanna drink?" The car rolled faster.

CHAPTER 10

MEET THE PARENTS

A NOTHER SEVEN HOURS on a bus led to an overnight train that delivered us to Beijing just in time for school on Monday. A thin envelope postmarked BERKELEY waited on my desk. I nervously broke its seal and read, "I am extremely pleased to inform you that the Admissions Committee is very favorably impressed by your application for graduate study . . ."

A rejection would have spared me a decision, but by then I already knew what I wanted to do: stay with Frances. I also wanted to continue writing about China, and learning Chinese. Berkeley allowed me to defer for a year.

Later that week the mail carrier, riding a green China Post bicycle fitted with panniers, delivered a wedding invitation from two former Peace Corps volunteers who had first met in Sichuan during our training. Three years later, they planned to marry in Wisconsin. I asked Frances to be my plus-one.

"I'll never get a visa."

"You will. You have a contract for next year at a school founded by an American diplomat's wife. You have a wedding invitation. It won't be a problem."

"I don't have a passport."

"You said it's easy to get one now." A recent change in rules had reduced the processing time from six months to one.

"I'd have to go back to my hometown to apply for it. If I did go to the wedding, I'd pay for myself."

"You always say that like I'm going to object. I'm hoping you start paying for me too."

Still she was not convinced. "You sound like my parents," I said, "declining the chance to come here. Who wouldn't accept an offer to see another country—any country?"

A challenge. I'd never seen Frances back down from one. Any suggestion that she was a stereotype—in this case, an inward-looking Chinese—roused her. "We'll visit colleges, we'll go camping . . . We can drive from Wisconsin to San Francisco and end at my grandmother's house on Monterey Bay."

At the moment her thoughts were on a place in China. Frances's family lived in a Manchurian coal-mining town located closer to North Korea's capital, Pyongyang, than to Beijing. "If I go home to get my passport, you have to come with me. I want you to meet my parents. My dad was born in Sichuan. He'll understand your accent."

The road to America was paved with forms. First, Frances needed an invitation letter, which my father wrote, confirming that she could stay at his home. The Chinese Consulate in Chicago instructed him to attach notarized copies of his bank statement. He Express Mailed these to Beijing. A China Post moped couriered the envelope to school. Frances had everything translated and notarized, again, for her passport application. She wrote my father a thank-you e-mail that began, "We are ready to go to my home. I hope it will be productive. I think your son is a little bit nervous about it. He's afraid that my father will not like him and kick him out of the house. Of course, he won't. Just make him drink."

Getting a train ticket north was simple: few people traveled the thirteen hours to Frances's hometown. Buying a return fare to Beijing would be harder: those trains were always full. On Thursday, she called her parents to tell them she was boarding a train home. Could her mother go to the station and buy two return tickets for Sunday?

"Two?" her mother asked.

Frances twirled the phone cord. "Um, Ma? One other thing . . ."

The smokestack skyline spewed ash, choking the rising sun. The train slowed under rusting pedestrian overpasses into Liaoyuan, a city of one million people whose name meant "Origin of the Liao River." I could not see the polluted water from the carriage, only the halted traffic as our train crossed Friendship Road: bicycles, horse carts, and Liberation trucks. This was as grim a city as I had ever seen. No wonder Frances had left home for school and work in Beijing. Liaoyuan's cooling towers belched clouds of steam, the smokestacks chugged out thick soot, and a slick coating of mud covered the station platform.

I liked her parents immediately. They stood waiting with smiles. Frances greeted them with a "Ma! Ba!" and laughter. No hugs or kisses, not in public. Her father, tall and rugged, patted my shoulder and said I should just call him Dad. He pumped my hand firmly, unlike most Chinese men, who cupped their palm when shaking, as if my hand was bleeding. Her mother was a short, round bundle of welcome. She handed me a large sack of hazelnuts. "You're hungry! These are from our city!" She couldn't stop smiling.

"Yes, I'm very hungry," I lied, and popped a few in my mouth. "They're delicious!"

"Oh! You like them? I'll buy you another bag! Wait here!"

Frances grabbed her arm and said the nuts would last a month. As the four of us walked away from the station, the three of them chatted about our trip. I wasn't the center of attention, and it felt wonderful. They didn't compliment my Chinese; they didn't ask if I could use chopsticks or how much money I made. They called me Sold Son instead of Heroic Eastern Plumblossom. Our first meeting had me wondering, as I had on rare and wonderful occasions in China, if they realized that I wasn't Chinese.

Dad had been a soldier and "barefoot doctor," as medics who delivered basic health care to villages were called. He had mapped the day's strategy: getting a passport was easy, he told us, but getting one approved in a single day might not be. We had school on Monday, leaving us only one afternoon to get everything signed and stamped. Dad knew everyone in town. This would speed things up. We would *zǒu hòumén*, go through the back door, into the shadow-bureaucracy his generation had perfected, circumventing Beijing diktat with on-the-ground adjustments. "We will begin," he announced, "at the office of *sǎozi*."

"It means sister-in-law," Frances explained. Misunderstanding the word, I greeted the young woman with a hearty smile and a bit of Sichuan dialect: "*Nǐ hǎo, sǎzi*," which meant "Hello, idiot!" Thankfully, the woman laughed.

We crowded into her office and stared at her desk, occupied by a laminating machine. *Sǎozi* was in charge of printing the city's identification cards. When she left the room, I asked to whom she was married in the family, considering Frances's brothers lived in Shenzhen, on the southern coast. "Well, she's not really my sister-in-law," she said. "But she and her husband borrowed our apartment for a time. In fact, she spent her wedding night in my parents' bedroom. So she owes us a favor."

I said that this was exactly how my passport was approved in America.

Sǎozi returned, confident that things would be done chop-chop. "There's this woman captain at the building across the way. She's in control of the cars that go to the city five hours south, where passport papers get the required special stamp of approval. Let's go ask her. I know her well." We walked downstairs and out the back door.

Frances used her bulky sheaf of forms to flag down a meterless Volkswagen Santana, and the four of us sailed across town between rows of peanut vendors. The ride lasted one minute. We bounded up five flights of stairs to the captain's small office. The middle-aged woman frowned. She was not expecting a foreigner.

Other city officials quickly filled the room—not to help with the passport but to confirm rumors of a *lǎowài* on the premises. They stared at me. I stared at them. Dad bounced back and forth from person to person, offering everyone cigarettes. Frances presented her papers: my father's invitation letter and bank statement, her Beijing residence permit, and her family's household registration. My stomach tightened and other parts puckered as the captain pawed through the stack, disinterested.

"Well," the captain exhaled. "I can't do anything."

I sank dejectedly into the pleather sofa. *Sǎozi*, however, argued, cajoled, and beseeched. The captain's stony face was the canvas upon which *sǎozi* Pollocked her pleas.

"OK, here's what I can do," the captain sighed at last. The room, filled with cops trained to listen in, leaned forward. "Pay me two thousand, and I'll put the application in the car going to the county seat. You can have the passport in two days."

It was wonderful news, had she accepted payment in lire. But she meant yuan, two thousand of which was five times Dad's monthly pension. He would lose face if he allowed his daughter to pay. My toes curled. Frances furrowed her brow. Dad stared out the window. The onlookers decided to get back to work. *Săozi* waited a beat, puffed her chest, and turned to the captain.

"But it's only a few papers," she announced. The captain glared. "In such a big car," *săozi* meekly continued. The captain frowned. "Surely someone could easily carry them." By now her voice had fallen to a near whisper.

The captain said *méibànfă*. Frances thanked her for her time. On the sidewalk, she said there was nothing left to do except try the official route and apply for the passport directly at the police station. My heart sank, as it always did when I heard those words.

Frances went to find a public phone to call the police and ask if the passport official was in that day. Dad and I shopped in Liaoyuan's outdoor market, sniffing melons, poking at meat, and bargaining fiercely. As in the Sichuan countryside, people in this town argued over pennies. A column of curious locals crowded around me. It felt like I was back in Neijiang. From the balconies of karaoke halls, hard-looking women in bright, tight tops tossed "Hello!" like confetti.

"Wow, [Hello!] what are [Hello!] those?" I asked Dad, pointing to a plastic bowl filled with squirming shells.

"Silkworms! [Hello!] You want some, right?"

"No, no [Hello!] silkworms, [Hello!] please."

"Aw, you have [Hello!] to try. They're [Hello!] nutritious. [Hello!] And a local specialty. [Helllllloooooo!]"

In small towns, the nicest buildings usually house government offices. The vestibule of Liaoyuan's police station featured a polished marble floor, a bas-relief of the Great Wall, and a young elevator operator in heels and tight jeans, whose job was to press buttons reading either "1," "2," or "3."

On the second floor, big letters informed in English that we had arrived at the passport office. The space was huge and well furnished, at least as far as I could see through its locked doors.

We rattled them, then retreated downstairs. The elevator attendant happened to know the number for the passport approver's pager. Frances headed outside to find a public phone. I sat on the floor underneath the Great Wall, watching a group of grown men, some with guns, bound into the new elevator. Surely they could press its buttons themselves. Instead, they teased the attendant, whose playful protests of *búyào* (don't) sounded practiced. After the empty elevator returned to the ground floor, she turned her attention to me.

"Where are you from?"

"America, but I've lived in China for yea—"

"You speak pretty good Chinese. Do you know Dashan? His Chinese is great."

The Canadian man, whose name meant "Big Mountain," often appeared on Chinese television. Foreigners were inevitably—and tiringly—compared to him, as if we all aspired to his level of fluency or his willingness to shill electronic Chinese-English dictionaries and appear on state-run television. "You look like him," the elevator attendant said. "But his Chinese is better."

Frances returned. "Mr. Wang went to another county today. He'll be back before four. He said we should get all the other forms stamped first, then come and see him."

We walked to a smaller, neighborhood police station, which had never processed a passport application. After pinballing between floors we settled into a bare office where a man and woman sat at facing desks. The woman thumbed through Frances's documents while the man studied my father's mutual fund statement. "Midcap," he asked in English. "What's meaning?"

With his stamp, the last one, in place, we moved across the street to make photocopies. Then it was back to the shiny new police building. We took the stairs. The wall clock said 4:00, but Mr. Wang wasn't there. Frances went to page him. I waited with a pleasant middle-aged woman who occupied the passport office's other desk. At her feet balled red yarn and two knitting needles.

I opened the conversation the Beijing way, by stating the obvious. "There is no telephone in your office."

She bounced off her chair in surprise. "Correct. You can read that magazine."

The glass tea table held a two-year-old publication whose cover showed smiling, white-coated women standing next to a row of canned peaches. I fit *Modern Living* magazine back into its frame of dust.

"Do you like your job?"

The worker bounced. "Your Chinese is very good. Almost as good as Dashan's."

"He's from Canada."

"I like my job." She said she handled the passport applications to go to "eastern" countries, like Hong Kong. Mr. Wang did the "western" countries, like Japan. She asked if I wanted some tea.

It had been a long day, but I couldn't help but ask. "Isn't Hong Kong part of China now?" Less than a year ago, in Lhasa, I had watched the handover ceremony.

She said Hong Kong was part of China, but Chinese needed a passport to go there. But not Tibet. "Tibet is part of our China."

Taiwan, too, she continued. But that required more than a passport: it barred entry to most compatriots from the mainland. The woman asked if it was difficult to get a passport in the United States.

"Sure! You have to find your birth certificate and bring it to the post office." I asked if she processed many passport applications.

"I knit a lot of socks."

I stopped pestering her. Throughout the day, no one had ever asked me to leave an office, instead permitting me to listen and observe Chinese bureaucracy at work. Slowly. How would the police in my hometown react if a local came in with a foreigner? Would they be as transparent, or would the visitor have to wait outside? I hoped their reaction would be the same: polite smiles, and perhaps the observation that the movie star Jackie Chan spoke pretty good English.

Frances returned with good news. Mr. Wang was on his way. He arrived, said hello, sat at his desk, looked perfunctorily at her stack of papers, told her she had filled out one form wrong and needed to make three additional copies of her dad's identification card. Walking back downstairs to find a copy shop, Frances wondered: Should she go through the back door and slip Mr. Wang a "gift" to speed the process? She had never offered money like that, and wondered how.

Handing Mr. Wang the photocopies to complete her application, she politely asked him if there was a fee she could pay to hurry things along.

Mr. Wang shook his head. He said it could have gone much faster; he was at his desk with nothing to do that morning—during which time, Frances realized, we were out trying to cut corners with sister-in-law. Mr. Wang accepted her papers, shook her hand, and said courteously, "I will ensure your passport will be issued within three weeks and thank you very much for your patience. Have a nice weekend."

On the walk to her parents' apartment, we passed Liaoyuan's new church, a white-tiled building squatting next to the railroad tracks. Red crucifixes dangled in the windows. A bell tolled. Inside, a gray-haired female minister spoke to a congregation of one hundred. At first I thought I was the only man, until I looked to the other side of the room. The men sat segregated in the opposite pews, all of them old enough to be Frances's father. I flipped back through a mental calendar: this generation had been educated by a faith that had promised validity and equality for all. Communism was officially atheist; yet, as part of Deng Xiaoping's reforms, the protection of "normal religious activities" was added to the constitution in 1982. The state, of course, was the arbiter, forbidding any practice that challenged its authority.

Frances whispered that the church had been built the previous year, when the closing of state-owned factories resulted in heavy layoffs. She thought the service reminded people of their old work unit's study sessions, when they would gather to hear the gospel according to Mao. Now they listened to the teachings of Jìdú, as Jesus was called. In a Beijing cathedral I saw an oil painting of him and Mary, sinicized and dressed in Chinese silks. In Liaoyuan, the church's only decoration was a digital clock whose red numbers counted down the time remaining in the service, by law restricted to one hour.

The minister's voice spooked Frances. "She's so angry," she whispered. "She's talking down to us. She sounds like a Red Guard. Let's leave."

Over dinner, Frances recounted her day for her mother, sǎozi, and the just-arrived uncle and aunt. "He's really my uncle," she said. "She's not really my aunt but the English teacher at the middle school who wants to meet you."

Dad worked the kitchen alone. With a cigarette clenched in his teeth and a wok over a single gas burner, he produced braised stuffed eggplant, sweet-and-sour pork, battered lotus root, pockmarked tofu, flash-fried green beans, corn with pine nuts, and fish dumpling soup.

The English teacher raised a toast to my "blue" eyes and eked out a "How do you do? Welcome you!" over a round of sorghum liquor. Two little-girl cousins climbed on my back, and uncle announced that I could use chopsticks. Frances's father brought out a steaming plate of black shells. Silkworms. The table's reaction—smiles in my direction—made it clear for whom the delicacy was intended.

I said I was honored. They should be honored as well, I slurred with the pasty worm meat on my tongue, because they got to see me eat the Northeast delicacy for the first and last time. Frances's father exploded in laughter and made another toast. More dishes appeared from the tiny kitchen. The aunt spilled her drink in her lap; a kid cousin fell asleep at the table; Frances's mother beamed at her daughter; her father sang a buoyant army song. I groggily woke the next morning on the sofa, feeling the relief that comes from passing an exam.

As our train pulled out of Liaoyuan, Frances's mother cantered alongside our window, advising us to "Learn from each other. Help each other. You're happy together! Happy together!" Her words trailed behind as we headed back to Beijing.

The journey to America began at the bank, where Chinese paid the visa application fee. Frances handed 430 yuan [$54] to the teller. The amount equaled half of her apartment's monthly rent.

The form asked for the expected information: name, address, employment, finances, family. In the eyes of the American consular officer, Frances was guilty before being found innocent, and she had to convince him that she would return to China. As a single woman in her twenties without a child or real estate, Frances was not optimistic about her chances.

"I don't think it's that fierce," I told her. "Show the wedding invitation, my dad's letter, your lease, your contract for next year: those prove you're coming back. You're not lying about anything. I'm sure the system rewards that."

We arrived at the American embassy on an early June morning. A line of document-clutching Chinese ran the length of the block.

The man waiting in front of us did business in the States. He waved his passport. It held four visas from previous trips. He boasted that it was easy to get approved; Frances had nothing to worry about. But his visits were classified as business, while she sought a tourist stamp. "Even easier!" he proclaimed. "I have a lot of friends who got those. Many of them never came back."

"That's why it's so hard to get a visa," Frances said. "People abuse the system."

The businessman disagreed. "It's because America doesn't approve more visas. If we Chinese do get one, it's very fortunate. Better take the opportunity: What if the chance never returns?" He shot a glance at me. "You should marry him, then no more problems!"

We noticed the line exiting through an opposite gate. "This is just to get our interview time," the businessman explained.

Frances drew number 128. She could expect to be seen before noon. Her nervousness turned to fear. "What if the officer asks if I'm traveling alone or with an American?"

"It's only a minute-long interview. Just be honest."

Inside the consulate, she slid her documents under the glass. The officer asked why she wanted to visit the United States. She pointed to the wedding invitation. He asked if she was going alone. He asked if the American was a man. He wondered if she planned to marry this American. "I don't want to get married," she replied truthfully.

On the street, I watched a stream of expressionless faces exit the consulate, leaving American soil and, with one step, returning to China. The business of Silk Alley was in full midday bustle, and the expressionless faces stuffed their rejection letters into the manila folders and DHL envelopes that held their passports, invitation letters, and bank statements. In sixty seconds they had been measured, weighed, and thrown back.

They dodged the roaming vendors who held out peacock feathers, video discs, and lighters bearing Mao's face that played "The East is Red" and who nipped at the heels of old pudgy foreigners whose tour bus had released them for an hour of shopping for silk scarves and Beanie Babies and cut-rate name-brand clothing bound for their mall back home. The foreigners carried camcorders and calculators and cans of beer, frowning, bargaining, demanding a better price, rolling their eyes, and sighing *The Chinese* except when they paid what they wanted and they smiled and said, *They're so nice; that one was lovely, wasn't she?* Rejected visa applicants shuffled past.

Frances walked up and said: "I didn't get it."

"You're too young and single," I teased.

Her face went blank. "No, I'm serious: he rejected me."

She showed the stamp in her passport: RECEIVED VISA SECTION AMERICAN EMBASSY BEIJING, and the date. The officer had canceled our summer with a forceful *ka-chunk* and handed her a letter explaining the basis for the refusal. He circled the paragraph about not demonstrating proof of return.

I wrote my parents the news. My mother said it was a shame the Chinese government wouldn't let Frances leave. But it was America's that wasn't permitting her to go.

Visa decisions sat in the hands of the interviewing officer. There was no such thing as *guānxi*, or a favor I could offer to get it approved, and it infuriated me. So this was why Chinese shrugged when I railed against going through the back door. When the rigid, official channels didn't work, you wanted the option of navigating the malleable, unofficial ones.

The officer was the first and only American whom hundreds of Chinese met each day, for an expensive, minute-long audience that could alter their lives. If his chop stamped a rejection, the faces fell stoically and thought: *The Americans.* If the officer met their demands, the faces smiled and reported to waiting relatives: *They're so nice; that one was lovely, wasn't he?*

Frances repeated the process. The bank, the fee, the forms, the line, the nervous wait, the interview. The second time was worse than the first. Her anger boiled over when the officer stamped her passport with the mark of rejection.

"You're not listening to me!" she yelled through the glass. The room of waiting interviewees went silent. She slapped her hand on the window. "Look at me! Why are you doing this? You're not being respectful! This is the American government? You think I'm lying to you, but I'm not! I work at an American school that teaches collaboration with China! You didn't even look at those letters! I'm just trying to go to a wedding!"

The officer did not shake his head and admiringly say, "You've got moxie. I made a mistake." Instead, he tore her application in two. Frances's face burned. "Asshole!" she spat.

The officer signaled for the next applicant to step forward. Imagine the look on that girl's face!

"I'm so sorry I put you through this," I said.

Frances shook her head. "*I'm* not. I'm reapplying next week." She loved a challenge.

Back to the bank to pay another 430 yuan. "I could get a bike for that," she fumed. We woke up at 2:30 a.m. and arrived at Silk Alley an hour later. At 3:45 a.m., sixty people already queued for interview numbers. Frances was number 560; she would be seen at 3:30 that afternoon.

At 3:36 she rejoined me in China. Her face was expressionless. I apologized.

"No, I got it."

I waited for her to say she was joking.

"The visa officer was great: he approved it immediately." Her voice was matter-of-fact. She nodded at my stunned face. "I started my speech, and he just looked at my teaching contract and said, 'I believe you.' Then he kept my passport. I pick it up in three days. Here's my receipt."

I whooped and wrapped my arms around her. Tears ran from my eyes in relief. But not hers. "I'm happy, but I feel more like I've been cleared of a crime I didn't commit," she explained. Stone-faced applicants stepped around us at the exit gate. Self-consciousness struck, and we walked the opposite direction. An auntie caught up and showed Frances a handbill printed with airfares. "Flying to America?" the auntie asked. Frances said yes.

President Clinton landed in Beijing the next day. The Chinese press was ecstatic that he agreed to be welcomed in Tiananmen Square by the men whom during his first presidential campaign he had called "the butchers of Beijing." The capital's newsstands were ordered to stop displaying a Chinese magazine that paired the president's face beside that of an intern whose name, in characters, was pronounced Mònǐkǎ.

On June 29, President Clinton gave an outdoor address to a large crowd near our school, at Peking University. He announced to the gathered students that he hoped "more and more young Chinese" would go to America. Frances and I laughed at that; had the president seen the predawn lines at the consulate? But over the next twenty years, the numbers would, in fact, rise, as Chinese income grew and more visas were granted.*

---

*In 2017, one out of three international students in the United States was Chinese, and China was America's second-largest source of tourism revenue. Chinese visitors to the United

The flight I had booked was full, so Frances flew to America on her own. She had ridden buses and trains her entire life; this was the first time she had been on a plane.

So this is what it feels like to be a foreigner.

Frances thought this as she moved through San Francisco International, unsure of where to go. She had to retrieve her bag, clear customs, make a phone call, and find her connecting flight to Minneapolis. Everything was so quiet and orderly; she couldn't even hear her own footsteps. Carpeting in an airport? She watched a row of fountains sending water in the air. How wasteful. Beijing could use that stuff.

The people around her were patient and pleasant. The customs agent brought over his friendly dog to sniff her. There was a red channel and a green channel. She didn't know which to choose. A white man in the arrow-straight line pointed to the green one and advised her to answer "No" to any questions.

A man in his seventies, well dressed and silver-haired, asked her if she could spare a minute. He stood on a platform that said something about free speech and the First Amendment. He told Frances she should donate money to the International Association for the Something-or-Other. She didn't catch the last part. She did as she would when a beggar approached her in Beijing. She pulled out a ten-spot and put it in his hand.

"Ten dollars? That's very generous. Thank you, miss."

She thought, ten yuan was the same as ten dollars; what was the big deal? The exchange rate said ten yuan was a little more than a buck, but in Beijing, ten *yuan* barely bought a Big Mac.

She asked him where she could find a public phone. He pointed to a row of them.

That's strange. No aunties standing beside them to take your money and

---

States spent $24 billion in 2016. Travel between the countries was eased by a 2015 agreement to issue visas valid for ten years instead of a few months. Still, even though the number has increased from near zero in 1995, two decades later only 6 percent of Chinese held passports.

watch the timer. No household phone sitting atop a handcart of cigarettes and beer. Just a bank of cold, shiny boxes.

She didn't have any change. The man using the phone beside her noticed her confusion. How embarrassing—can't even figure out a telephone! "Can you help me?" she asked.

"You need to put coins in there, then dial the number."

She showed him the wad of bills in her hand.

"I think tens and twenties are too much," he said. "Here, you can use my phone card. What's the number you're calling? I'll dial it for you."

My father answered in Minneapolis. He was very excited to meet her at the airport, he promised her. I was down swimming off his dock, but he would tell me she was on her way. "We'll be waiting for you at the gate with bells on."

"No, no bells, I'll be embarrassed," Frances pleaded.

He thought she was in on the joke. "And horns too! Lots of horns! We'll blow them to welcome you!"

"Please don't, please." Her voice turned serious. She listened to the uncertain silence on the other end of the line. "Wait, you were joking, weren't you?" As she walked away from the phone she had a realization, one that I had said, to her disbelief, that I felt every day in China: *They think I'm a moron.*

She bought cigarettes to calm her nerves. Wow, only six dollars for Marlboro? Ten yuan for a pack in China! She flicked the lighter and managed one blissful drag before a security officer approached.

"No smoking? What? I'll go out there, got it. Thank you." So you couldn't do whatever you wanted in America.

Frances boarded the connecting flight, only to find a man in her seat. She checked her boarding pass. She had specifically asked for the window so she could watch America from above. Now an Asian man was in her way.

"Excuse me, I think you're in my place."

The burly white man beside him, in the middle, turned his sunglasses to her. "I'm sorry, you can't sit there."

She didn't know how to reply. Was this the culture? Did airplane seats in America work like hard seats on a Chinese train: first come, first grab?

"I don't mean to be rude, but I don't understand."

"I'm an immigration officer," the man said. "And I'm transporting him.

You can sit here." He motioned to the aisle seat. Frances looked at the Asian man. His left hand was cuffed to the officer's right.

She took her seat, terrified. She'd never been close to a criminal before. What if he planned an escape? With explosives! Her mind replayed the more fiery scenes from Air Force One. The Asian man, however, looked resigned. The officer looked tense.

The plane left. The beverage cart came around. Frances asked for a beer. The stewardess rattled off a list. So many choices! It was a confusing blur. "I'll have the first one you said."

For the entire summer Frances subsisted on "first ones." America was a land of decisions. A restaurant meal was an interrogation: Eating in or taking out? Booth or table? How would you like your chicken burger? Roasted or barbecued? *The first one.* Whole wheat, sourdough, or French roll? *Yes.* Those are breads. *The first one.* And what would you like on it? *Less choices.* The waitress just kept coming: sides selections (potato salad or fries; home-style or curly?), salad dressing decisions, and several soups of the day.

Later, when she retreated to allow Frances to ponder the dessert menu, I opened the newspaper to a page filled with movie listings. "What would you like to see?"

"The first one," Frances said.

She reminded herself to leave a tip and also noted that the check included tax: two added costs compared to a meal in China. Also new: customer service. Walking into stores actually intimidated her. It was uncomfortable wandering through them. The workers approached you and asked, "Can I help you?" Why did they do that? Did they think she was going to steal something?

We watched the Independence Day parade in the small farming town of Delano, replete with floats, clowns, ROTC cadets, and Shriners in miniature cars. One of the first things Frances noticed in the U.S. was the number of flags—on homes, over restaurants, on T-shirts, flying over stadiums—and that at baseball games you rose and sang the national anthem before the first pitch. In China, one rarely saw the flag outside of government buildings or a schoolyard. The parade and displays surprised her. "I thought America didn't like nationalism."

"No, we just don't like other countries to have it," my dad said. "Hey,

Frances, you should be in the parade! We could put you in one of those mini-cars."

She looked at me, uneasy. "Um, sure, I guess I could do it. Where do I go to introduce myself?"

In China, it was common—polite, some would argue—to invite foreign guests to participate in festivities and perform. Frances thought my dad was serious, and froze with fear at the image of her being announced as a "Very Special Guest, from Far-Away China, Land of Fireworks!" and then paraded before an applauding throng. She began crossing the invisible borders I navigated in China, the ones she had never seen.

Frances looked forward to stepping outside her culture for a while. But China was everywhere, even in rural Minnesota, especially on the shelves at Target. It was strange to come across an island of her culture—a product emblazoned with MADE IN CHINA, a baseball cap on a white teenager that displayed the Chinese character 爱 (ài, love) or tattoos of characters their owner didn't know how to say. "How do you pronounce it?" a waiter asked her, showing off inked lines that sort of resembled the Chinese for "brave loyalty." "It means what? I just thought it looked cool."

Frances realized why I never wanted to watch Dashan on Chinese television, why it exhausted me to explain again that my eyes were brown and that I could use chopsticks, and why Beijing teens wearing caps announcing nonsensical English phrases such as LOVE KITTY TRUCK still made me laugh.

She wondered why Chinese restaurants in America had names like Lucky Jade Dragon Fortune Golden Wok and a banner trumpeting a $6.95 lunch buffet. Restaurants in China didn't sound so unappetizing, and what was a buffet? And, now that she knew what a dollar was worth, why the hell did a plate of garlic-fried broccoli cost six bucks?

Fortune cookies were hysterical. The shell tasted bland, yet better than that mysterious orange syrup that coated America's sweet-and-sour dishes. But the messages within were overoptimistic and American. We played a game. I read the fortune, and Frances corrected it to sound authentically Chinese.

I read: *You are one of the people who "goes places in life."*

"You're not so bad," she edited. "Better than some, worse than others."

Your present plans are going to succeed.
"No plan is the best plan."
The current year will bring you much happiness.
"This is as good as it gets."
You will step on the soil of many countries.
"The best thing to do is to stay home and serve your parents."
You have an ambitious nature and may make a name for yourself.
"You're a woman. Be chaste and stop dreaming."

She liked my parents. My parents liked her. My mother said I looked happier than she had ever seen. But what about her grandchildren? How would she see them if we lived in China? Frances's mother wondered the same thing, only reversed. We shuttled between my parents' homes, and Frances watched me balance our time equally between them. I'd been doing it since I was a kid; to me it was just part of being back. It amazed her. "I don't ever want to be divorced," she said. I agreed.

She noted that my voice had changed; in Minnesota I spoke with flat *a*'s and round *o*'s; the accent came back on landing, just as at home she reverted to the Northeast's dialect. She opened her jaw wide and mimicked me. "Would I like a glass of malk? Oh, yah. You bet."

After attending the wedding—as culturally fraught for her as being the guest at a Chinese one was for me—we bought a tent and prepared to head west. A friend of a friend sold her Mercedes to a buyer in Salt Lake City and needed the car driven there from Minneapolis. Instead of seeing big cities, Frances wanted to hike and camp in the Black Hills, Montana, and Yellowstone. Growing up, she had always thought of the United States as the world's most developed country. Yet, from Minneapolis to Cheyenne, she moved across a dispersed, quiet, underpopulated land. This was the culture shock: seeing all that beautiful yet eerie space.

In Cody, Wyoming, the rodeo town where Jackson Pollock grew up, a waitress asked what she thought of it.

"From what I've seen, I think it's quite primitive." Frances meant it as a compliment.

The waitress nodded. "Why do you think we live here? Wyoming's got the smallest population of any state. Four hundred and sixty thousand people and all this land."

Our far-corner district of Beijing exceeded that figure. Frances said she could get used to all this space.

We crossed Beartooth Pass and camped in Montana, where people talked about wild animals like Beijing cabbies joked about traffic. One guy at the bar in Red Lodge chuckled as he told us, "Yesterday on my hike, my dog Bo rustled a grizzly out by the stream and he charged me. I had to go up a tree." The lead story in the local paper told of an eight-year-old boy who had been bitten by a mountain lion. Did the survivor harbor any malice toward the creature? "Aw, no," the boy was quoted. "The fella was just hungry." When Frances told a park ranger she wanted to avoid bear areas, the woman laughed and said, "Leave Montana."

On the drive south to Yellowstone, the final fifteen miles of the Beartooth Highway dropped down into the Clarks Fork Valley. We stopped at Crazy Creek Falls, a mountainside of waterfall, and went for another walk.

"This is so different than a Chinese waterfall," Frances said. "There's no carved rock to stand beside for pictures, no entrance gate where you have to pay a fee, no guide telling you what animal the falls look like or the legend of how they were made." She breathed in its mist. "It's just . . . a waterfall."

In Salt Lake City we delivered the car and waited at the Amtrak station past midnight. The train was five hours late. Frances refused to believe it. Trains didn't run late, especially by five hours. Every half hour she rose from her bed of spread-out newspapers and woke the lone station attendant to see if the engine was nearing.

The only other waiting passenger was a grandmother who sat, placid as a Buddha, drinking cocoa from the vending machine. "The train's always late, it's coming from Chicago, you have to understand. There's nothing we can do about it."

I taught the woman *méibànfǎ*—nothing can be done. She watched Frances anxiously pounding on the stationmaster's door, demanding the train. "You said the Chinese usually say it in situations like this?"

At one o'clock in the morning, we finally arrived in Emeryville, California, where the car rental office had closed. We needed to get to my grandmother's house on Monterey Bay, eighty miles south. The kind Amtrak clerk issued us a taxi voucher.

Our older cabby admitted she couldn't see well, especially at night. She said this as she went through a red light. The driver somehow—it was actually sort of impressive—managed to get not *on* the Bay Bridge but beneath it. We crawled along a frontage road that disappeared into the ocean before us. A plunge? No, the road was blocked. Our headlights stabbed at the eyes of a man standing by two parked cars. A bandana covered his head and a gun rested in his hand.

The driver squinted and wondered, "Now, what do you think those boys are up to?"

Frances sat, oblivious, behind her. The driver slowly reversed and found her way back to the freeway.

The trip was a crash course in America. Later that week, my aunt took Frances on a visit to a Santa Cruz elementary school. The environment reminded her of her own classroom in Beijing. Except everything was padded. There were no sharp corners, no iron scissors, no disease-carrying pet turtles. She asked why Americans were so afraid of kids getting hurt. My aunt taught her more new vocabulary: *negligence, litigation.*

We spent our last days at the beach and with my eighty-one-year-old grandmother, a draftsperson who designed her home and whose art hung on its walls. Despite this, Frances felt she was just like a "Chinese grandmother." Perhaps this is true of all Americans who lived through the Depression. Her own family had emigrated from France, and her father was a San Francisco baker. She still cooked all of her meals, squeezing the last drop out of every ingredient, usually purchased using a sheaf of clipped coupons—the impersonal American equivalent of Chinese market bargaining. My grandmother grew up sewing the family's clothes and raising her younger siblings. She had a chance to study piano in Paris, but her father forbade her to go, saying, "No girl of mine is running around Paris. You'll stay and keep the books."

"He sounds Chinese," Frances said. My grandmother's brother, meanwhile, got to train as an artist, becoming an Oscar-winning production designer on such films as *The King and I, South Pacific, Cleopatra,* and *Ghostbusters.* I had heard only bits of my grandmother's life while growing up, and through Frances came to know her anew as the two chatted while pulling garden weeds, chopping mustard greens, and sitting on her bed, watching her favorite show, the Food Network's *Iron Chef*.

San Francisco's Chinatown was the only place, in the entire summer, that disappointed Frances. "It looks so different than Beijing. It's dirty and crowded, the stores sell cheap souvenirs, and the restaurants look dirty." I laughed; that was exactly how many Western visitors described Beijing.

"You could also look at it historically," I said, "like why Chinatown is there, who founded it, the Exclusion Acts, how immigrants fought to keep it, how it still functions as a landing zone for recent arrivals." In this, it was similar to Beijing's *hútòng* neighborhoods, where migrant workers occupied the divided, dilapidated courtyard homes as they sought a foothold in the capital.

"I know all that," Frances said. "And I know that half the students at Berkeley are Asian-American, and that Chinese in the Bay Area have a high economic standing. But do non-Asians know that? Or do they know these roast ducks hanging in the windows, and that's 'China' to them?"

On the sands at Ocean Beach we watched the container ships creeping toward the Golden Gate. This was the end of our road, the end of America. China waited on the other side. I asked: "Are you ready to go back?"

"Of course," she said. "Aren't you?"

"I wonder where we'll be a year from now."

"Maybe here."

I was relieved; she had decided to apply to colleges, visa and finances be damned.

"Or maybe there," she added, looking to China. "It's not our decision to make."

We leaned against each other, and held on tight.

CHAPTER 11

SIGNPOSTS

DURING OUR SUMMER away, hands had been busy planning, shaping, and erasing Beijing. Where the Han tombs had been unearthed a few months before now stood rows of look-alike white apartment blocks. They reminded Frances of the lines of tombstones at the Presidio's San Francisco National Cemetery.

What the Western media had expectantly called "Beijing Spring" never really came to pass. Contrary to rumors that Tiananmen Square would be restored to its imperial-era leafiness—when it more resembled a garden than a gathering place—Chairman Mao remained there, in a mausoleum displaying his gray-suited body in a crystal coffin, tucked beneath a red flag. He didn't look peacefully asleep; he looked gravely ill. Mourners paced past silently, and some left flower bouquets at the feet of his statue. After the shuffling queue passed out of the room, a guard scooped up the accumulated flowers and carried them back out front to be sold again. Nothing went to waste in China. Even mourning could be recycled.

By the Tiger Autumn of 1998, Beijing started looking as if its planners had been handed green crayons. Gone went the row of restaurants and stores lining the southern wall of the Language and Culture University. No more fried squid on a stick for Frances, no more cold noodles for me. No more jobs for hundreds of entrepreneurs, mostly migrants, who had opened clothing stores, music shops, and bars. In place of the uprooted lives went lawns. Whose signs said KEEP OFF. The McDonald's, however, could stay.

Weigongcun, the neighborhood around the Foreign Studies University filled with restaurants owned by Uighurs, Muslims from China's far west, came down next. "I could not understand why the imperial authorities got along poorly with the Moslems," the Beijing writer Lao She wondered as a child, during the last days of the Qing dynasty. "Moslems in Beijing were restricted to selling mutton and sesame cakes, opening small shops, or at most running a small-scale Moslem restaurant." Even after the emperor fell and China was "liberated," that was still, de facto, true, though no longer on Weigongcun. Atop the ruins of restaurants, grass seeds had already been sown.

Then fell South Haidian Street, the diagonal, tree-shaded stretch between People's University, Book City, and Peking University. Its land was in the way of a new grid of wider streets. Diagonals didn't fit the plan. Xizhimen, the former West Gate of the old city wall that had become a thick, steaming soup of migrant-run restaurants and outdoor clothing stalls, got erased. Even the venerable downtown neighborhood of Xidan couldn't escape improvements. Billboards posted at the spot promised a bigger, better Xidan. But today it only got worse: the painting showed a row of towering shopping centers surrounded by cars. Not *miàndi*—the cabs were banned as dangerous, polluting eyesores—not red taxis, but privately owned sedans. One stretch of this road had just been closed to bikes, because they got in drivers' way. The state-run *China Daily* ran a story headlined "Bicycle Kingdom Rules No More."

Beijing's streets had suddenly become viaducts between Point A and B, not destinations unto themselves.

My hearing had faded to the point that I could sleep through the jackhammer bursts from neighboring construction that had become my alarm clock. I wasn't sure I wanted my ears fixed, but Frances took me to a traditional Chinese medicine clinic.

The doctor, an old man in a white lab coat, took my pulse and looked at my tongue. He didn't look into my ears. He wrote out a concoction of herbs, instructing me to boil them in a clay pot for twenty-five minutes on low heat. At home I measured, sorted, and simmered. For six days I pinched my nostrils and gulped the bitter black slime. It did not improve my hearing; it made me gag at the sight of coffee.

At a Western-style clinic, the nurse actually gasped when she peered into my ear canal. She irrigated; she mined. Two years of Sichuan coal smoke and a year of Beijing dust had filled them to the brim. The contents were so disgusting that the nurse walked away with the tray full of ambergris to show others. Down the hall, I heard fascinated yelps of "*Āiyā!*"

I walked outside a new man, into a new world. My balance was back. My hearing, remarkably acute. A taxi honked its horn and it sounded like it was on the sidewalk right behind me—which it was. I also picked up, from a not-too-distant neighborhood, the cries of a *hútòng* being attacked with sledgehammers. Over the next four years Beijing would relocate a half million people from its center to the suburbs, the equivalent of giving the entire population of Washington, D.C., its packing papers.

Already the signposts of my and Frances's courtship were vanishing. That favorite restaurant, that field where we watched the stars, that bar and cinema where we spent our first dates—all gone. Individuals have landmarks too; without them it is so easy to forget, so simple to lose one's way.

I dog-eared and annotated the thick booklet that was China's national train timetable, seeking to answer the question *How can we get there fastest?* From Beijing Station, I set out on weekends with Frances to visit places that sounded like potential travel articles. I never queried editors, but sent the finished story, having learned to never wait for permission to write. I kept pieces circulating, tracked on a corkboard above my desk, until they found a home. Before the Internet took off, it was possible—with the editor's blessing—to sell a story several times, so long as the outlet's readership did not overlap, as in Hong Kong, Los Angeles, Chicago, and New York.

Fact checking provided a glimpse of how Western readers paused and questioned observations that I took as prima facie true. The process made me realize I was catching details about China that were new to them and thus likely to readers. This was allowed; I was not required to churn out new versions of standby stories from coastal cities such as Shanghai or from atop the Great Wall.

"Is there really a cigarette brand named Famous Dogs?" an editor asked. "Send us the package."

"You mention the restaurant featuring scorpions: on the menu or on the floor?"

"You said that next to Friday's a new Chinese restaurant opened, named 'Saturday's.' Is this a joke?"

"Is the book of Confucian sayings 'from my hotel' standard issue, like Gideon Bibles, or did you buy it?"

After I submitted an item about the first Starbucks opening in China, in downtown Beijing, a London-based editor asked, seriously, if it served coffee. "Chinese drink coffee?" he replied, surprised. "Can we fact-check this?"

I faxed a snapshot of its menu. (That verb is as outdated as the fact that a Starbucks opening in China once counted as news.*) I didn't think the brand would catch on; its coffee was expensive. A "small" cup—mercifully, there was no "tall" on the Chinese menu—cost the equivalent of two dollars in an era when people still sipped penny-pinches of tea leaves steeped in jam jars.

Before e-mail and cell phones, being an unaccredited writer, without a fixer or translator, reporting a story on, say, underground coal fires meant riding a sixteen-hour train to a brutish Inner Mongolian town named Wuhai, dodging local police and talking my way through the gate of the state-owned company and onto one of China's largest coal fields, then wandering its forlorn fifteen square miles (picture the Badlands, only on fire), looking for a quote.

"This is a dangerous fire zone," said an official sent out to rope me away from the blaze. I quickly transcribed his Chinese into my notebook in *pīnyīn*. Translation into English would have to wait; my coal-dusted notebook pages of hastily written romanized Chinese looked like rubbings of runic tablets. Orange dump trucks bounced past over rutted dirt tracks between open pits, trailed by donkey carts whose drivers shoveled spilled chunks of coal. Under hard helmets, smeared black faces stared at us from straw-and-mud huts. The land was bleached of life; even the company's statue of Chairman Mao looked pallid, flaking in the lashing wind.

The official knelt beside a crack in the sandy, smoldering earth. Suddenly

---

*In 2016, a new store opened at the rate of one per day. China had 2,300 outlets; Starbucks planned to open 500 stores annually for the next five years, making China its largest market.

he disappeared, shrouded by sulfuric smoke. "Currently," he yelled, "this is China's most destructive coal fire." Wuhai was in the running for the unenviable crown of World's Worst Ecological Disaster. He said 16 fires burned 250 feet deep here, advancing 100 feet per year. The official compared the fire to a dragon whose head—its path—he aimed to chop off. The coal company lacked resources, however, and so the fires burned, pumping ash from 20 million to 30 million tons of smoldering coal into the air each year. I asked him to repeat the number; Chinese calls one million "*bǎiwàn*," literally "100 10,000." It always threw me off. Wuhai's hazy air held five times the standard amount of carbon monoxide, and its decrepit buildings were pocked from acid rain. An eight-square-mile sinkhole slowly swallowed the foundations of schools, homes, and hospitals. I filed the story with the dateline HELL, realizing there were easier ways to earn $1,000.

I sent a note to the guidebook whose distance error, compounded by my foolishness, nearly stranded Frances and me in the blizzard atop Mount Wutai. An editor replied with a job offer, updating the next edition of the Rough Guide. The catch: I would have to cover the Northeast. No other writer wanted to go there, she said. The previous edition began its section with a quote from a French Jesuit who had visited in the nineteenth century: "Although it is uncertain where God created paradise," the priest wrote, "we can be sure He chose some other place than this."

The editor allowed that "perhaps we have presented too negative a picture." In truth, the Jesuit's description still applied to the Manchuria I had seen on my visit to Frances's hometown. The region extended north of the Great Wall like a swollen thumb, pinched between North Korea, Siberia, and Mongolia, and was often dubbed China's Rust Belt. But updating its guidebook chapter would get me off the beaten path and into places few travelers went, all while learning more about where Frances came from.

In the Northeast's large cities, stepping off the train each time was to step into the same town, in perpetuity. The view showed a characterless, sooty line of smokestacks staining matchbox apartment buildings. I created a template to begin each chapter's "Arrival" section. Simply circle the correct words:

> In front of the station stretches [Liberation/People's] Street. [Culture/People's] Square sits in the heart of town. Rusting children's rides and a mangy petting zoo await in [Labor/People's] Park. The only affordable lodging for foreigners can be found at the [Friendship/Railway] Hotel.

Away from the metropolises, however, the region's countryside reminded me of the American Midwest, with a wide-open prairie sky and rows of corn stretching to the horizon. We visited the rice farm where Frances's grandparents had cared for her as a child, in a village whose name, Wasteland, belied its natural beauty. Its paddies ran from a bend in the Songhua River clear to the foothills in the distance. The flat, fertile land closer resembled Northern California's Sacramento River valley than the mountain terraces of southern China. The trip planted a seed, an idea to one day move here and explore the region in full.

In the meantime, traveling the Northeast with Frances was a mobile history lesson. Uniquely for China, where the past is usually narrated in that cocksure voice bellowing how all roads led to the Communist revolution, I had to do the work, to make sense of the sites that lay scattered across the Northeast like playing pieces on a board game called Empire. We could sleep in former Russian and Japanese hotels, embark at Russian- and Japanese-designed train stations, walk through pistachio- and lemon-painted Russian and Japanese ministry buildings that looked like they rode the train in from Moscow or made the crossing from Tokyo and decided to stay. In the future, some of these would be protected and marked as "patriotic education bases." In 1998, however, administrative offices or tenants often occupied the sites. Harbin's onion-domed St. Sophia Russian Orthodox cathedral—later restored as a city museum—was being used as a department store's warehouse.

Much of this information was new to Frances: as a schoolgirl she had been taught not regional but national history. She of course knew that Japan had invaded the Northeast in 1931, the start of what China called the War of Resistance. She did not know the extent of Japan's ambition. In Changchun, the former capital of the puppet state Japan called Manchukuo (1932–1945), axial boulevards lined with Japanese pine trees still led to roundabouts such as the former Unity Plaza—renamed People's

Square—ringed by steel-frame bulwarks of buildings designed to evince Japan's inviolability. The former Central Bank of Manchukuo was now the People's Bank of China, the Manchukuo Telephone and Telegraph Company was a branch of China Unicom, and the Police Headquarters had become the Public Security Bureau.

Frances and I slept at Changchun's former Yamato Hotel, built as part of a chain that dotted the region's former South Manchuria Railway, which Japan had controlled. The room had clean sheets and a television, but otherwise its floor-to-ceiling windows and claw-foot bathtub made a 1930s time capsule. The front desk said that Chinese preferred to stay in the hotel's characterless new wing, which cost double this room's 240 yuan [$30] tariff. The room was comfy and quiet, save for the old steam radiators that ran along one wall. At night they hissed low, as if urging us to keep this place a secret.

Traveling together on long, slow train rides across the prairie was far more enjoyable than disembarking at our destination. Most Chinese businesses did not have webpages; I had to tromp around town to ask suspicious hotel clerks if we could inspect their rooms, and find good local restaurants whose staff might comprehend a guidebook-toting customer who could not speak Chinese. This being the Northeast, we ate a lot of boiled dumplings. Waitresses recited a list of fillings that included cabbage, corn, pork, fennel, mushroom, lamb, celery, eggplant, shrimp, egg, and onion.

"The first one," I started replying.

On weekend trips and school holidays, we covered an area the size of France and Germany combined, from the Yellow Sea port of Dalian to the Trans-Siberian Railway border station of Manzhouli. In Dandong, the Chinese city that faces North Korea across the Yalu River, Frances taught me the words to the song that welcomed visitors to the Resist America, Aid Korea War Museum. The ditty was titled "Defeat Wolf-Hearted America." As I listened, a vendor in an army jacket asked if I wanted to buy a cold can of Coke.

Chinese and South Korean tourists crowded Dandong's riverfront prom-enade, Korean barbecue restaurants, and karaoke halls. Monuments to North Korean–Chinese friendship served as backdrops for photo poses.

Tourists paid one yuan for a minute of peering through binoculars at the North Korean shore. They called out what they spotted. It was I Spy with Chinese characteristics.

"I see a soldier!"

"I see a man on a bicycle!"

"I see someone waving!"

"Is he starving?"

The promenade's bestselling souvenirs were North Korean currency, acorn wine, and stamps with slogans such as BECOME HUMAN BOMBS.

Dandong's televisions picked up North Korea's station, a parade of programs devoted to the myriad achievements of then leader Kim Jong-il. In one fifteen-minute program, I watched him bottle beer, map an army exercise, compose a symphony, and fix a tractor. An exuberant chorus of soldiers sang behind the images. The narrator used the Dear Leader's name as punctuation between heralds of his deeds. "Blahblahblah KIM JONG-IL! Blahblah KIM JONG-IL blahblah KIM JONG-IL!"

Newlyweds walked about in wedding dresses, and touts called people to ring-toss games. A park by the river charged one yuan to sit on the grass, a downy blanket of green rare in China. Picnickers packed the knoll. A neighboring gate's sign said, in Chinese: HUNTING PARK. For some reason, this made me say, "Come on, Frances, this should be interesting."

Our entrance ticket said that ten yuan bought us four arrows, to be aimed at live rabbits, ducks, and chickens. We could carry away whatever we killed.

"Just like in America!" the attendant said, cocking an air pistol. He fired a shot at a limpid bunny. Missed. "Your turn." He held out the gun.

Instead, Frances and I walked out on the "broken bridge," bombed in 1951 by U.S. planes, which President Truman had forbidden to cross into Chinese air space for fear of sparking World War III. Navy pilots dropped the spans leading from the North Korean side to the midway point of the Yalu. Now a man with a telescope sat perched at its end, charging customers to peer into the Hermit Kingdom. The man said that China wanted North Korea to remain a buffer zone from the American-allied south; it would always support the Communist regime. The telescope's view showed rusting fishing vessels, an old truck, a lone soldier, and a Ferris wheel that looked like it had not turned since before the war.

Finally, to update the Rough Guide's Dandong section, we boarded a speedboat that sliced across the Yalu, buzzing within meters of North Korean soil. Cruising the breakwater of Sinuiju city felt like paying money to shoot at an exhausted bunny. I thought back to the propaganda around the Resist America, Aid Korea War Museum swearing eternal China–North Korea goodwill, and the most ironical of punch lines surfaced: With friends like these, who needed enemies? This was car-crash tourism.

As the boat circled back to Dandong, we saw what the North Koreans looked at all day: a bustling new city of high-rises, green grass, and trees. The Resist America, Aid Korea obelisk high on the hill, ten thousand war graves behind it, the half-bombed Yalu Bridge, the café umbrellas advertising Budweiser, and the throng of colorful brides and fun-seekers. And rows of telescopes, where people paid to stare at an empty shore.

Over our school's winter break, Frances went home to her parents in Liaoyuan while I bundled up and set out to finish updating the Rough Guide's Northeast chapter.

Due to its recent past as a colonial prize, the region's museums told a gruesome narrative, and one that evinces China's continuing mistrust of Japan. I spent Christmas Eve morning outside of Harbin city, looking at pictures of Japanese wartime medical experiments on the grounds of its former military base. After buying a ticket ("You're the only one today") to the Japanese Army Unit 731 Museum, I learned what happens when you inject a deadly virus into prisoners, or freeze them, or heat them, or dissect them alive.

Outside in the minus-30-degree air, my beard beaded with frozen breath. The sun set at 3:45 p.m. I couldn't stand the thought of another night in the coffins that were state-run Friendship hotels, and when I called Frances, she told me to come to her parents' house. "It's Christmas. I can't imagine being alone on Chinese New Year."

I bought a train ticket and arrived in Liaoyuan before midnight. Never had its cooling towers looked so good.

Frances led me from the station. Everyone at home was asleep, she said, so I had to be quiet when entering the apartment. We crunched through the silent snow and up four flights of stairs, opening a door to a yell: her parents, grandparents, and uncle all cheered. They led me across the cold concrete floor and into the dimly lit living room. I remembered that this was an apartment without running water and with a temperamental flow of electricity. Her father said, in halting English: "Merry Christmas!"

And there it was. A Christmas tree. An actual, living tree: one that looked remarkably similar to the waist-high ones that lined the road to the apartment from the train station. The branches held lights, silver tinsel, and ornaments of wrapped boxes, Santas, and candy canes. A star crowned its top. How they had managed to find these items and assemble them so quickly baffled me, until I remembered they were all made in China, perhaps even this town. I breathed in the scent, then started to cry. Frances's father looked worried that he had offended me.

I said it was wonderful, the best Christmas tree I'd ever seen. He told me to look beneath it. Presents.

"*Èr rén zhuàn!*" her father shouted before I could get the tissue wrapping off. "They're cassettes. Last time you were here you kept asking about the Northeast's traditional music. Well, this is it! It's called *èr rén zhuàn*. It's like opera. They make fart jokes too. It's funny!"

I had no cassette player, but still I teared up. The room looked extremely worried until I said, "I'm not homesick. Thank you."

Frances's father unscrewed a bottle of rice wine and raised a glass in a toast, saying, "That's because you are home."

CHAPTER 12

THREE PROTESTS

H EADING BACK TO school, Frances and I exited into a Beijing Station ringing with pounding hammers. The crowd of passengers pushed us through the cattle bars and out front, where the apron of cement normally dotted with blue-suited migrants asleep on their bedrolls had become a roped-off construction site. Workers installed cream-colored tiles. Another bunch laid pipes. "A fountain," one answered in a Sichuan accent when I asked what he was building. "And over there will be a lawn. It's 1999."

The makeover was part of the preparations to celebrate the fiftieth anniversary of the founding of the People's Republic, as well as Portugal's handover of Macau, its small colonial foothold on China's southern coast.

Frances and I walked the long Beijing block—five hundred yards—to Chang'an Jie, the capital's central boulevard. Workers there tore up the sidewalk to stripe the curb with sod. Soon after the Communists took Beijing in 1949, the American writer David Kidd recorded the first time this ancient axis had been redrawn. Kidd watched workers raze a grove of silk trees to make the bleachers that still stand, nearly always empty, facing Tiananmen Square. Kidd noted that the men wore blue suits with numbers whitewashed on the back: prisoners.

Fifty years later, the second, (paid) shift wore loafers, slacks, flimsy plastic helmets, sport coats with the tags showing on their sleeves, and matching T-shirts that said McNUGGET BUDDIES. Later, when the sod died, a new shift of workers arrived to actually paint the grass green.

Teaching in a collaborative bicultural school meant observing two sets of holidays. Before classes broke in mid-February for the Chinese New Year, our students organized a temple fair with a nearby Chinese public school. The fair blended Ping-Pong and baseball, Chinese and Western chess, calligraphy and comics, folk dances and hip-hop, and a singing performance by Frances's kindergartners. I tried to get her to teach the new song by Cui Jian, China's rock godfather whose anthems had scored the demonstrations at Tiananmen Square nine years earlier. His latest album, *The Power of the Powerless*, shared its name with a Václav Havel essay. It would have warmed my heart to see five-year-olds chorus the words to "Spring Festival":

> The cycle is not long, just over three hundred days
> No long-term plan is the best insurance
> Hold up a fortified defense since fear is right in front of you
> Only one thing left—keep saving money.

The New School of Collaborative Learning wove themes across its courses each semester, such as "interdependence." Starting in March, teachers were to guide students to draw connections between their lives and the larger world: their families, their neighborhoods, the environment. In science class they researched Beijing's watershed and plummeting water table, whose overuse caused some parts of the thirsty city to sink four inches each year. In social studies class the kids wrote clean-water resolutions to present at Beijing's Model United Nations conference.

Interdependence, I would teach them, sustained us. When it came to the environment, to world affairs, to the forging of peace itself, we humans were all in this together, I'd cheer. But I couldn't lie to them; kids know when teachers are faking. I'd had enough of interdependence. As the teenagers might put it, I thought interdependence sucked. I was sick of depending on others, of having my life hang on admissions decisions, on the yuan-dollar exchange rate, on a visa officer's frown or grin. I wanted a normal life free of all that, where Frances and I could map our own future. I wanted to be selfish, to be free. I wanted independence.

Frances, meanwhile, learned a new English word: *deadline*.

She came across it on March 15 while filling out her application to San

Francisco State University. The top of the page warned that international students *must have their forms postmarked by March 1.*

She had been waiting on her Test of English as a Foreign Language results. Frances's relief at seeing that her score exceeded the university's requirement vanished when she looked at its forms. She walked into my classroom to ask if *deadline* really meant what the dictionary said.

"I thought you mailed everything in last month!"

"I told you," she said holding back tears, "that I had to wait for the damn test score. And my mom had to gather all my records. The schools had to look up all my classes, write a transcript, get it stamped by four or five different people, then give it to my mom. She had to pay too. Then she mailed everything here, and I had to pay to get them all translated into English, and stamped again, which took another two weeks. I can't just call someone and ask them to send me a copy. You know how sacred documents are in China."

She handed me a page of San Francisco State's thin application, which an American could have submitted in under an hour. Today when I hear American politicians and British Brexiters say the word *immigration,* I don't see people "taking our jobs" but picture, with great empathy, piles of paperwork, long waits, and lives in limbo.

"I have all my transcripts," Frances said, "and my test score, finally. I filled out the employment history and everything else. I just have to do this statement of finances."

Like most American colleges, San Francisco State required international applicants to verify that they had enough funds to cover one full year of study. It was assumed that they could find gainful work on campus to cover expenses. Although tuition cost $7,808, estimated living expenses meant that Frances needed to present a bank statement showing she had at least $18,860 in cash or equities.

She stared at the paperwork between us. "I hate it. I'm tired of people telling me what I should do. Maybe everything happens for a reason, and I missed the deadline, so that's it. Maybe we weren't ever supposed to meet, that all these decisions that brought us together turned out to be the wrong ones. I won't get the student visa anyway."

I began a pep talk in the same tone I used when sermonizing about interdependence to my students.

"Speak Chinese!" She gathered the nest of papers. "I'm not afraid of anything. Well, ghosts."

She would have to ask her oldest brother for support; he was a stockbroker, and had done well. But he also had a mortgage and his own family to support, in addition to their parents. That responsibility fell heaviest on firstborn kids, who were expected to fill the large gaps in China's social safety net.

Her brother answered at his desk. He said he'd have to get a bank official to verify the value of his investments in dollars. Frances's hopes sank. She asked how many weeks that would take.

Her brother laughed. "It will be done in an hour."

He worked in Shenzhen, in the south. Everything was different down there. He said he would courier the papers to her overnight. After she hung up, she started to cry.

"Oh, no," I said. "Did he refuse?"

"No, he's my big brother."

She phoned San Francisco State. I was outside, trying to teach my students baseball, when Frances came out with the news. "They said it was no problem. I can turn in the application by April 1."

We still had a long way to go—acceptance and a student visa—but at least the wheels were turning. My multinational students, meanwhile, argued over a close play at second base: "Out! *Bùdùi!* You were out!" "What's 'out'?" Teaching them "interdependence" was much easier than explaining the rules of baseball.

NATO began bombing Serbian forces in Kosovo in late March, 1999, just as my high school students began reading the classic Chinese novel *The Water Margin* (also called *Outlaws of the Marsh*), translated by Pearl Buck. The action followed a ragtag band of brigands who are eventually corralled by the emperor to fight crime and repel foreign invaders.

Outside our school gate, students noticed that the neighborhood bulletin board, which usually displayed the daily newspaper, now showed photographs of Serbian innocents ducking. Others showed tanks and the Serbian president, Slobodan Milošević, whose resolute face was undermined by a gray crew cut that bolted from his scalp in upright shock.

The Chinese media reported that if the West backed Kosovar

"separatists" today, tomorrow it would support those trying to split regions from China, such as Tibet. In print and on newscasts, the Western military alliance was dubbed "U.S.-led NATO." It echoed the "U.S.-led UN forces" I had read about in the Northeast's Resist America, Aid Korea War Museum.

By mid-April, "U.S.-led NATO" was a new bit of Chinese vocabulary I'd memorized despite myself. I had to look up how to say *genocide* and *ethnic cleansing*—and also Operation Noble Anvil, the American mission, whose name evoked an image of Wile E. Coyote as its commander, dropping an iron anvil off a cliff. My students had never heard of the character. Only one had ever heard of a place named Kosovo.

On a bright April Sunday, I woke early and laced up my skates. Not since my first weekend in Beijing, eighteen months before, had I rolled from my suburban corner of the capital fourteen miles to Tiananmen Square. I skated past the honey seller's beehives beside the Old Summer Palace and out of my low-rent residential quarter, past Tsinghua University. Traffic thickened, so I hopped on the sidewalk and skirted the ruins of the Yuan dynasty city wall, built in the thirteenth century, when Kublai Khan held power. Marco Polo visited Beijing then and noted how its trees grew in straight lines. The khan had ordered them planted two paces apart "so that any wayfarer may recognize the roads and not lose his way." That tradition continued across China; in Beijing, I glided through a gauntlet of symmetrically spaced cottonwood poplars. Their fluffy white catkins cascaded to the ground like fat flakes of snow.

They swirled around the dancing traffic cop on Xueyuan Street, shimmying and jiving as the traffic followed his instructions. Come summertime, his venerable act would be replaced by a mute traffic signal that drivers blithely ignored, steering headlong into the honking gridlock.

I turned east and exited the university district, passing under the Second Ring Road to genteel Beijing, the courtyard homes that fronted the central chain of lakes. The water looked clean but cold. I thought of the writer Lao She, whose body was fished out from a former pond near here. On this morning, in the West Lake, an old man smoothly breaststroked through the pond scum.

The courtyard homes grew grander as I moved south, entering the *hútòng* that once housed imperial gentry and now belonged to high-ranking officials. Barbed wire and security cameras topped their gray walls; plainclothes police stood in the lane, fooling no one. They were always men, they always dressed in white dress shirts, and they always looked uncomfortable. I wondered who trained them; in Neijiang there were farmers who could teach them how to stare with less affect.

I had to step around the rubble at a new east-west thoroughfare that bulldozed across Beijing's historic core. It was named Ping'an Dadao, Safe and Sound Boulevard; it would turn out to be neither. Now I neared the city's administrative center. Strangely, however, the usually busy Wenjin Street was completely empty. I looked ahead to Beihai Park's thirteen-story white stupa, bobbing over the vista like a buoy. No vehicles blocked the view. Then I noticed the people. A line of them stood on the sidewalk at the road's northern side. They weren't doing anything except looking at the tall foreigner skating down the middle of the vacant street, past the gate of Zhongnanhai, the lakeside garden adjacent to the Forbidden City. The former imperial playground was now a palace, of sorts: Mao made Zhongnanhai the seat of the national government, and where its supreme leader lives.

I made a U-turn. I thought I'd interrupted a coming parade. I waited on the lake bridge for five minutes. Not a single car approached. I retraced my route, skating west down the empty boulevard. Never had I seen such a barren Beijing street.

The crowd still lined the road's northern edge. They stood in orderly rows, two or three people deep. They all looked to be women in their fifties and sixties, the people you addressed not as "ma'am" but as *āyí* (auntie). A few pushed up the sleeves of their hand-knit cardigans and waved as I glided past.

Israeli flags flew from the light poles of Zhongnanhai's fifteen-foot exterior wall, painted the same deep ochre as the Forbidden City. I remembered reading that an Israeli minister was visiting Beijing; this must have been the "voluntary" greeting line for his motorcade, but there were no police in view.

Zhongnanhai's gates stayed shut, and so I luxuriated on the rare, carless stretch of pavement. I skated the half mile, swerving back and forth past the silent aunties standing still in the cool spring air. I wished I had a camera: they made the most orderly crowd I'd ever seen in China. Finally, I skated south, along the Forbidden City's moat.

A canopy of locust trees shaded me all the way to Chang'an Jie. It, too, was nearly empty. At the approach to Tiananmen Square, an officer held up a white-gloved hand.

"The square is closed," he said gruffly in Chinese. In the air his glove traced a wide loop around Tiananmen. I unlaced my skates at the subway entrance, took the flip-flops from my backpack, and rode the subway closer to home.

Cell phones were still an expensive novelty. The landline rang just as I opened my front door. Pete Hessler had recently moved to Beijing after finishing his first book, *River Town: Two Years on the Yangtze*. The only media outlet that offered him a job was the *Wall Street Journal*, where he worked as a barely paid clipper.

"Did you see the demonstration?" Pete asked.

"No, but I saw a waving party for Israel at Zhongnanhai."

"The aunties? That was a demonstration."

"Against Israel?"

"For Falun Gong. I'm at the *Journal*. Last week there were smaller demonstrations in Tianjin because a magazine wrote that Falun Gong caused mental disorders. It was a complete surprise today."

As Pete talked, my mind replayed scenes of elderly aunties practicing Falun Gong exercises at dawn. I had seen them in parks around the capital and even in front of the embassy district's Dunkin' Donuts, moving through a series of languorous movements that resembled *tàijí*. The dozens of aunties—they were almost always older women—followed instructions playing from a boom box set to an ethereal Chinese flute.

Now these *āyí* were calling on the government to protect their freedom to exercise? Aunties knit socks. They babysat. They manned the public phone and cigarette stands. They gossiped and, somewhat incongruously— given that they were New China's first generation of "liberated" women—formed the ratting ranks of the Neighborhood Committee patrols, which leapt at the chance, endemic in nondemocratic societies, to play a part, to serve the state, *to be of use*. Pete told me that ten thousand of them had stood in front of Zhongnanhai. "Then they all just left," he said. "That was the end."

He noticed a nice detail: the protesters had cleaned up all their trash when their wordless assembly dissolved that afternoon. "Hey, jackass," Pete said. "You skated through China's largest demonstration since Tiananmen."

Stories in the Western press before the protest had painted Falun Gong as a cult, reporting that its Chinese founder had fled to America and refused to disclose his finances or respond to charges that he grew rich by demanding his followers purchase his books, cassettes, and posters. He claimed he could levitate through meditation and taught that interracial marriage was a sin, that homosexuality was impure, and that the Earth would soon explode.

But if believing what a charlatan told you was a crime, China would need to build more jails. No one, I thought, could consider Falun Gong a "threat to social order." These "rebels" looked too much like family.

In another two months the government would brand Falun Gong an "evil cult." And then the government banned it, arresting and torturing unrepentant practitioners. At the end of April, however, the whole thing sounded like an old Beijing tall tale: the Day of Ten Thousand Aunties. You had to have been there to believe it. Local press chose not to. The next day the front page of Beijing's papers ran stories with Belgrade datelines and photos of the damage caused from bombs dropped by "U.S.-led NATO."

The following month, in May, I scanned Chinese headlines that showed the usual appearance of *Belgrade*, *NATO*, and *bomb*. My eyes widened at the words *Chinese embassy*. Stories reported that three Chinese journalists were killed when "joint direct attack munitions" struck China's embassy in Serbia.

Please let it be the Brits, I thought. At least then Frances and I could commiserate; after all, they once burned down the White House. I couldn't imagine that the United States would deliberately target an embassy, especially one belonging to a Security Council member with the world's largest market. *Titanic* still played in Beijing's cinema; Hollywood, like the rest of the West, wanted to market to, not moralize, the country. China's premier, Zhu Rongji, had just returned from Washington, D.C., drumming up support for the country's pending application to join the World Trade Organization. Relations between the two countries were the most cordial since I had arrived four years earlier as a "Friendship Volunteer."

Frances read the news and hoped the bombing was an accident. We had plans to meet a group of my high school students to go ice-skating at a mall near the embassy district. From the subway, we walked through the knockoff market dubbed Silk Alley, squeezing past tourists clutching North Face jackets and Beanie Babies. It looked like any other Saturday.

We left the rink at sunset, parting from my students. On the walk to the subway, we noticed a small crowd gathered around the fresh edition of the *Beijing Evening News*, tacked up in a display case. The entire issue looked devoted to the embassy bombing. I recognized strident characters and the words "deliberate attack" by a "U.S.-led NATO" plane.

"The tone of this is pissed off," Frances said, sounding worried. "I've never seen anything so strong before in the paper. I don't think it was an accident."

"You think that after reading one article?"

"You thought it was an accident after reading one article."

Oddly, Silk Alley was now shuttered. We exited onto the narrow road that fronted the American embassy. Holding a skate blade-up in each hand, I passed through a line of soldiers, wondering what they were doing there.

A hundred young men had gathered in front of the embassy. Now we saw that three rows of soldiers faced them, blocking the compound's perimeter fence. As the only visible foreigner on the scene, I wondered if I was on the wrong side of the barrier. Frances said we should keep walking.

I asked a pair of young Chinese men why they were there. They were members of the Communist Youth League, they said, from two universities. "The authorities" had rounded them up and brought them here by chartered bus. What authorities? They pointed behind me, to a professor slapping the back of his hand into his other's palm, yelling "Exchange blood for blood" in Chinese. I gripped my skates tighter. Frances said we should leave.

In preparation for the nation's fiftieth anniversary, new grass had been ordered planted throughout the embassy district. Earlier that week its sidewalks had been broken up, but the rubble had yet to be carted away.

Cairns of rocks and palm-sized paving-stone chunks stood around us. As the professor railed against American aggression, a student grabbed a rock and punctuated his remarks with a throw that nailed the lamp beside the consulate's gate. Shards exploded. The second lamp shattered next. The crowd cheered.

A young man grabbed another bit of stone and let fly. It sailed over the gate and into the embassy's plate-glass window. The cairns became squadrons. One sortie after another attacked the building's façade. The soldiers stood rod-straight as the rocks whizzed over their heads.

The students wore sport coats and, despite the tight material at their shoulders, threw hard. They moved around me, to the stones, then past me, running into a heave. No one said a word to me or even made eye contact. Maybe they thought I was a Serb, or perhaps by standing still with a blank expression I had at last mastered the Chinese Stare, achieving the moment of nonexistence that rendered me transparent.

As the rocks flew, I realized that politics and everyday life rarely intersected more tangibly than when you were in a foreign land, watching your embassy get stoned.

What I didn't know then was that, unlike the aunties' protest a few weeks earlier, this entire display of outrage had been orchestrated from above. Its inception, and its end one week later, formed a template that Beijing would use repeatedly to ramp up patriotic fervor, often timed to divert attention from sensitive anniversaries, man-made disasters, lax food safety enforcement, toxic pollution, or calls to reform the government itself—causes, all, of the 180,000 protests it admits occur nationwide each year.

A CNN crew arrived, and we walked away as the sun set and the stones rained down.

I awoke Sunday expecting to read that the Chinese and American presidents had held a historic joint news conference explaining everything and swearing friendship. Instead I read an e-mail from Tom, a Peace Corps friend who had gone on to work at the consulate in Chengdu, Sichuan. There, a mob of rioters overwhelmed the guards, scaled the perimeter fence, battered the building's door with a bicycle rack, and set fire to the consul general's home. No one was harmed, but at one point Tom entered his kitchen to find two protestors had broken in through his back door. They demanded he come out to "control the crowd." He told them to put down his Pop-Tarts. By dawn, soldiers cleared the grounds.

In Beijing, police sealed the embassy district, allowing only buses bringing more university student protesters to pass. On state television that night, a man named Hu Jintao, Jiang Zemin's second-in-command—and the future president—sat at a desk. He clasped his hands and repeated the charge that an American bomb hit China's Serbian embassy, killing three journalists. He did not say that their job was likely a cover for intelligence work, and that the United States had issued an apology, as limited as it may have been. Hu concluded that the attack "incited the fury of the Chinese people" but that law, not mobs, ruled the country.

The Americans still trapped inside the embassy destroyed documents through the night. Outside, protesters held professionally printed signs insisting NATO = NAZI. Leaflets bearing that slogan littered the streets, showing Bill Clinton's head superimposed on Adolf Hitler's body.

The next day in class, my Chinese high schoolers said that the West was always pestering their country about human rights and freedom of speech. "Or does that only matter if Chinese criticize their government instead of support it?" one boy asked.

The other international schools had closed, but as ours was located far from the embassy district and founded to teach collaboration between East and West, we remained open. The Chinese students were heady from a rush of national pride. The non-Chinese thought the whole thing was a spectacle. An eighth-grade girl from Albania, whose uncle lived in Kosovo, had been in a car with her father as they returned to their apartment. Three demonstrators stopped the vehicle, with stones in hand, before her father, a stout ex-wrestler, rolled down his window and said they had five seconds to move before he ran them over. I asked if she was scared. "I was scared of my dad," she said. "He drove away yelling to himself how 'that idiot Hoxha insisted Mao and China were our brothers!'" Her classmates asked what a Hoxha was, having never heard of the Albanian dictator.

Outside, during lunch, Frances pointed out that the teachers at the new Chinese kindergarten who shared our building had taped a white paper banner to the school's wall. Its black brushstroked characters said: STRONGLY CONDEMN U.S.-LED NATO INVASIVE ACTIONS.

Frances said there was nothing to worry about. "Black writing on white paper means mourning. Red characters on yellow paper means anger." She had her kindergartners retort by decorating the banner with colorful crayon strokes approximating hearts, cats, houses, and butterflies. Her mom called to tell me that she didn't think I was responsible for any of this, so I should not worry. (Her dad, a former army medic, advised me to stay away from crowds.) "Are you eating?" Frances's mother asked in Concerned Chinese. "Have you eaten today? You should eat more. Keep eating." I handed the phone back to Frances, who rolled her eyes while waiting her turn to speak. Finally it came: "Yes, Mom, he's eating."

In my class, we watched the demonstrations on CNN—which, for a change, was not suddenly blacked out when it went to live China coverage. The news network showed a map of China marking cities where protests were taking place. However, the graphic had most of the city names in wrong locations. Southern, coastal Guangzhou had been relocated to the far northwest.

"Another bad map," Frances said. This was pre-Google; the U.S. blamed the bombing on an out-of-date map that showed an ammunition dump on the Belgrade lot that actually held the Chinese embassy. Many Chinese, and most of their media, rejected this excuse, just as they had President Clinton's initial apology. After criticism that he sounded insincere, Clinton apologized two more times, finally adding the words, "I regret this," which in Chinese raises the level of contrition to include personal responsibility.

China's president, Jiang Zemin, accepted Clinton's conciliatory phone call two days later. The delay signaled a possible tension in the Chinese government between reformists and conservatives, or it signaled absolutely nothing at all. As usual, China watchers read the tea leaves and came to no consensus. Reading the news while living through the event being reported brought not clarity but confusion. At school, students passed around the *tīngshuō* (heard-said) gossip, but none of it changed the fact that their homework was still due and required grading.

Six days after the bombing, coffins carrying the three victims' remains arrived in Beijing. The nation's flags were lowered to half-mast, an honor usually reserved for political leaders. The protests ended that day. Any belief in their spontaneity was erased when signs began to appear demanding the Chinese government take a stronger stand against the U.S., against the West. Those chartered buses reversed course back to campus, where classes reconvened.

On their return to Peking University, the students would have passed the poster painted by protesters who pledged to turn down their admission to American graduate schools. Their demonstrations, and rocks, closed the consulate's visa application section, which would likely stay shuttered through June 4, the tenth anniversary of Tiananmen. Rumors circulated that students would again protest on that day—in front of the American embassy, where their peers had fled a decade before, when the United States represented safety and the rule of law.

Frances received the letter admitting her to San Francisco State. Her whoop of excitement was muted, however, by the recent protests. Under normal circumstances, the chances of the consulate approving a student visa for a single woman with no binding ties to China was a long shot. Now she faced the additional obstacle of applying at a building still scarred by protesters' stones.

"Things will be back to normal then," I said.

"You don't know that." She said I sounded like the strangers who kept promising us we would have beautiful children.

I offered extra credit for going to Tiananmen Square. Three high school students rode the subway with me after school. The kids talked about their upcoming Model United Nations conference. They had maneuvered through police cordons and debris to interview diplomats about their nation's position on water conservation.

I worried they weren't sufficiently prepared. But as the subway rattled beneath Beijing, my students debated a more pressing matter.

Masanori, a seventeen-year-old from Japan, knitted his brow and said, "Mr. Meyer, China doesn't have any doorknobs, right? I don't get it. All the doors have handles. They don't turn. They go left-right. Open-close. I don't get it." He studied an advertisement over the door. "It's all red bulls running in the same direction. What is it?" He swiveled his head to the next attraction. His body percolated with hormones, caffeine, sugar, questions.

He asked: "Why do we get extra credit for going to Tiananmen Square?"

"You're kidding," I replied. "What day is today?"

He didn't know. I told him to ask the middle-aged man sitting beside us.

In fluent Chinese, Masanori asked, "Sir, excuse me, what's today's date?"

The man's eyes stayed on the newspaper he was reading. Its front page still had U.S.-LED NATO in a headline. "June Fourth," the man said.

Masanori stared blankly.

"The tenth anniversary," the man said into his newspaper.

The students and I stood beneath the portrait of Chairman Mao. I asked them to look around and try to imagine, just try, what the scene sounded like ten years before. Masanori said it probably sounded like it presently did: silent; the military operation had actually begun the night of June 3, and much of the shooting happened on the western approach to the square.

We watched tourists line up for photographs, and men sidling beside them. The men talked into rolled-up newspapers.

"Mr. Meyer, look!"

A shower of white paper rained onto the sidewalk. A young man darted for Chang'an Jie but police quickly pounced on him.

Masanori hustled over to grab a leaflet. But not before the men with rolled-up newspapers converged to wipe the ground clean.

He looked to me. "I wonder what it said?"

For the sake of the young man who had tossed the leaflets, I hoped NATO = NAZI.

At the start of the year, I thought June 4 was going to be The Event, but the day would bring no surprises. Instead, standing with seventeen-year-olds, I remembered how I felt when I was the same age, on this day a decade earlier, hearing the news on my Beetle's radio in Minnesota. China felt as far away from my life's orbit as Mars; never did I suspect that I would have ties to the country, let alone even visit it.

We walked west, past the epicenter of a previous wave of demonstrations that ended—with a wave of arrests, but no bloodshed—twenty years ago, in 1979. What had been dubbed Democracy Wall, named for the posters pasted there calling for political reform, was gone. In its place stood a new mall. The students and I cooled off at its Dairy Queen. In the middle country a decade was a generation, and a lifetime, away.

CHAPTER 13

ARRIVALS AND DEPARTURES

A T THE STONE-POCKED and paint-splattered consulate, Frances stood in line with a bookworm wearing thick glasses who had consulted a fortune-teller about his student visa application. The palm reader said if the sky was clear, he would succeed. Frances looked up. Overcast.

"Maybe the sky is clear, but we can't see it," the man suggested. "It's behind the smog, you know?"

The clerk told her to get in this line. Frances did as she was told, then slowly raised her gaze. Her visa officer was a man who smiled as he greeted each applicant. She slid her documents under the glass. The officer kept his head bowed. He thumbed through her passport, pausing at the previous year's tourist visa to America. *See, I came back,* she wanted to say. The officer pushed Frances's document pile, her life, aside. She watched his hand scribble two illegible lines on a piece of paper and pass it beneath the glass.

That was it. It was over. Frances blinked and stared at the paper.

"Hello?" the officer said. "Take this receipt and go to window twelve."

She wasn't sure what had happened. In a second, the pieces assembled: *He kept my passport . . . receipt . . . window twelve.* Blood soared to her head, a rush overtook her, months of pressure, worrying about this moment, exploded from her mouth.

"YES! OH! YES!" Her laugh erupted into the silent hall. "Thank you, thank you, thank you so much!" Her feet attempted a shuffling jig. "You don't know how much this means to me!"

The officer said, "Next." But not before he smiled.

Frances rode cloud nine to window twelve. She wished she could bottle the sensation. Now the bookworm, standing behind her, tingled with it too. "The palm reader was w-wrong," he stuttered. "I was *approved*."

Those three wonderful words. Frances gathered her papers and stepped through the gate. The smog had, in fact, cleared. She shielded her eyes from the sun, searching for a pay phone. Where had all the aunties and their curbside landlines gone? Where had the curbside gone? Chucked over the fence by protesters. She weaved around the piles of rubble, behind the soldiers, past the embassy's scarred façade, and down a locust-tree-shaded street before stopping to use the phone at the Friendship Store. Did the salespeople and shoppers there hear my yells and her mother's applause? Frances hung up and floated down the Avenue of Eternal Peace, westward to America.

We moved to San Francisco in the summer of 1999, renting an apartment near Golden Gate Park and Clement Street, the "new" Chinatown of middle-class families, Good Luck Dim Sum, and Green Apple Books. I commuted across the Bay to Berkeley, majoring in education and earning a reading specialist credential while working one-on-one with "underperforming" second graders at an "underresourced" public elementary school. What code words! Whenever I saw a Berkeleyite wearing a T-shirt that said FREE TIBET, I wanted to add: AND ALSO OAKLAND.

The Rough Guide hired me to update its guide to Northern California, which introduced Frances to the region the way researching the north-eastern China chapter had done for me. On weekends we drove to the coastal redwood forests, to Mount Shasta, to the remains of the Japanese internment camp at Manzanar, to Yosemite National Park, and across the Salinas Valley, the setting of John Steinbeck's great books, such as *East of Eden*, which Frances read with a clearer sense of place, just as living in Beijing finally made the classic *Dream of the Red Chamber* more vivid for me. In the Sierra Nevada mountains we walked the railroad tunnels blasted by Chinese workers a century before, running our fingers over chisel marks made by her countrymen.

I kept writing travel articles, approaching subjects as I had in China by simply showing up and asking for permission later. For a story on a bar pilot crew that steered ships under the Golden Gate Bridge, I boarded the boat without being asked for identification or signing a waiver; the sailors didn't hand me a life jacket or harness as I climbed a Jacob's ladder forty feet up the side of a swaying container ship in frigid open ocean. "Oh! I thought a bar pilot was like a Sausalito sailboat pub crawl captain," the magazine editor said when I filed the piece. "This isn't about beer at all."

After two years, Frances transferred to UC Berkeley, whose fat acceptance packet included a letter that began, "This is the big envelope. The good one." She continued her art major but took elective courses in legal studies, as she was curious about how the law worked in America. Her interest snowballed into adding it as a major. In some ways we were flipping places, diving deeply into each other's home culture. She soon knew more about America's constitution than I did; in its entirety I had read only China's, sold in state-run bookstores in a cloth-covered hardcover edition. It was the country's twelfth constitution since the end of the last dynasty in 1912, and the fourth of the People's Republic since its founding in 1949.

The current version dated to 1982 and was more aspirational than enforced. The document said that "all citizens are equal before the law," that Chinese over age eighteen had the right to vote, that citizens enjoyed "freedom of speech, of the press, of assembly, of association, of procession and of demonstration." Chinese also had the "right to criticize and make suggestions regarding any state organ or functionary" as well as the "freedom of religious belief." It sounded like a wonderful country to live in; in reality, the Party's control of the press, clergy, courts, and government undermined these freedoms.

In addition to rights, the constitution also enshrined citizens' obligations. Chinese had the right to rest but also the duty to work. Women enjoyed equal rights with men "in all spheres of life," but families were obliged to practice family planning. Children "of age" should support their parents.

All Chinese were enjoined to "safeguard the unification of the country and the unity of all its nationalities"—meaning prevent ethnic unrest—and to "keep state secrets" and "observe public order." In other words, not airing grievances in the media or on the street, as the Falun Gong aunties did when they surrounded Zhongnanhai.

Back in the States, I wrote op-eds about witnessing their demonstration, but like my travel articles the pieces felt thin. I feared I "had the experience but missed the meaning," as T. S. Eliot wrote in a poem I once inflicted on my bewildered teenaged students. I didn't want to become the "Old China Hand," the type of person who, the writer Lin Yutang lamented, returned to the West and signed his letters to the newspapers, "An Old Resident Twenty-Five Years in China." It read impressively, Lin said, yet was usually only more "gossip along the world's longest bar."

I wanted to write more deeply about China but wasn't sure how, especially without a journalist's accreditation. Not that having one granted any special insight: after the aunties' demonstration, *Newsweek* had breathlessly reported that they had "changed China's political landscape"; in fact—like the students at Tiananmen a decade before—they were brutally repressed. Forecasting Chinese politics seemed akin to covering a casino. At any given moment there were losses or gains, but in the end the house always won.

Two years later, in July 2001, the International Olympic Committee selected Beijing to host the 2008 Summer Olympics. "We Win!" Chinese headlines trumpeted. Immediately the capital—and the country—mobilized for what the government was calling China's coming-out party to the world. Beijing had already been playing catch-up, remaking itself from an inward-looking Communist capital to an international global city; the Olympics announcement just accelerated its transformation. In Qianmen—at six hundred years, the capital's oldest *hútòng* neighborhood, adjacent to the southern edge of Tiananmen Square—I saw a banner hanging over a fresh pile of rubble that said PROTECT THE ANCIENT CITY'S APPEARANCE. Below the empty slogan, characters read:

再现古都 (The ancient capital reappears.)

At least it did, until the following night, when an anonymous hand neatly excised part of the second character, changing the revel to a lament:

再见古都 (Farewell, ancient capital.)

The altered sign was pulled down within hours, but no matter: Beijingers saw it firsthand, every day.

I traveled back in 2002 for a job updating the next edition of *The Rough Guide to China*, four years after my previous rounds through the Northeast. Now my territory had expanded to include Inner Mongolia and the Yellow River region as well. Only after landing did I realize that this covered one million square miles of land, an area nearly as large as India. I had budgeted four weeks.

At night in a *wăngbā*—a "Net bar," or Internet café—I squinted through cigarette smoke at the screen to read Frances's e-mails about studying Cézanne at Berkeley. I replied that I had exited the Xi'an train station to see two people costumed in gigantic inflatable Wuliangye-brand liquor bottles square-dancing on the street as a brass band played an out-of-tune "Jingle Bells." Frances said spring had bloomed in Berkeley; I trudged through a blizzard to former Japanese military tunnels on the Siberian border. She made salads from organic produce purchased at the Berkeley Bowl; on trains I ate bowls of instant noodles whose packaging assured consumers they were "ISO 9001 certified"—the global quality control standard whose label was omnipresent in China after the country won approval to join the World Trade Organization. (The noodles still tasted like cardboard.) Frances spent a day reading on a sun-splashed patch of Berkeley grass; I sat in a Changchun *wăngbā* trapped by a massive dust storm. Its customers played the video game *Counterstrike*, whose refrain echoed across my travels: "Terrorists win. Terrorists win."

Chinese called the Yellow River the cradle of their civilization. It looked exhausted: dust-blown fields, soot-stained brick houses, unregulated coal mines. In comparison, the Northeastern prairie looked like a promised land; no wonder millions of Han Chinese, including Frances's maternal ancestors, passed through the gate at the Great Wall to settle there in the nineteenth century, a migration that at its peak exceeded even the number of Europeans coming through Ellis Island.

My route took on Homeric proportions, but in place of *The Iliad*'s lists of kingdoms, I logged cities, marching through Linfen and Yuncheng, Baotou and Xinzhou, Weihai and Yantai, Anyang and Shijiazhuang. I made sure the terra-cotta warriors were still there, copied the ticket prices and opening hours at Buddhist grottoes, found the cleanest hotel in Hohhot, and walked the winding hilly streets of former German colonial Qingdao, drinking beer like the locals: through a straw, from a plastic bag filled from kegs delivered by the town's Tsingtao brewery. On its outskirts, I got trapped in a gas station bathroom stall whose lock had jammed, pulled myself atop the thin plywood door, and—hearing that horrible creak as the stall tore from the wall—rode the entire structure down to the floor. I exited briskly, hailed a passing cab, and watched from its window as uniformed pump attendants headed for the source of the clatter. In arid north-central Datong, I wandered around China's last steam engine factory, a plant large enough to have its own hospital and schools. The engineer idling on a siding understood my universal gesture and tooted the big train's steam whistle. On a train from Inner Mongolia back to Beijing, I turned thirty. Confucius said at age fifteen he had set his heart on learning; at thirty his character had been formed, and he "firmly took my stand." As ever, his 2,500-year-old lesson sounded like practical advice.

As Frances finished her last semester at Berkeley, I looked for an apartment in Beijing, where she would join me after graduation to work at a firm while preparing to apply to American law schools. If my two years in Neijiang were elementary school, and my two-year stint teaching in Beijing equivalent to middle school, then I intended this next stage to be high school, with a goal of graduating from a freelancer to a full-time journalist.

I thought: *I can do this, I don't need her help.* I bought my first cell phone, using it to call a woman who advertised a one-bedroom apartment in a 1950s walk-up building on Wěikēng (Duckweed Hollow) *hútòng*, near the city's chain of central lakes. The monthly rent was the equivalent of $200, cheap for Beijing. The owner admitted her elderly mother had recently passed away inside the home. I debated whether to share this news with Frances, knowing that she—like many Chinese—feared ghosts.

In truth, I was creeped out too: the deceased's bedding and clothing still filled a wardrobe, and the television automatically tuned in to Beijing's opera station when it was switched on. I couldn't read the on-screen menu's instructions to change it, so every time I pressed POWER, the performers' plaintive wails reverberated off the cement walls. One was decorated with a wall calendar whose page had not been turned from the previous October, when the woman had died.

Still, the kidney-shaped West Lake and the delicious dumpling restaurants at Xinjiekou were a short walk away, while the view from the sunporch looked over a Buddhist temple's tiled roof. I spent the first afternoon standing at the windows, watching flocks of pet pigeons swoop in loops over the *hútòng's* courtyard homes. The bamboo whistles tied to their feet made a mournful sound, which dipped and crested with their wings. I was back in Beijing, and it felt like being home.

The next morning I woke in the musty bedroom's spectral sunlight and thought, *So now what do I do?* For the first time in China, I did not have a classroom of students waiting. In exchange for spot work as a stringer— doing interviews and research for stories—*Time* magazine's Beijing bureau let me use their office to work on a comparatively fast Internet and secure landline. I was not an official employee, or accredited, but Matt Forney, the bureau chief whom I had met playing basketball, nonetheless looked the other way when I regularly phoned Frances, back in Berkeley. The office had formerly been a diplomatic apartment, so it featured a full kitchen; Matt used one bedroom as his office, while two staffers worked at desks in what had been the living room. Framed issues of the magazine hung on its walls. I often worked at a desk beneath the exhausted gaze of Chiang Kai-shek, on the cover for September 3, 1945, shortly after Japan's surrender and the end of the Second World War. Farther down the wall, the December 1, 1958, issue featured "Red China's Mao" and Napoleon's alleged admonition, "Let China sleep. When she awakens the world will be sorry."

I had heard that prediction repeated ad nauseam; in 1997 the *Economist* recommended the line—whose second sentence is more commonly rendered as "When she wakes she will shake the world"—be put to sleep. It was the cliché "that launched a thousand articles." Since then it has launched at least a thousand more. In fact, Napoleon probably never said it: the quote appears in none of his writings, and according to a leading Napoleon scholar its contemporary users never cite a source.

Yet since 1895, when a British field marshal wrote that a slumbering China will awaken and "become a Frankenstein monster," Napoleon's apocryphal line has been invoked to cast "a rising China" as a threat to the global order, and Western exceptionalism. In his 1958 book *Scratches on Our Minds: American Views of China and India*, *Newsweek*'s former Asia correspondent Harold R. Isaacs noted that the preceding fifty years produced sixty articles and thirty books in which "China, or the giant, or the dragon, has awakened, is waking, or is stirring, rising, changing, or being reborn."

Time's Matt Forney repeated the old joke that "There are no new stories on China, only new journalists." I took this two ways. First, for the past century, the country has cycled through a loosening and tightening of central control, of progression and regression, which leads to coverage tinged with a sense of déjà vu. Second, foreigners' China reporting tended toward extremes, leading to stories capturing either the awful or the enchanting. This explained why an editor at a hallowed American news magazine advised me: "An article from China requires an ending that makes the reader feel either: We're all gonna die, or We're all gonna get laid."

A short time later, a *Time* editor suggested that I travel to Sichuan to report from a village where he had heard that prostitutes desperate for customers were digging ditches across roadways to slow truck drivers and even throwing themselves in front of the moving vehicles.

I didn't go: these types of stories seemed a little too pat, especially when a reporter could only spend a short time—sometimes less than a day—on it before deadline, and then move on to the next assignment. In a country in so much flux, a story often became clear only over time.

Four years previously I had taught the Beijing writer Lao She's novels and taken my students to the theme restaurant that was then the capital's de facto memorial to the Cultural Revolution. Now, after waiting years for approval, Lao She's widow was permitted to open their former courtyard home on Fēngfù (Bountiful) *hútòng*, just east of the Forbidden City, as a museum of her husband's life and death.

On the day I visited, sunlight bathed the persimmon trees Lao She had planted in a south-facing courtyard. Displays in Chinese told how, in 1900, European forces breaking the Boxer Rebellion's siege of Beijing killed Lao She's father, a Manchu soldier. He had grown up dirt poor in the inner city of Old Beijing, born, as he wrote, "just in time to witness the flickering candles of the funeral rites of the Qing Dynasty." Still, at the age of twenty-five, Lao She managed to move to the West, teaching Chinese literature at the University of London and, later, working with an American woman in Philadelphia to translate his novels into English. His best-known book, 1936's *Camel Xiangzi* (also titled *Rickshaw Boy*), describes the hopeless travails of a Beijing laborer on the eve of Japanese occupation. It ends so devastatingly that the American publisher changed the ending without telling him, allowing the title character to live happily ever after. Lao She was a Beijing native and knew better.

Pearl Buck wrote about hosting Lao She during his stay in America, calling him "a sensitive man, oversophisticated perhaps, instinctively avoiding anything painful, even in conversation," including politics. Instead of delivering lectures about the Japanese occupation of China, he charmed audiences with quotidian topics such as "Crickets, Kites and Pekinese Dogs and Their Significance in Chinese Life."

Buck was sad to see him return to China in 1949, after the Communist victory: "Now he is an exile of a sort, living in Peking and speaking what he is told to speak and writing what he is told to write . . . I marvel at his obedience. But I know he has compensations. He is in Peking, he is in China, and his heart is free."

I am always drawn to people's bookshelves, especially authors', curious what they might reveal. Lao She often wrote satire, and so I wasn't surprised to see English-language editions of *Damon Runyon Favorites*, Carson McCullers's *The Heart Is a Lonely Hunter*, and *The Prince and the Pauper* by Mark Twain. Lao She had often written of his love of Shakespeare, but only one of his works was here: *Antony and Cleopatra*. The tragedy looked incongruous on the shelf, until I remembered that Shakespeare's play is steeped in betrayal. Instead of being paraded before Rome's "shouting varlotry," Cleopatra chooses suicide.

Beijing museums are usually emptied of personal effects, and staged like an Ikea showroom. Lao She's widow made this exhibit feel intimate, as though the writer had just stepped outside to pick a persimmon. His chair was pushed away from his writing desk. An enamel tea mug rested on a blotter next to his spectacles. On the daybed was spread an unfinished game of Solitaire. The tear-away calendar sat there like a clock hit by a bullet, showing August 24, 1966. On that day Lao She rose early, stepped over the courtyard's threshold, and walked to his favorite pond, never to return.

Time wasn't interested in that story, but did publish my visit to Beijing's largest brewery. "How do you get to our factory?" the voice on the line repeated my question with a laugh. "Just show the cabby a bottle of Yanjing and say, 'Take me.'"

And so it was, down Twin Rivers Road, beneath the bellies of incoming planes, where the billboards all urged YANJING and the air reeked of roasted barley. The empty boulevard carried us in efficient quietness to the gates of Yanjing's Beer Science and Technology Mansion. The guard saluted the car around the fountain and under a granite colonnade. The lobby's clocks told the time in Paris, London, and New York City. A man in a suit waited with his name card. I wished I had worn a tie.

In the Beer Exhibition Hall, sweeping his arm over a model of the factory, the grandly titled "general manager work vice director," Zhang Erjing, narrated Yanjing's success. Founded in 1980 by the Beijing municipal government with $770,000, two decades later the brewery boasted assets ten times as large. Its ubiquitous bottles of beer accounted for 85 percent of the Beijing market, and 10 percent of the nation's. The secret to its triumphs? WINNING CREDIT FROM THE PEOPLE WITH ITS EXCEL-LENT QUALITY, read a display. PLEASING THE PEOPLE WITH ITS UNIQUE FLAVOR, AND SERVING THE PEOPLE WITH ITS SINCERE ATTITUDE.

It's cheap too. "Our signature brand is affordable," allowed Zhang, leading me to shelves of Yanjing's fifteen varieties. The stuff from a local *xiǎomàibù* (corner store) costing two yuan (about 25 cents) was the Refreshing brand.

According to Zhang, each Beijinger annually quaffed fifty liters of beer, half the amount the average American drank. His job was to increase that figure, both by acquiring regional breweries and by introducing new prod-ucts. Yanjing also produced soft drinks, mineral water, soy sauce, and vinegar. All without a foreign partner—not surprising, from the official beer of the Great Hall of the People. Although, Zhang admitted, the brewery imported all of its malting barley from Canada and Australia. My eyebrows arched in surprise: communism was a foreign import, and so was Buddhism, but I had assumed Beijing's beer was a wholly local recipe. In fact, China did grow barley, but the demand for beer outpaced acreage as Chinese farmers switched to planting crops such as corn and wheat, for which the government guaranteed a minimum-price subsidy.

Zhang led me upstairs to the "production dispatching center," where a worker straightened at his console and began pushing buttons. "We have eighteen thousand workers," Zhang said. On the factory floor below us, I counted six. "But mostly we are automated using modern German equipment."

As we walked above the assembly line, Zhang reeled off stats as quickly as the robots were fastening caps on newborn beers. After an hour of admiring shiny tanks and blinking switchboards, we made for the Yanjing Bar. EACH GUEST IS ENTITLED TO ONE GLASS, read a sign. Zhang signaled for a pitcher and recounted the day he drank here with boxing promoter Don King. "Big hair," he remembered. We tapped our steins and savored a malty freshness that forever spoiled my appreciation of the bike-transported local stuff.

Zhang lit a Red Pagoda Mountain Gold and wanted to talk about the business plan, "about strict control over rate of charges on assets," but I had some nagging questions: Favorite Yanjing? "Draft brand." Brown bottle or green? "Doesn't matter." Pineapple beer: Why? "Refreshing." The growing red wine market? "No problem! Wine's not as good for you as beer." Then Zhang pointed to his cheeks and mine, declared them pink, and ordered tea. The tour was over. He had to get back to work.

Complaining about the Western media's coverage of China is not new: "It is surprising to discover the number of Americans who have a genuine interest in the Chinese people," Pearl Buck wrote in *China As I See It*, "and who would like to have sound information upon which to base their own opinions . . . True, it has not been easy and until recently it has been impossible to get reporters in and out of China proper. But one must assume that the news media themselves are also at fault for underestimating the general intelligence of their reading public and the range of its interest."

Her observation, from 1970, remained valid, but I saw how correspondents worked under pressure from faraway editors with their own agendas— and around an at-hand regime that obfuscated and impeded their reporting. I couldn't change that, so I pointed the finger at my own nose, as Chinese do when singling out themselves. *I can do better,* I kept telling myself, but my stories from this time were trifles: features for in-flight magazines, city guides for premium American Express cardholders, food items for *Reader's Digest.* These publications paid $1 per word; I wrote a lot of unnecessary words. Once for *Time* I filed an article from Hainan island's Sanya city beach on the new trend of body painting. It included the line: "As Mei Mei's nipples hardened under painted cherry blossoms and she awaited her souvenir snapshot, scuba divers and snorkelers shared space with jet skis in the warm South China Sea below. China felt very far away."

So did the word *dignity.*

Despite knowing better, I accepted an assignment for a piece called "Luxe Lhasa." Gone was the old fighter jet in the square fronting the Potala Palace. In its place stood an obelisk named the Tibet Peaceful Liberation Monument. Even Swiss engineers had said it was impossible to build a railroad to Lhasa. The Chinese government loved that sort of challenge; it had nearly finished building the line that would connect "the roof of the world" to Xining, the capital of neighboring Qinghai province, a mostly barren plateau twice the size of Germany. It had once been Tibet's Amdo region, until the Republican government subsumed the land into greater China in 1928. Not all of China's domestic strife was created by the Communists.

The editor of the glossy travel magazine was not interested in that. He asked about Lhasa's tennis courts. I had not seen any; volleying at twelve thousand feet above sea level was a recipe for pulmonary edema. *How about the wineries?* I described a thin-air hangover from *chang,* the local liquor often served from empty gasoline cans. *Are there beaches?* I recounted my afternoon squatting on the sandy banks of the Lhasa River, counting bloated cow corpses as they floated past. Seven. *What about festivals and holidays?*

I advised travelers to avoid the "sensitive" anniversaries: the historic dates of uprisings, ethnic riots, and military reprisals. There were nine! *Any spas worth recommending?* I contracted giardia and spent the night tethered to an intravenous drip in an empty hospital ward whose fluorescent lighting intermittently flickered, as in a horror film. This was a low.

After landing back in Chengdu from Lhasa, I decided to visit Neijiang for the first time since leaving, six years before, thinking that the trip would be restorative. The two-hour bus journey was still a knee-hugging ride, filling my head with thoughts of *plunge* as the speeding vehicle keeled into the expressway's S-curves, skirting the wreckage of overturned trucks. When the green sign announced the exit to 内江 NEIJIANG, my spirits didn't rise, but suddenly sank at the memory of torpid days, when even the cicadas seemed to buzz *lǎowài* as I plodded to the dirt-floored No Big Deal stall for a bowl of radish-pickle fried rice. I remembered the smell of vinegar and mud.

"Are you sure you lived here?" the cabdriver asked, looking for the teachers college. "Your directions got us lost!" Even beyond Neijiang's new McDonald's, I recognized nothing. A new bridge had replaced the ferry to the far shore of campus. The former bamboo-shaded mud road had turned into a wide, paved boulevard. No Big Deal was gone, as were all of the other lean-to restaurants and small businesses. We stopped beside billboards advertising high-rise apartments named SEATTLE GOLD MOUNTAIN and CALIFORNIA BLUE HARBOR. Well-dressed women walked past, carrying umbrellas to shade themselves from the sun. (Farmers had tans; sophisticates stayed pale.) I watched them walk toward signs promising yet another new development, its slogan receding around the bend: VIP VIP VIP VIP.

The taxi dropped me at a decorative fountain spuming high in the air. Previously, this water would have irrigated crops, but instead of rapeflowers the air smelled of fresh paint. The college had been upgraded to a university. My old teaching building became a place for furniture storage, and my former apartment was mothballed too. Teachers now lived in high-rises built where I once walked through sugarcane.

I looked for Mr. Wang, my former supervisor, but he had realized his dream, winning a government scholarship to spend a year studying British

Romantic poetry at Cambridge University. "What has surprised me most," he replied by e-mail, "is that people aren't embracing or kissing passionately on the street, as you see in Hollywood movies."

They were in Neijiang, however: students walked together holding hands and embraced by the new basketball courts. Previously, public displays of affection earned the offender a steep 50-yuan fine. Now unmarried couples were permitted to live together off campus. A chime dismissed class, and hundreds of well-dressed young people walked past, laughing or staring at their phones. No one yelled *lǎowài*. Did anyone even notice me? Had I become the Ghost of Peace Corps Past? Even when standing before familiar buildings, such as the library (and spotting the ceiling panel that concealed the ladder to the attic), I found it hard to believe that I once spent two years here.

The librarian led me to the new teaching building, where we dropped into an Oral English class being taught by a Chinese professor I had never met. Politely, she welcomed us inside, although I already felt in the way. At first glance the students seemed unchanged from those I had taught. They also chose inimitable English names, such as Season, and Friday. But the seniors said that after they graduated—in cap and gown, a new trend on Chinese campuses, mimicking the Western tradition—they were free to choose their career. Some planned on teaching English in their hometowns, where they could take care of their parents. Others said they wanted to travel abroad, to open a flower shop, to write a book, or to go on to graduate school. One student, named Sajone, said, "I want to be a teacher as a volunteer to work in the poor places." That was the first time I had heard a Chinese person say that. After winning its Olympic bid, Beijing promoted volunteerism, adding community service to the national high school curriculum.

The class shook their heads disbelief when I described my former life on campus. No cell phone! A three-week wait between letters home? *Beatles songs in class?* They listened to Beyoncé.

Outside the post office, I ran into a former student, a young woman who worked for the city government. We chatted in Chinese after she admitted she had forgotten most of her English. As I walked a final lap around the campus, a drunkard ordered me to go home. OK, I replied. In English he cursed fluently. I said I used to teach here. "I was your student," he lied.

He kept walking away, gathering courage as the distance between us increased. Over his shoulder he let out a yodeling yawp, the longest and loudest "*Lăooooooowài!*" I had ever heard, transporting me right back to my volunteer years. I flashed with anger, and then let it go and laughed. I had returned to Neijiang for a glimpse of the past, but left happy to find it all but erased. China was changing so fast that even the nostalgia wasn't as good as it used to be.

CHAPTER 14

DIGRESSIONS ON THE NEW FRONTIER

R ATHER THAN RUSH back to Beijing, where a story would be assigned
to me, I decided to slow down and stop reporting on China to instead
just experience it. As a volunteer in Sichuan and a teacher in Beijing, the
moments I most remembered happened not by appointment but by chance.
I had lived here long enough to know that whenever I didn't know what I
was looking for, I should stop the search. Soon enough, someone would
approach and tell me why I was there.

In Chengdu I bought the only available ticket for a northbound train
that day, a slower line that would take twenty hours to reach Xi'an. After
clearing Chengdu's exurbs, the train's pulse—*click-cluck, click-cluck*—
resounded off tunnel walls and into the window below my upper berth. I
rolled over to watch the approaching magic trick, when, with a bang caused
by the pressure change, the train shot from the tunnel's darkness back into
broad daylight.

We entered a plush valley hugged by jagged peaks. All down the compartment corridor I watched stocking feet jerk awake. Passengers rose to see
pink orchid sunlight fill the open windows.

The Min River spun far below, the color of turquoise and completely
still, save for a flock of paddling white geese. Rice paddy terraces scaled
the mountainsides, illuminated by bonfires of burning stalks. A temple
stood high over the valley, keeping watch on a young girl tending a row
of waddling ducks. Ahead, the engine car entered a curve, presenting a
fleeting glimpse of the train's twenty-five cars uncoiled.

A tap on my shoulder came from behind. A man demanded, "*Lǎowài!* Hey, how tall are you? Where are you from, *lǎowài?*"

The smell of feet filled the air. The *click-cluck* of the wheels grew louder, and the train plunged back into darkness, roaring and smoking all the way.

China's railroad (*tiělù*, "iron road") ties together a nation nearly as large as the entire United States. For most Chinese, the train is not a romantic mode of transport but an affordable one, and safer than the highways. The regular, non-high-speed lines usually have three classes—my hard sleeper berth to Xi'an cost the equivalent of $15—and run around the clock to every province. "Except Taiwan," Party officials hasten to add. Although blueprints for a tunnel to the "renegade province" are said to exist.

Unlike other Chinese routines—posting a letter, banking, paying utility bills, job-hunting—riding on a slower train remains all but unchanged. Even in the shiny new stations, the boarding process can still resemble the crane shot of *Gone With the Wind*'s battlefield hospital. In the common class compartments, you still sit facing and touching knees with other passengers. You still are encouraged by the anonymity of strangers to talk, and to complain about family, work, and politics. You still, if you are a foreigner, recite your height, salary, and chopstick proficiency.

"The only bad moment the train passenger has is on the platform, when the other passengers are boarding," the travel writer Paul Theroux wrote in *Riding the Iron Rooster: By Train Through China*. "Which ones will be in your compartment? It is a much more critical lottery than a blind date, because these people will be eating and sleeping with you."

As I made my way through the cars of Train 530, I passed grandmothers and old men and children, all smiling warmly at me, and I at them, hoping that they were my bunkmates. Instead, I found myself billeted with five slimy-looking guys smoking Famous Dog cigarettes.

I put my backpack up on the shelf of steel bars and sat on the foldout chair bolted beneath the window.

"Sure is hot," a man said.

"No mistake," I replied.

"Your Chinese is great!" the man exclaimed, and the four others lobbed questions. Where was I from? What was I doing in China? Did I want a smoke? Did I play cards? How many beers could I drink? How much money did I make? What did I think of Chinese girls? And would I trade my lower bunk for the top one? The questions were punctuated with a symphony of cell phone rings, tinny imitations of Beethoven's Fifth Symphony, "We Are the Champions," and also "Mary Had a Little Lamb."

I thought: *I bet these guys snore.*

The train creaked into motion and we pulled out of Chengdu as platform attendants stiffly saluted our passing faces. I opened the lavatory door. After one full minute of travel, the floor toilet was clogged with a collage of feces, sanitary napkins, and a 40-watt light bulb.

My bunkmates settled into a routine of phlegm clearing, money arguing, and cell phone shouting, all punctuated with "*Tā mā de*" (literally, "His mother's"). Often used as flexibly as the f-word in English, the vulgarity was so ubiquitous that even a century ago the famous essayist Lu Xun wrote, "If the peony is China's national flower, then '*Tā mā de*' has to be considered its national curse word."

The men dressed alike, in polo shirts tucked into slacks cinched by designer-label belts. They played poker with cards featuring naked Western women, and their Famous Dog smoke obscured the NO SMOKING sign hanging above them.

We chatted about unimportant things and got along fine. I told them I was a teacher, as benign, boring, and impoverishing a profession as you can have in China, but one that allows a comfortable distance between yourself and others. Teachers might be toothless but they are still respected. I could read a book or write notes quietly; that was typical antisocial teacher—not just foreigner—behavior.

A conductor wearing a navy-blue uniform a size too large came around and exchanged our paper tickets for plastic chits. No bunk swapping was allowed. Everybody took off their shoes. I filled the thermos from the car-end samovar and made jasmine tea. The *click-cluck, click-cluck* of the wheels became the soundtrack for a movie of water buffaloes, smokestacks, rickety bicycles, and children waving at the train while their parents waded in paddies planting rice. A moped puttered along the thin road with a live hog lashed between the driver and the handlebars. It did not look upset.

Our compartment hummed with chitchat, movement, and tea slurping. The pajama party had begun.

You knew when a station approached, because the blue sky began to cloud and then darken. Dirt roads changed to fetid canals. The smog seemed to brake the train on its own. City names—Eternal Spring, Auspicious Forest, Precious Chicken—sound inviting or intriguing on maps, but—from the railway, at least—often do not look as advertised. A forlorn stop named New Happiness made it hard to imagine life in Old Happiness.

As the train slowed, the car's interior energy subsided. We crept past concrete buildings covered in white bathroom tile and into a characterless station whose loudspeakers blared a dirge-like tune. Platform attendants saluted our frowns, and a phalanx of food vendors converged on the cars, pitching apples, beer, and hot dumplings. Passengers bargained until the end. As we departed, vendors panted, running to close one more sale, tossing bananas into the windows.

I felt a sore throat coming on; my bunkmates' cigarettes weren't helping. "Have one," a man suggested helpfully. "Then you won't notice the smoke so much." I thought: *If Frances were here, she would snap,* I'll show you the colors! *and scare these men into submission*; she never backed down from bullies. I considered upgrading my ticket to a soft sleeper, but past experience had taught me that inhaling secondhand Famous Dogs in an open compartment with my own class of passenger beat inhaling secondhand Marlboros in a closed-door compartment with Party cadres.

Instead, I spied an open top bunk at the end of the car. I scaled the thin ladder and found it empty, so I squatted there instead. It was a fortuitous move. I was trying it out for size, when a young man on the lower bunk introduced himself in cheerful Chinese. He was a software developer returning home to Xi'an after a Buddhist pilgrimage to Mount Emei. He wore glasses and a long-sleeved cotton shirt tucked into blue jeans. He didn't want to know how much money I made. He asked if I was "lost in the red dust of the world."

I climbed down and sat beside him.

I had won the seating lottery. Sharing this six-bunk area was a young woman with pink-tinted hair wearing pink clothes and pink platform shoes and holding a pink plastic purse. She did not miss a beat when I asked, deadpan, her favorite color: "Pink."

Across from her sat an old man wearing a mesh baseball cap with the logo WELCOME BACK MACAU! The old man stared quietly out the window. His only luggage was a small knapsack with a hand towel tied to the outside. The cloth showed a drawing of a yellow duck walking with an umbrella under the rain and the caption OK. Next to him sat a thin man in a tank top undershirt with a bad case of bed head. He gave me an open-palmed salute and said in English, "Hello, my American friend!"

Introducing himself last was a stocky man with glasses who extended his hand and gave mine a firm shake. "Bob Chen," he declared. "That's my English name. Computer engineering. Would you help me with my English?" He dug out a thick tome titled *e-Business 2.0: Roadmap for Success* and read: "'Supplier integration'—how do you say that in Chinese?"

"I can barely say it in English."

Bob Chen blinked.

"I'm just an English teacher," I said apologetically.

The others smiled. I was harmless. Over roasted watermelon seeds, we exchanged names, birthplaces, and major life events. The train rushed along out of the plains and into the steppes. There was nothing to see out the window save for kids playing basketball on a dirt court with backboards made from stacked railroad ties. The man with bed head wanted to know how much money I made, but Bob Chen looked up from his book and scolded him for being so rude. I told him it was OK: officially, since I was actually a freelance writer, my salary was zero. I showed them my notebook, filled with scribbles. Bob Chen returned to reading *e-Business 2.0*, then asked, "How do you say 'aggregation of information assets' in Chinese?" Bed Head giggled. The girl in pink had fallen asleep, snoring soft pink breaths. The old man stared out the window.

The train bounced on. We rolled through rough terrain that nonetheless produced those bumper harvests the state press reported every year. I wondered what these farmers, whose technology was limited to a water buffalo, put on their wheat fields. I flipped through a Chinese dictionary, trying to find the word for fertilizer. The Buddhist interrupted me. "Do you want to look for it on a website? I know a good online dictionary." Sure, I said, but I didn't have a computer. No sooner had the words left my mouth than he had dug out his laptop and dialed up the Internet. Bob Chen sprang up and fetched his. They were both scanning dictionary pages and quizzing each other on their machines' technical specifications. This was a new vocabulary lesson too. I only understood bits: "How big is your battery? How much memory does yours have? You got a big processor in that thing?"

It took a few seconds to turn the pages of my pocket dictionary (*fertilizer* was under F, *féiliào*), but it seemed rude to interrupt. Bob and the Buddhist showed me their favorite websites, including ones they had designed. We checked for www.famousdogs.com.cn but came up empty. Bob said I should register the domain.

The food cart rattled by, selling three kinds of cigarettes, one brand of instant noodles, and five kinds of beer. The press cart followed, pitching state-run newspapers and a novel whose cover had a photo of a sexy woman, $100 bills, and cigarette smoke. I half expected the title to be a translation of Dale Carnegie's *How to Win Friends and Influence People*. Instead it was the type of lurid novel usually sold not in bookstores but from blankets that vendors spread on the sidewalk outside Beijing subway entrances.

Bob and the Buddhist realized they had the same Chinese chess program. They played fifteen minutes on one machine before the battery conked out, then moved to the other computer before that, too, drained itself. The Buddhist dug into his suitcase and produced a chess set of round wooden pieces and a paper board, the kind that Chinese had been playing on for millennia. They spread the game out on a lower bunk and lost themselves in the competition. Bob Chen looked up once, wondering how to say *checkmate* in English.

I went back to reading Theroux's *Riding the Iron Rooster* by the window, but my eye kept being drawn to the poster on the bathroom door. One half of it showed a peaceful railway station. The other half depicted a flaming inferno with people on fire running for their lives. The caption warned: DON'T BRING EXPLOSIVE FERTILIZER ON THE TRAIN. A photo below it showed why: the gruesome aftermath of an explosion that made blood run down the compartment walls. Why did I always look?

Outside, the trees stopped growing in straight lines, meaning we were far from any town. The settlements under the spruces grew thinner, and I welcomed the sight of shingled roofs and asymmetrical rice paddies, separated by winding ridges and occasional graves, whose rounded soil stood in the fields like pitchers' mounds. The vista signaled a lack of central planning and also a portrait of the past, when much of China looked this poor. We rumbled past two men playing chess along the train tracks, maneuvering pebbles on a board scratched into the dirt.

The train groaned as it slowed, as if saying that it, too, wanted to keep going. Instead we pulled in to another town. I caught the girl in pink staring at me. Her blush matched her clothing and she asked, "Do you really understand Chinese?"

She was awake and ready to join the group, stretching her body over the men as they played chess, asking questions and sighing, "I don't understand!" Her midriff showed and her voice was coquettish, but on a Chinese train she was everybody's sister. She leaned back and sang a pop song's chorus, "*Are you happy or not? Do you love me or not?*" The old man stared out the window.

She loved this guy at her college, she announced, but he didn't love her. It was because she was short. The boy said she was 1.5 meters, but he wanted a wife who was 1.7 meters. The men, all married, advised her to forget the jerk.

"I've been eating tall pills," she said. "But they're not working. Sometimes I spend 600 yuan on them, other times 400 yuan, but they don't work."

"You're being cheated," Bob Chen said. "That's fake medicine." He turned to me and asked how to say *jiǎyào* (literally, "fake medicine") in English. "Quack, like a duck?" he wondered with a laugh. English coinages sounded illogical.

"I wish I were 1.7 meters," the girl pouted. "Then he would love me."

The Buddhist looked up from the chessboard and said, "Life is a sea of suffering. As soon as you look back, you will see the shore."

The ride grew monotonous into dusk. We entered tunnel country, making the climb from plains of rice paddies to plateaus of wheat. Bob Chen and the others lay in their bunks. It felt like nap time at kindergarten. The old man remained sitting by the window, but with his eyes closed. I climbed the metal rungs up to my new squatter's berth and squeezed in, burrowing beneath what could have been the same scratchy horse blanket that Theroux complained about a decade before.

By 8:00 p.m. the compartment found its second wind. The drinking and card playing began, and passengers roamed the aisle, looking for new faces to meet. They passed our group without pausing; we had closed ranks, like wallflowers at a dance who had found a safe corner to share. This was one benefit to traveling alone, without Frances. Couples can become their own impenetrable units on the road. Here, I had been adopted into a new one.

In the fading light I saw only wheat, growing thickly and forever. The homes became lean and red-tiled, and then there were no houses at all. On trains you realized China's vastness; the widened perspective of leaving its cities showed, too, the long-view insignificance of headlines' "momentous events," such as the Olympics, whose opening ceremony was being counted down to on clocks displayed in city squares. The only clock on the north Sichuan plain was the harvest moon, fattening into view. Time to scythe the fields.

For the first time I spotted birds: black sparrows that raced the train, gorging on the bugs it swirled skyward. Bob Chen filled a thermos at the samovar and then poured steaming water into our Styrofoam bowls of Third Wife-brand instant noodles.

Bed Head returned my book, saying in English, "Thank you, my good foreign friend!" His English seemed to be improving with every passing station. I had stopped reading Theroux to pay attention to my own journey. Bob Chen and the Buddhist debated if Falun Gong was a religious cult or a harmless sect. Bob said the former, the Buddhist the latter. The girl in pink slept narcotically, again; I wondered what was in those tall pills. The old man stared out the window.

At precisely 10:00 p.m. the train's interior lights clicked off and we all climbed into bed.

"Hey, why didn't you change your ticket? Hey!"

The conductor had a hold on my toe.

We had stopped in some town, and I was in a new passenger's assigned bunk.

"I'm sorry, I'm sick," I mumbled. "They're smoking. I'm a teacher . . ." Why wasn't anyone sticking up for me? Bed Head? Bob? Were they all really sleeping through this racket?

"Give me your chit!" The conductor studied my berth assignment under her penlight.

"I'm a teacher," I protested meekly.

The train shuddered to life. "*Tā mā de!* OK, you stay." Pointing to the smoking end of the car, the conductor told the new passenger to go and sleep there. Down the corridor, I heard my five former bunkmates slapping down trump cards in the dark, swearing loudly. "You're lucky," the conductor told the silent man. "It's a lower berth. That's better. It costs more." I felt bad, consigning him to that. But not bad enough to climb down from my bed.

But I was awake, and suddenly aware of the snoring. Sucking, snorting snoring. I envied that depth of sleep. I made a clamshell of the thin pillow, inserting my head into its mouth. Snoring! I put on my headphones and played a CD by the Jon Spencer Blues Explosion. It drowned out the snores, but still I could feel my bunkmates' wheezes. The music also, of course, blared so loudly that I lay awake for hours, inhaling the fug of feet.

I awoke from a watery sleep at 5:00 a.m., flopping down from the bunk and landing on a floor littered with beer bottles, cigarette butts, seed husks, orange peels, and gobs of spit. The lavatory looked even worse.

The view outside, however, was spectacular: dawn, glimpsed twenty seconds at a time through a screen of mist as the train exited tunnel after tunnel. Plump raindrops thudded on the car's roof, and cascades tumbled off the mountains into the fog.

"Excuse . . . me . . . what . . . is . . . your . . . name?"

The old man, silent for the entire journey until now, enunciated his Chinese slowly and loudly to help me understand.

"Sold Son," I told him, but he didn't understand. "Heroic Eastern Plumblossom." The old man smiled.

"Good friend, good friend," he replied in staccato English, patting the open space on his berth. I sat beside him. He grabbed my hand and did not let go. Then he flashed a toothless smile and asked me to fill his teacup with hot water.

His name was Mr. Li. He was seventy-seven. He had been watching me write in a notebook and wanted to show me that he was writing too. On every page of his tattered journal I saw an entry headed by the date, weather condition, place, and a one-character description of how he felt.

We looked out the window together. For the weather, Mr. Li recorded: *Fine*. The place was: *the train*. He felt: *good*.

His wife had "left the earth" the year before, he said, and now he was fading too. This was his last tour of China. He had begun in Shanghai and traveled to the karst hills of Guilin and then to holy Mount Emei and now was stopping in Xi'an to see the terra-cotta warriors before eventually ending his trip in Beijing. He was really looking forward to Beijing. He wanted to pay his respects to Chairman Mao. I advised him not to buy the repurposed flower bouquet on sale outside the mausoleum.

Mr. Li sat on the edge of his berth with his hands on his knees, dressed in a faded blue "Mao suit" and yellow mesh cap. When it was time to drink his hot water from his tin cup, he blew on it tenderly, like a child.

I liked Mr. Li because he looked me in the eye when he talked and he gently touched my forearm to make a point. "Heroic Eastern Plumblossom, you come with me when we get to Xi'an. We'll see the terra-cotta warriors together." I did not tell him I had been and vowed to skip mass tourist sites; I flash-forwarded and pictured our adventures. We'd be a sort of a bilingual version of *Harold and Maude*.

By 8:00, the compartment stirred. Famous Dogs smoldered and so did muffled farts. A line formed to lay waste to the toilet.

I stayed next to Mr. Li. We stared out at broad fields of wheat planted on reddish soil. "So bitter, Little Plumblossom," he said. Yet I thought the scenery was breathtaking. Mr. Li meant that it was one thing to look at, another to live off of.

We crossed a tributary of the Yellow River, here just a trickle of muddy water. It was Sunday morning and no one was out. I liked that, the idea of Chinese people for once sleeping in. There was nothing to see except the smoke from a few cooking fires and the reflection of light on rain-slicked roads.

The breakfast cart rattled by, selling cans of rice porridge mixed with peas. The train passed through an apple orchard and past inhabited caves dug into hillsides. I pointed out birds to Mr. Li; he pointed out modern farm equipment to me. The rain stopped and the sun broke through the clouds. We had settled into a rhythm, a rhythm we six passengers had created and one different from the compartment next door. The ride's momentum had grown, and I didn't want the trip to end.

But outside, the trees began growing in straight lines, and the train slowed into smog. As we creaked into the Xi'an station, Mr. Li tucked his duck-decorated towel into his knapsack and straightened his mesh cap. The other passengers were disembarking farther down the line. Bob Chen and the Buddhist gave me their name cards. Like me, Bed Head didn't have one, and so he just saluted with an open palm and a wide smile. The girl in pink slept soundly. I had planned to tell her she looked a little bit taller than the day before.

I helped Mr. Li off the train and onto the platform. All around us, people battled to squeeze onto the idling train. The platform attendants stood in rigid rank, and barkers pushed carts of hot dumplings along its length, steaming the compartment windows.

Mr. Li grabbed my hand and held on tightly. He looked a little unsure, and I pretended not to be. Nobody paid us any attention as we sought our bearings. The train rumbled back to life and blew its air horn long.

"Ready, Little Plumblossom?" Mr. Li whispered. We walked together slowly, into the tunnel marked EXIT.

My onward ticket said JIAYUGUAN. In the past, a one-way fare there portended very bad things. At the Great Wall's western end, the Gate of Hell ushered criminals and dissidents to banishment into the Gobi Desert. "One more cup of wine for our remaining happiness," lamented a poem about the place. "There will be chilling parting dreams tonight." China proper once ended here.

My visit made a bookend of sorts: with Frances, I had stood fourteen hundred miles east, where the wall stepped down mountains and descended into a Pacific Ocean bay. Jiayuguan, "Excellent Valley Pass," was named for the last Chinese oasis on the ancient Silk Road. I saw dust. The Gobi Desert, more gravel seabed than sculpted dunes, ran table-flat to snow-capped mountains. Jiayuguan town still resembled an extended caravansary: a few hand-pulled beef noodle restaurants, Internet bars, and a hotel huddled around its single intersection, unregulated by stoplights or signs. Eddies of pebbly sand swirled along its sidewalk.

A gang of taxi drivers swooped toward me, honking and yelling, "*Great Wall! Great Wall! Great Wall!*" Across the road I spotted a pink Suzuki Alto City Baby with a furry pink steering wheel. The driver, heavily made-up with hair piled atop her head, silently nodded. Female cabbies were as rare and fortuitous as four-leaf clovers. They seldom smoked, they never erupted in road rage, and they rarely interrogated their passengers. A cabby once told me she empathized with the exhaustion from justifying my existence, since she endured harassment and backseat driving from fares throughout her shifts.

The City Baby's driver introduced herself as Wei *xiǎojiě*, Miss Wei. She had moved from Chongqing, in southern Sichuan. Reflexively, my mouth started speaking Sichuanese; the muscle memory still remained. Jiayuguan was a good place, she said in dialect. It had two dance halls. You could eat lots of different food. On the other hand, she had never realized how many handsome men lived in Chongqing until she moved to a town with so few.

Miss Wei would take me wherever I wanted to go for 80 yuan ($9.75). There was one condition. She looked me over and made a face. After a sleepless night riding the stuffy train, I looked like the sort of black-bearded barbarian the wall had been built to keep out of China. Miss Wei said I looked like I had just ended a shift at Jiayuguan's largest employer, the steelworks. Before I could thank her for the compliment, she gently asked, "Can I bring my brother-in-law?"

We picked up a stocky man, who squeezed into the City Baby's backseat. "He knows the interesting places around here." I admired her tact; usually in China people instantly trusted a foreigner, but perhaps this was because the foreigner was always outnumbered. Not out here.

We drove through the Gobi on a washboard gravel road. The wall ran parallel beside us, looking as low and rounded as a burrowing gopher's wake. The City Baby slid to a cloud-billowing stop. "*Dàole*," said Miss Wei: "Arrived." The pressed-earth remains of the wall ended at a canyon's edge, teetering over the shallow, sand-colored Taolai River. I climbed atop a dirt mound that a sandblasted stele identified as the wall's first tower. Centuries of wind had rounded it down to a nub.

That something so historical, and of such interest to tourists, sat in this solitary, unreconstructed state was something of a small miracle. No nosy auntie rushed from a tin booth to sell us overpriced tickets or socks. No row of stands selling identical souvenir kitsch blocked the view. But as Frances pointed out on the phone that night, Chinese tour groups flocked to pose for pictures on sections of the wall that evoked China's grandeur, not its decrepitude. Plus, Jiayuguan was out in the middle of the Gobi; the nearest big city, Lanzhou, was nearly five hundred miles away.

Miss Wei apologized that there wasn't more to see, as if the Great Wall's terminus weren't enough. She suggested visiting the steelworks, when her brother-in-law offhandedly asked if I wanted to visit the petroglyphs. The word went over my head several times, even after the man traced its characters with his finger on my palm. Finally the words for stone and carving made a mental click. Sightseeing in China was often a dubious proposition, but when a local casually mentioned anything old, let alone ancient, I knew to say yes.

The carvings, he said, could be seen on cliff faces above the shallow, sandy river. Its water, and not an entrance gate, barred the path. As the driver and her brother-in-law remained in the car, I hiked into the valley, tied my running shoes over my neck, took off my shorts, and waded across the current, chilling me to the waist. A short walk ahead, groups of small carvings of deer, fish, and birds, powdered with white chalk, shone from the walls of black rock. Etched by pastoral nomads before the first emperor unified China in 221 B.C., they had outlasted Jiayuguan's Great Wall, extended here by a fourteenth-century emperor. I ran my fingers beside the chiseled flint marks and then sat beneath them in the setting sun, listening to the timeless river rush by.

I should have quit while I was ahead and ended the trip there: I had met the unexpected people and places that I had hoped would find me. I did not yet understand that these encounters didn't have to end, that sticking with the elderly Mr. Li on his travels after Xi'an or lingering in Jiayuguan with Miss Wei and her brother-in-law was worthwhile, and could lead to a deeper, more intimate story than the sort I was accustomed to filing. A daily journalist excelled by being in the right place at the right time; a book writer knew to remain there. But I hadn't grasped this, and the compulsion to keep going, to see more, to cross a fabled city off my wish list pushed me farther west, into Xinjiang—"New Frontier"—a province the size of Alaska that makes up one-sixth of China's total area.

Kashgar (Kāshí in Mandarin) had long been one of the ancient world's most anticipated cities. To reach it from Jiayuguan's oasis, Silk Road travelers first had to cross Earth's largest shifting-sand desert after the Sahara. The Taklamakan Desert's Turkic-derived name means "place of ruin," and I was glad to be chugging along its northern edge on a train, and not on camel or foot. Compared to these wastes, the Gobi was a child's sandbox. All day the unchanging view showed scalloped dunes undulating to the horizon. I hypnotically stared from the corridor windows alone; the Chinese passengers hung the horsehair blankets on the windows and bunched at the carriage's opposite side, where the vista showed civilization: truck stops, oil derricks, and the occasional town. Signs pointed the way to Kazakhstan and Kyrgyzstan, which bordered most of Xinjiang.

As the train slowed, I stood at the exit door, eager to end this twenty-four-hour journey and explore the medieval alleys of what Beijing friends had called "the least Chinese of Chinese cities." From the train I squinted for a glimpse of the former oasis, wondering if Kashgar was like Marrakesh, with a medina crowned by minarets and a bustling souk. Instead, the station's exit led to a wide sidewalk and vast parking lot. Oddly for China, both were empty. Lines of sand whipped along the concrete, attempting to become a dune.

The bus into town puttered along wide, vacant Liberation Road, passing rows of look-alike buildings covered in white tile: the Bank of China, Air China, the New China Bookstore. Government offices were distinguishable by the long, rectangular white-painted boards hanging vertically next to their doors. In brushstrokes of black, Chinese characters announced them: FAMILY HEALTH BUREAU. TAX BUREAU. POST OFFICE. More than even the red national flag, it was these signboards, the same-size planks seen across China, that reminded me I was still inside the empire, no matter that Kashgar was closer in distance to Moscow than to Beijing.

At People's Square, Kashgar's Mao statue faced the vacant, treeless plaza. The Tiananmen replica wasn't a surprise; after all, Lhasa had one, too. Chairman Mao, however, looked incongruous; most Chinese cities had pulled his statue down. His raised hand waved west, over the poplar trees, at the Pamir Mountains in the far distance. Behind Mao loomed the oddest sight of all: a Ferris wheel. I asked a Uighur (pronounced "wee-ger") man what the locals called it. In Mandarin he replied, "We call it the 'Chinese wheel.'"

*

Marco Polo needed three years to reach Kashgar in the late thirteenth century. He spent only 250 words on his stay in "Cascar," calling the Uighurs "a wretched set of people who eat and drink in a miserable fashion." History does not record what they made of him.

I paged through his *Travels* while sitting cross-legged on the veranda of Kashgar's main teahouse. The manager carefully set a willow cage on a large hook above my head, and soon birdsong scored my thoughts. The tune competed against the tinny tinks of copper being pounded into teapots and tools below. Glowing in the sunlight spreading across the bazaar, veiled female merchants sold melons, grapes, and *doppa*, the hand-embroidered four-corner hats Uighur men balanced on their heads. In Chinese, I ordered mint tea and a plate of *pilau*, saffron-and-mutton rice. The man, a Uighur, looked at me expectantly. I tried again in telegraphic Uighur, and he understood.

Over my shoulder, a voice said in Chinese, "It's good you're trying to speak our language."

Mahmud, also a Uighur, had a wispy white beard, a mouthful of gold teeth, a flowing robe, and a bald head covered by a *doppa*. He was seventy-five years old. "I used to be a journalist," he said. "Then at age sixty-five I realized that journalists don't make much money. Retired journalists make even less."

Mahmud said he started a second career that had netted him more wealth than a lifetime writing articles: selling life insurance. "Uighur life expectancies keep rising," he explained. "So the policies mature."

Mahmud had lived his entire life in Kashgar. I wondered if he had grown up hearing stories of the First East Turkestan Republic, an independent state declared in Kashgar in 1933 and crushed by Republican Chinese forces the following year. Mahmud asked if I would like some more mint tea. I asked what topics he had been forbidden to cover as a journalist. Mahmud asked if I would like some more mint tea.

He ignored my questions and asked his own. What did young people have to complain about in Kashgar? Health care had improved, food was clean, and the economy was developing. Where I was staying? Had I registered with the police? Yes: the same Kashgar cop had already stopped me twice on the street, asking to see my passport. That had never happened even once in another Chinese city, not even in Lhasa. Didn't he recognize me? Or in his eyes, did *lǎowài* all look alike?

I had found the teahouse while wandering the Old City, searching for my hotel. Bulldozers had recently chewed through the core of the narrow alleys, leaving a trail of concrete named People's Avenue. The wide road did not appear on my map; I was adrift until I saw the yellow-painted brick walls of the Id Kah, one of China's largest mosques. It looked more like a municipal meeting hall than a masterpiece of Islamic architecture.

I ducked behind a billboard showing a Uighur girl using a trash can (PAY ATTENTION TO SANITATION) and into the twisting maze of trellised alleys lined with open piles of garbage. The terra-cotta houses' roofline rose from one story to two and dipped again, unlike Beijing's congruent courtyards. Missing, too, was the capital's rigid street grid. I passed one small mosque, then another, and yet another. Cheerful children emerged from a doorway and waved, a scene that was repeated after passing each mosque. After fifteen minutes of this, I finally realized I was walking in circles; they were the same kids, at the same doorway, next to the same mosque.

I exited onto People's Avenue and flagged down a cab, telling the driver to take me to the Qinibagh Hotel. He just laughed.

"Are you sure that's where you want to go?"

I nodded.

The Han Chinese man flipped on his meter, drove diagonally across the street, and stopped at a pair of tall white gates. "Here we are. That's six yuan."

As in Tibet to its south, the government promoted Han Chinese migration to Xinjiang province. In the 1990s, Uighurs made up 90 percent of Kashgar's population; a decade later, as the city grew and emigrants arrived, their number fell to around 75 percent. In the province as a whole, Han Chinese now constituted nearly half of the populace; the number is likely higher, since Chinese census takers do not count military personnel. As in Lhasa, soldiers were a common sight on Kashgar's outskirts, where Internet bars and remittance offices linked Han migrants with home. If I closed my eyes and listened to the beeping taxis, "The East is Red" ringtones, and the cheerful Mandarin chatter of grandmothers sitting on storefront steps, I could imagine I was anywhere in China.

But the heat and unforgiving sun told me otherwise. New Kashgar's trees were mere seedlings; propaganda billboards cast the only sidewalk shade. People walked too close to the signs to read slogans such as SWEAT THE REAL SWEAT, WORK HARD TO CREATE A CLEAN AND CIVI- LIZED CITY.

Many billboards showed ruddy, happy locals waving or dancing, a reflec- tion of the Han Chinese notion that China's fifty-five ethnic minorities are excellent singers and dancers. I have never seen them depicted as bankers, doctors, or even life insurance salesmen. Nor were they shown on their state-allotted plots of farmland, scraping out subsistence in the most unforgiving, isolated nooks of the country. The women were usually shown wearing flimsy, bosomy dresses, and the propaganda never depicted the men as I saw them: bearded, strong, restless.

Instead, the slogans said: EACH NATIONALITY IN XINJIANG SHARES THE SAME DESTINY.

I saw this chalked on a cinema's sidewalk signboard. Below it were the characters that mean "ice-cold air-conditioning." I had nowhere else to be, and bought a ticket.

Heart to Hearts was based on the true-life story of a Han doctor sent to the remote Xinjiang plateau. As the movie told it, he worked tirelessly for the betterment of the village at the cost of his marriage. He never complained. Instead we watched the doctor tap his own vein to donate blood, razor off his own calf skin to perform a graft on a local boy, and raise his only daughter to fill his shoes and continue serving the village. In the film's final act, she rushed a mining accident victim to hospital, only to be buried by a landslide. The closing scene, scored by high-pitched wails and throbbing orchestration, climaxed with a group of Uighur women dancing at her funeral—in flimsy, bosomy dresses.

The film was not distributed nationally: this was a production for local audiences only. Before the credits rolled, an epilogue narrated in Haughty Chinese reminded Han viewers that they should love locals like their own family, and told the Uighurs that the Han migrated there to bring "civilization." The lights flicked on. Nobody clapped. I noticed the theater sat divided: Han on one side, Uighurs on the other. Each side silently filed out into the blinding Kashgar sun.

The Qinibagh Hotel retained none of the historical intrigue from the early twentieth century, when it was the British consulate. The former Russian consulate, now the unfortunately named Seman Hotel, looked even more forlorn. Both had become standard state-run lodging whose best feature was their absence of character, which compelled guests to remain outside, exploring.

Officially, Kashgar's clocks were set to Beijing time, even though it was 2,700 miles away, the distance between San Francisco and New York City. The sun rose at 7:00 a.m. and set at 11:00 p.m., making some locals turn their clocks back two hours, diktat be damned. Bus stations ran on Beijing time, movie theaters on Kashgar time, hotels on Beijing time, restaurants on Kashgar time. But the one true clock was the Id Kah mosque's minaret, calling the penitent to prayer five times each day.

Built in 1442 and since remade several times, the mosque had been raised from the ashes of the Cultural Revolution and expanded to hold ten thousand worshippers (and, it seemed, an equal number of closed-circuit security cameras). At the entrance, young boys sold butterflies crafted from wire to clip onto clothing. They patiently taught me how to pronounce the food listed in my Uighur phrase book. Their fingers traced the words from right to left as they read *apricot, grape, mutton, mulberry.*

Over a week, I became, in a sense, that ever-present policeman, ghosting around Kashgar, surveilling people's routines. Every morning I began at the teahouse, wishing Frances were there and not sitting in UC Berkeley's History of Art 130A: Early Chinese Art. I ended each day at Id Kah's square, watching my solitary shadow blend with the ones cast by its minarets. Scribes wrote letters for illiterates, and artisans shaped metal, sewed hats, and trimmed bright bolts of silk. Scenes repeated themselves, the sun shone hot, and meals rotated between saffron rice and hand-pulled noodles. This was life at an oasis. And yet, the world pressed in: Uighur teens, by Chinese law too young to pray at Id Kah, crowded me with questions about the NBA, Britney Spears, and international currency exchange rates.* As much as I enjoyed chatting, I also wondered what these fleeting conversations revealed about Kashgar. Travel writing, and indeed much journalism, put characters onstage, let them exclaim a line or two, then shunted them off, never to return. What did the dialogue amount to; what pattern would form after immersing oneself here for years? Short articles also made a narrow window through which to view a place, crowding out archival research that showed how history shaped its present state. I began to dream about researching and writing a book, not about Kashgar, but about workaday life in Beijing's oldest *hútòng*, before it vanished forever.

On Id Kah's square a Uighur engineering student named Omar who freelanced as a tour guide said that business was slow; fewer foreigners traveled to Kashgar. More Chinese came, but they hired Chinese guides. Omar liked leading Japanese around; they were the best tippers. Their tour groups arrived on minibuses chartered in the provincial capital, Urumqi, nine hundred miles north. In Kashgar they asked Omar where the Japanese restaurant was. "Urumqi," he told them.

The next day, I shadowed Omar as he led a group of Danish women wearing "local" baggy embroidered pants (the kind, Omar noted, that Kashgarites had abandoned for jeans) to the International Trade Market of Central and Western Asia, a sprawling Sunday bazaar. It was a Uighur Ikea: in one area you could buy sheep and donkeys, in another harnesses and carts, and then you could trot over to the section selling hand-carved furniture and woven carpets. Thousands of shoppers arrived at the field on horseback and foot. There were few bicycles and even fewer Han Chinese. I spotted Mahmud, the life insurance salesman, handing out pamphlets that pitched new policies.

Omar left the Danes to browse on their own, and brought me to a domed cement building whose English sign said SPORTA CITY. On Fridays and Saturdays the venue was home to the Shake Your Soul! Disco. On Sunday it became a cockfight arena. Its bar sold Sprite and Remy Martin XO cocktails, but I bought a Fēicháng (Extraordinary) soda, whose label

---

*In 2014, young Uighur men attacked Id Kah's imam as he left the prayer hall, stabbing the seventy-four-year-old to death. His assailants said the state-appointed imam was a government stooge; the government called him a martyr.

exulted that it was "the Chinese people's own cola." The bottle's red-and-white packaging looked exactly like Coca-Cola's.

Sixty middle-aged and elderly Uighur men stared at the dance floor, littered with droppings and feathers. The men wore long robes and four-corner *doppa* hats, and smoked loose tobacco rolled in torn scraps of the *People's Daily*, the Communist Party mouthpiece.

Omar and I took our seats in the first row. Scabby roosters strutted past, crowing peevishly. The crowd leaned forward. Omar said that the government had recently allowed the fights so long as the cocks didn't kill each another. The mashed-up man asleep in the chair on the dance floor was the state-appointed umpire. He would call the fight when blood was drawn and declare the winner.

Across the arena, a man raised a rooster high into the air. Omar poked me and we got up along with everybody else to stare. The bird looked like an assassin: black downy feathers, sharp cream-colored beak, and sturdy yellow legs. He didn't have a scratch on him. Omar called him Tyson. His challenger looked like he had been pulled off a PETA poster: blood caked its feet, a scab sealed one eye, and hunks of feathers were missing. Omar named him the Big Pif Paf, after the popular roach repellent sold in Kashgar's bazaar. Only one of us was having fun.

Two handlers entered the ring and washed their hands in a bucket of water. They tenderly scooped up each bird, rubbing water over the wings. The umpire snapped awake, lit a cigarette, and stood.

Bettors exchanged 10-yuan notes. Tyson was the underdog. The umpire slumped back into his chair. The crowd fell silent. The handlers squatted in the ring near their birds. The fight began. The Big Pif Paf pecked at Tyson; Tyson bobbed and pecked the air; wings fluttered, feathers flew, the umpire declared the winner but did not raise the bird's wing. I asked Omar who won; he nodded toward the Big Pif Paf with a look that said I was a moron. The handlers scooped up their birds and exited the dance floor cradling their partners gently as the sound of paper money being exchanged filled the stands.

"This is an old Uighur tradition," Omar said. "This is the real Kashgar." The Beijing-scripted billboards lining Kashgar's roads, commanding SANITATION and CIVILIZATION, felt very far away.

CHAPTER 15

COUNTDOWN CLOCKS

W HEN I RETURNED to Beijing in early 2003, a loud rap on my Duckweed Hollow *hútòng* door startled me, as if the woman who had died in my apartment had come to collect her things. I warily unbolted the lock. A uniformed policeman asked to see my household registration document. Suddenly, I regretted trusting the landlord when she had told me I didn't need to visit the neighborhood police station after moving in. In fact, foreigners were required to present their passports and leases to the police, who recorded the details and issued notecard-size pieces of thin paper that looked worthless but whose red-star stamp officially permitted residence.

It turned out that my old flat was still owned by my landlord's *dānwèi* ("work unit"), which had assigned it to her. She hadn't yet bought the deed from her employer, and state-owned homes could not be sublet for profit. That rule made sense, I told the policeman, who, like most of his Beijing brethren, carried himself more like a put-upon village constable than a body-armored disciplinarian.

Nevertheless, the cop gave me three hours to gather my belongings and leave. Otherwise I would be fined. Either way, I could no longer live here. I didn't negotiate; any amount higher than one yuan was more than I could afford. That was all I had in my pockets, having burned through my savings while traveling.

I packed my duffel bag, tied my pillow and kitchen tools in a bedsheet bindle, and slinked down the dark *hútòng* like a tramp. I crashed on Pete Hessler's sofa and called Frances in Berkeley, where she was writing her senior thesis in legal studies. Not since admitting teenage screwups to my mother had I felt this sense of shame. I half expected Frances to say that she wasn't angry at me for renting an illegal apartment, just *disappointed*. When it came to making a solo go in Beijing, I wasn't as grown-up and independent as I thought.

Instead, she called her older brother, who happened to be in town on business. Within two days he helped me find a cheap place in a new high-rise a few blocks away, on the other side of the West Lake in a neighborhood named Xiaoxitian. The apartment was bone stock—unfinished cement floor, unpainted walls, unhung doors—but the monthly rent cost the equivalent of $250. I thought I was getting a deal.

But at what price? Coming home meant passing through a perimeter fence's guarded gate, stepping into a silent elevator, stomping a foot to activate the corridor lights, and passing through a multi-lock, reinforced steel front door. Unlike in the *hútòng*, I knew none of my neighbors and seldom even saw them. I could feel them in my bones, however, since workers spent the day renovating their apartments, percussively thudding through concrete walls and powdering my hair with flakes of fine white ceiling plaster.

I thought I could never feel more isolated in Beijing than in the spring of 2003 on the twenty-second floor of that lonely apartment.

I was running down my savings just as *Time* began whittling down its Beijing bureau. By then, however, I had realized I was not cub correspondent material. I didn't like cold-calling experts and stopping strangers on the street to quote their quick takes on complex issues. Was the yuan undervalued? *It depends, says Morgan Stanley analyst Andy Xie.* Is China protecting American intellectual property rights? *Yes and no, says a U.S. Consular official in Beijing.* Should the West fear a strong China? *No, says Guo Hong, a fifty-four-year-old bicycle parking attendant.* But I had asked her the wrong question: Mrs. Guo wanted to know why the price of chives in her *hútòng*'s wet market kept going up. Her off-topic quotes stayed in my notebook, hinting at a story I was more interested in reading than the one I had been assigned.

Matt still gave me spot work, including squiring visiting *Time* executives around town and to the Great Wall. My teaching credentials opened the door to a gig that better suited me. Beijing's international schools often needed substitutes; the largest paid $200 cash per day. A sixth-grade teacher there was about to go on maternity leave, so I could sign on for the entire semester, saving money toward Frances's summertime, post-graduation return.

I gratefully accepted the job without realizing that now I had to get there. *Time*'s office was in the embassy district, a short bike or subway ride from my apartment. The International School of Beijing sat sixteen miles northeast from home, a quick commute in many cities, but not in a town where peak-time traffic averaged five to eight miles per hour. More than two million cars clogged Beijing's roads, double the number that planners had forecast for seven years hence.* As a result, making it to class for the 8:00 a.m. start meant boarding a school bus two hours earlier, in the dark. The drive from downtown to the airport's suburbs passed under a bridge showing a digital clock counting down the seconds until the 2008 Summer Olympics. One morning I read 165,456,718; the next day it showed 165,369,211.

The red numbers moved as unceasing as a river's current. And yet, for a few months in the spring of 2003, it appeared they might be halted by an ominous cough.

In southern China, doctors initially diagnosed a farmer's muscle pains and high fever as pneumonia. But then more patients presented similar symptoms. And still more: in Hong Kong alone, hundreds of people sought treatment. After monitoring news of the "flu outbreak" on the Internet, the World Health Organization (WHO) asked Chinese authorities for further information. Their requests went unanswered until February 2003, when China reported 305 probable cases of a new virus called severe acute respiratory syndrome (SARS). In fact, there were three times as many patients. Chinese officials—no doubt with an eye on the Olympics count-down clock—ordered a media blackout; WHO epidemiologists who had landed in Beijing were prevented from traveling south to investigate.

In March, when reported cases were still limited to Hong Kong and

---

* By then, the number had more than doubled again: five million cars crammed the capital's roads in 2010.

southern China, the *Beijing Evening News* ran a story on the front page using the English acronym SARS, informing readers the letters could also stand for *Smile And Remain Smiling*.

Events accelerated quickly. In April, the government reported Beijing's first SARS case. But soon it emerged that authorities had suppressed the epidemic's extent. The chief physician of the capital's central military hospital, seventy-one-year-old Jiang Yanyong, leaked the actual tally of patients in an e-mail to Beijing and Hong Kong media.

Overnight, the number of Beijing's reported SARS cases jumped from 37 to 407. The scandal made the government barely flinch, at least outwardly: the capital's mayor and the minister of health were sacked, replaced by the next party cadres waiting on its deep bench. For the moment the whistle-blowing doctor was exalted as a patriotic hero.

Beijing announced that patients showing pneumonia-like symptoms would be quarantined in six city hospitals. From my uncurtained bedroom windows, I stared at one of them when I tried to fall asleep, glowing silently across the Second Ring Road. The shelves of my neighborhood super-market, like those across Beijing, went bare. Traffic thinned. Schools were ordered shuttered for two weeks. Even construction halted. A city of 15 million people suddenly stopped.

Because this was late April, the annual spring blizzard of cottonwood pollen snowed down onto the now-empty streets. My neighborhood pool hall closed, as did the barbers, and cinema, whose marquee had promised *Lord of the Rings II*. The plate-glass window of the only restaurant that remained open usually displayed a list of dumpling flavors; now it held a poster painted with the characters 消毒—*xiāodú*, disinfected.

The cottonwood tufts made people sneeze, which made bystanders jump away. Soon there was a run on surgical masks. Beijing became a city without lips or noses; the few folks I saw on the street looked like they were heading for the operating room, albeit wearing green plastic eyeshades, button-down shirts, and nylon pants that covered all exposed skin. Fear of potentially infected surfaces extended to doors—pushed open not with hands but elbows—and elevators, whose button numbers chipped off from people using house keys to press them. In my building, I watched an auntie hoist her Pekingese and use his paw to choose the floor. The next day a taped notice said: NO DOGS IN THE ELEVATOR.

The woman was upset; after all, dogs couldn't get SARS. I questioned her source. She asked how many canine cases had been reported. She had me there, but she also couldn't tell me how the virus was transmitted. Even though Beijing's news channel broadcast the government's daily press briefing live—a rarity in a country where news was shown with a delay, in case anyone veered off-script—people still gossiped and turned to folk cures.

The lead story of one evening's newscast made me scramble for the little red dictionary I had carried since my Peace Corps days. What word did the reporter keep repeating? *Honeysuckle*. Rumor had it that drinking tea steeped with the herb would protect you from SARS. In a Beijing market, the reporter's hidden camera captured price-gouging honeysuckle sellers. "Be careful when shopping for honeysuckle," the reporter advised viewers. Then she said something more familiar: "Don't believe rumors, and listen to the government." The market she reported from looked strewn and barren, as if everyone had just fled. I half expected a zombie to clomp slowly into the frame behind her.

The city smelled chemical; I exited my apartment's elevator to the alarming sight of yellow, hooded hazmat suits worn by men dousing the sidewalk with bleach. The fumes smelled more menacing than the unseen SARS.

The one novelty of this fraught fortnight was the suddenly wide-open roads. I flagged down a cab and for the first time said my destination was the Second Ring Road.

"What exit do you want to get off at?" the driver asked.

"I don't. Just go around the entire loop."

The driver laughed. "I've never been asked do this. *Hǎo wán'r!*" The words meant "What fun!" I had not often heard them since Beijing went on lockdown.

As we cruised unobstructed around the Old City's perimeter, I asked the driver if his water bottle held honeysuckle tea. He snorted. "If you want to protect yourself from SARS, you better drink something stronger."

I sniffed the liquid. Clorox? No, 112-proof sorghum liquor.

"I take a shot every two hours," the driver said. I tried to make a joke that it disinfected him, but it's hard to translate a pun. He took a long swig, and I was happy that for once on the Second Ring Road there were no other cars to hit.

The International School of Beijing remained open—even as the villages the morning bus passed had sealed themselves off behind plowed mounds of dirt. Could a moat and drawbridge be far behind? The school bus detoured around the makeshift roadblocks through a new villa development named Merlin Champagne Town. Its billboard showed happy people clinking glasses under the caption, HERE'S TO CHAMPAGNE, THE DRINK DIVINE THAT MAKES ALL OUR TROUBLES SEEM FAR AWAY. It looked like they were mocking me; I lived in an unfinished apartment that reeked of vinegar, since the neighbors mopped their floors with the disinfectant, which was cheaper than bleach.

Even worse, my electricity was out. New Beijing apartments required a smart card—charged with cash at an Industrial and Commercial Bank of China branch—to be inserted into the electric meter. My landlord had neglected to give it to me when handing over the keys; now he had left town. I came home depressed each night to darkness, until a struck match flared to light candles. Never in my life had drinking by candlelight been less romantic.

Still, I remained in Beijing for the pay, and also because I had grown attached to my sixth-grade students, who, throughout the tense weeks, acted as if we were on a marvelous adventure. As ever, I admired children's resiliency. The school told teachers to send kids to the bathroom to wash their hands after coughing or sneezing, but the decree was quickly amended after it became clear that kids were not above faking an *ah-CHOO* to meet their friends in the lavatory. Instead, my desk filled with bottles of Purel.

I had begun the semester's history class explaining the causes of war. We ended the school year on disease, learning about the discovery of coronaviruses.

Despite the government's avowal of a new era of openness and transparency, by May, after the outbreak had been controlled, Beijing returned to its old ways: prerecorded newscasts, underreporting of bad news, and plummeting honeysuckle prices. People stopped flinching when someone sneezed, ceased using their keys and dogs to press elevator buttons, and once again filled the roads, bringing traffic to a standstill. As the school bus idled on the airport expressway, the Olympic countdown clock hanging from an overpass kept moving: only 157,680,394 seconds to go.

*

When the school year ended and SARS did too, I wanted a change of scenery and some fresh air, or at least a place that didn't smell of bleach. I took off from Beijing Capital Airport at breakfast and by dinner stood sixteen hundred miles southwest in the fresh, thin air at the entrance to Tiger Leaping Gorge.

Its name sounded just as alluring in Chinese: hǔtiào xiá. The characters' dipping, falling, and rising tones mimicked the thirty-mile mule path that unspooled like a dusty rope through the world's deepest canyon, at 12,870 feet, situated at the headwaters of the Yangtze River. The gorge's name was what had drawn me to it as a Peace Corps volunteer—and to Frances as well, when she had hiked it the summer before we met. The tan she carried back from Yunnan province to Beijing had drawn my attention to her; one of our first conversations was about the gorge's spray-painted rocks pointing hikers to guesthouses. That blemish was nothing compared to the development to come—a new road ran alongside the river, I had been told: tour buses rumbled in, guesthouses mushroomed along the trail, and power lines rimmed the path, bringing refrigeration, floodlights, and the Internet. Two hikers had been robbed. It sounded bleak yet believable. Nearby Lijiang, once the wood-and-cobblestone seat of the Naxi kingdom, had turned twee. Now its twenty-thousand-resident Old Town hosted five hundred thousand visitors annually, mostly Han Chinese on package tours to a region of their country that local officials had named Shangri-La, from James Hilton's 1933 novel Lost Horizon, which was set in the vicinity.

I had mentally downgraded Tiger Leaping Gorge, but I was also curious to see what had become of the place. It had been the subject of my first published travel article, a genre of China writing that I had just about outgrown. Coming back felt like closing a loop.

On a clear June morning, I had a pre-hike breakfast at the Gorged Tiger Café, run by an Australian named Margo Carter. She had first visited Tiger Leaping Gorge six years earlier and was so taken by it that she decided to stay. But now, she said, paraphrasing a disappointed customer, "Ecotourism in China is walking all day to a remote waterfall, then finding someone pissing in it." I asked how the hike had changed. Carter's tone signaled caution: "See for yourself."*

---

*In 2010, Carter died while trekking solo in remote northwestern Yunnan.

But once I paid the new 30-yuan [$3.50] entrance fee, turned off the paved road, and walked through the grounds of the middle school (where kids still hollered "Hello!" from the classrooms), to the gorge's high path, little seemed different. In fact, the trail looked better. Formerly it wound past those spray-painted rocks touting two competing guesthouses in a hamlet named Walnut Grove. Posted signs for the new hotels—the Half-Way, Tina's, and the Naxi Family—looked politely muted in comparison. "We are a home in the mountains having silence with beautiful scenery, but not nothing commercial," read a small ad enticing hikers in Chinglish to the Old Horse Inn.

I arrived on the high trail at the same time as another man. I had traveled all this way to be alone with memories. Now there was no way around the fact that I'd have a walking partner.

If Coen Weddepohl was as disappointed, he was polite enough to not show it. The twenty-eight-year-old was on a long Asian vacation from his job in the City of London. Dressed in a Fire Department of the City of New York T-shirt and hiking pants, he stopped to ask me to snap a picture of him against a backdrop of the Jīnshā (Golden Sand) River. Before hitting a bend and becoming the Yangtze, the lime-green water funnels through black cliffs striped with orange lichen and alkaline tears—part of the legend of the river-crossing tiger that gave the gorge its name. After passing a farmer's home, Weddepohl asked me to photograph him beside a wheat field. I framed the lens, fearing I was in for a long day. Three times in the next mile, my backpack's zipper broke, spilling my laundry along the path. I saw his face register the same worry.

We made small talk for the two hours leading into the high trail's 24 Bends, a grueling series of switchbacks that took us to 8,800 feet. Weddepohl mentioned needing to get into shape. It looked impossible for him to get any more sculpted. As I panted up the dusty path under the unclouded sun, I remembered that a younger me could make this climb without pain. A middle-aged farmer descended, leading a donkey. "You're not even close to the top," he said.

Three hours into the walk, Weddepohl and I parted—he to eat lunch and be alone with his thoughts, me to collapse beside a waterfall. An hour later he caught up. We continued down a perfect path: cushioned by pine needles, shaded by bamboo, crossing frequent creeks brimming with melted snow. The hike felt exactly as I remembered it—grueling, isolated, uplifting.

As the day wound down and the sun arced behind us, we threaded our way along a cliff face toward a waterfall. Over his shoulder, Weddepohl mentioned that he'd been diagnosed with "a condition." A moment passed. On the road, solitude with a stranger can be freeing, a safe zone to talk without consequences. And Weddepohl was the kind of guy with whom you wanted to chat, preferably over pints. He talked about growing up in the Netherlands, about being held in a Congo jail, about managing hedge funds. (These events were not unconnected.) He made me laugh out loud by confessing to substituting Chinese currency for absent toilet paper: "And all I had were tens and twenties!" So I decided not to let it go. I asked about his condition.

While watching a goat teeter on a tree limb, he said he had leukemia. This trip was part bucket list item and also to strengthen his body for the bone marrow transplant scheduled in England. He described the operation and recovery details with the same confident optimism he brought to calculating how long our hike would take. We made it to Walnut Grove in eight hours, just as he had predicted.

The next day's leg would take another four hours—out from the shade of the walnut trees and into the hot sun, descending far down to the river, then up again to a waiting bus that would rattle all afternoon into Lijiang town. Weddepohl's chemotherapy pill made him too fatigued to continue. He had a long journey ahead: on to Bangkok, north to Pyongyang, south again to Hanoi. They were places he always wanted to see but had never had the time. That was the one good thing about being diagnosed with a terminal illness, he said: you suddenly became very aware of how you spent the seconds that remained. He kept his eye on the countdown clock that we all carry within.

The guesthouse called him a cab, which arrived ten minutes later via the new road. I continued down the old trail, past the explosions detonated by dam surveyors. At the river crossing, the ferry sat anchored but unattended. Spray-painted instructions on the landing stone said to phone for a lift. The ferryman used to wait in his boat, but the new road made his once-profitable job obsolete. Now he left his farm work and descended the steep switchbacks only when hikers called. After a dozen rings, the answering voice asked how many passengers were waiting at the river's edge. I didn't know that Weddepohl would go on to survive his marrow transplant, and so my voice broke when I said I was alone.

But not for long: Frances graduated and flew back to Beijing. A Berkeley law professor introduced her to a Chinese lawyer who worked in a British corporate firm's capital branch. After interviewing there, she was hired as a legal researcher. Four years earlier, when Frances last worked in Beijing, she had been a kindergarten teacher, walking a short distance to her classroom wearing casual clothes. Now her standing had changed, although she wasn't convinced it had improved. "Welcome to the corporate world," she e-mailed me from her Central Business District office, thirty minutes after leaving our apartment. "I have a secretary, and *āyís* attending me with coffee. The computer is brand-new and beautiful." Her dress shoes, however, hurt. "They are very tight. I feel like Cinderella's stepsisters trying on the crystal slippers to please the prince. I am pleasing no one."

By week's end, she said it was the first job where she felt she was being treated well, and fairly. Research assistants, even Chinese nationals, received the same health care benefits as lawyers. She found us a better apartment, one with working electricity, located on the eastern edge of Beijing's old city, just inside what had been the city wall. Now the Second Ring Road expressway and the number two subway line traced its footprint. The complex was the rare development that, after dilapidated courtyard homes were razed, permitted their tenants to remain, in new, city-subsidized walk-up apartments. The alleys that ran between the buildings retained the former *hútòng* names: Carrying Pole Lane still adjoined what had once been the imperial docks where Grand Canal barges deposited grain at the *hútòng* named Hăiyúncāng, or Sea Transport Storehouse. A few of the six-hundred-year-old brick warehouses stood shuttered and neglected there.

Directly opposite our building, a woman ran a *dìdao* ("typical," meaning authentic) Sichuan restaurant. I recognized her accent; she had emigrated from Neijiang. Now Frances and I had the neighborhood meal base that solved the perpetual argument of where we should go for dinner. We usually ate there: *mápó* tofu, fish-fragrance-sauce eggplant, spicy steamed fish, and cellophane noodles topped with lean pork and spring onions were a welcome change from Beijing's heavy, oily northern cuisine, such as fatty duck in plum sauce. Plus, the owner never asked if I could use chopsticks. Often she complained about the prices of ingredients in Beijing. Chives, for example, cost twice as much as in Sichuan.

Crossing the narrow street from our apartment's entrance gate brought us into the city's longest contiguous warren of *hútòng*, running three miles west to the central lakes. Frances and I spent our weekends just as we had when we first lived in Beijing, biking and walking and wandering the lanes, reveling in our reunion. Some nights we tossed a Frisbee on the small square between the Bell and Drum Towers, the fifteen-story imperial timekeepers that dated back to Kublai Khan's reign in the thirteenth century.

When Marco Polo visited the capital at that time, he marveled that "the whole interior of the city is laid out in squares like a chessboard with such masterly precision that no description can do justice to it." Old Beijing is so flat and geometric that locals often say the cardinal directions instead of left and right: "*Wàng běi zǒu*" ("Go north"). Hugged close by the narrow backstreets, we felt cut off from the city's accelerating transformation. But even in the *hútòng*, propaganda posters promised NEW BEIJING, GREAT OLYMPICS!

The Beijing journalism professor who had coined the catchphrase said it was misunderstood. "In the face of modernization, globalization and the 2008 Olympics," he lamented, "Beijing seems to be prepared to turn itself over to real estate developers. By 'new Beijing,' I meant we want to have a new humanism in Beijing, a new humanistic city. But the local officials and planners took this slogan literally. They think 'new Beijing' means destroy old Beijing and build a new Beijing."

On countdown clocks across the city, the seconds ticked away.

CHAPTER 16

DEFENDING THE GHOSTS

D URING NAZI RULE, Albert Speer, the "first architect of the Reich," drew up plans for a postwar Berlin renamed World Capital Germania. His design included monumental architecture such as the domed People's Hall, a victory arch, and a massive Chancellery, situated along a broad, three-mile-long axis called the Avenue of Splendor, modeled after Paris's Champs-Élysées. Only one of these projects was realized: the stadium built to host the 1936 Summer Olympics.

After the war, Speer was imprisoned for twenty years in Spandau Prison and in 1981 died of a stroke on a trip to London, aged seventy-six. He had six children; his son, Albert Speer Jr., became an architect, founding the firm AS + P, which stood for Albert Speer and Partner. In 2001 it opened an office in Shanghai. In 2003 the younger Speer was commissioned to design a promenade connecting Beijing's Olympic stadium in its north to the Forbidden City at its center.

"We're even bigger here, much bigger," Speer Jr. said, comparing his Beijing plan to his father's for Berlin. "But the two are not comparable. This is an idealistic axis. This is not an axis representing power. It's an axis that looks back to two and a half thousand years of Chinese history."

AS + P's plan featured not an Avenue of Splendor-like boulevard— Beijing already had Chang'an Jie, bisecting the Forbidden City and Tiananmen Square. Instead, Speer Jr. pitched a landscaped corridor linking the stadium via the city center to a high-speed rail station to the south.

"The officials' eyes glazed over at his mention of the train station," Johannes Dell, the head of AS + P's Shanghai office, told me. "Speer grew frustrated and told them to imagine it as an *airport for trains*. Officials perked up when they heard that word; trains are old, airplanes are modern."

Dell was not surprised by the officials' infatuation with the new. "Cities are like people," he said. "They don't learn from others' mistakes, they learn from their own mistakes. I hope Beijing does it quickly."

I had taken an overnight train to Shanghai to visit AS + P, curious what was being planned for the "New Beijing," and if there was more to the story than the flashy new buildings that dominated media coverage of the capital's $200 billion makeover, including Frenchman Paul Andreu's National Theater (nicknamed the Egg), Briton Norman Foster's dragon-shaped airport, the Swiss-designed "Bird's Nest" Olympic stadium, and its neighboring aquatics center, called the Water Cube, planned by Australians. The world's most expensive office building, imagined by the Dutch firm OMA, formed a loop of six sections. Beijingers called it the Big Pants; actually it was home to the decidedly less playful state-run China Central Television.

Most of these projects went up outside the capital's historic heart, but still its *hútòng* fell. Even before the Olympics were awarded to Beijing, a decade of urban renewal had already destroyed 80 percent of the lanes; by the late 1990s an average of six hundred *hútòng* were pulled down annually. Beijing's district governments held title to the state-owned land's "usage rights," which they leased to developers for a fixed amount of years. The government received a windfall; the developers, naturally, did not construct low-income housing to replace the working-class neighborhoods it paid top dollar to raze.

Many *hútòng* residents, who had been assigned to live in subdivided, dilapidated courtyard homes lacking heat and private toilets, were happy to move. However, they were not pleased with the developer's offer of an apartment outside the city center, far from their jobs, social networks, and their children's schools. A common refrain I heard in the *hútòng* across from my apartment was *Pàn chāi, pà chāi*: Hope for demolition, fear demolition.

Above all, Beijingers wanted transparency. Who was making the decisions to shape the city? It wasn't the plebs: planning meetings were not open to the public, and there were no referendums, either. When Frances and I visited the new Beijing City Planning Exhibition Hall that had opened near the southeastern corner of Tiananmen Square, we found a

extreme242 THE ROAD TO SLEEPING DRAGON

sign taped to the ticket window. Frances translated the characters aloud: "Please buy your tickets with prudence. The exhibits do not concern the topic of razing."

Previous visitors had demanded refunds after the exhibition hall's displays of flashy new projects did not reveal the government's plans for their old neighborhoods. Who could say what the landlord was up to? Decades of living in nationalized housing had made most Beijingers tenants in their own town.

In 1935 the writer Lin Yutang had asked who would be China's interpreters. "But do the Chinese understand themselves?" he continued. "Will they be China's best interpreters? . . . In [a Chinese person's] breast is concealed a formidable struggle, or several struggles. His soul is torn by a conflict of loyalties belonging to opposite poles, a loyalty to old China, half romantic and half selfish, and a loyalty to open-eyed wisdom which craves for change and a ruthless clean-sweeping of all that is stale and putrid and dried up and moldy. Sometimes it is a more elementary conflict between shame and pride. To escape that is indeed a delicate task."

Lin said that writing about one's own culture was like sorting family treasures: "even the connoisseur's eyes are sometimes deceived and his fingers sometimes falter."

That recalled the contemporary writer Feng Jicai, who wrote, "When describing a place, the best position an orator can take is from the threshold, with one foot in and one foot out. If both feet are out, you might be gossiping about matters. If both feet are in, you might not be able to see the whole picture. In a more modern phrase, I could say that one must have a 'sense of distance' when talking about a place."

In Neijiang, I taught sections of his Cultural Revolution oral history, *Ten Years of Madness*. As a child, Feng had wanted to be a painter. The Cultural Revolution canceled his studies, so he turned to writing. By his estimate, Feng wrote a million words during that decade, on onionskin paper hidden in his bicycle tires and glued behind the newsprint that papered his apartment walls.

Instead of blaming leaders for the destruction, in *Ten Years of Madness*

Feng recorded individuals' feelings of guilt and their desire to take responsibility for their actions. Were it fiction, the book would have gone on the long shelf of the genre China called "scar literature," but my students had never read contemporary Chinese history written this way. Feng interpreted China differently.

He had spent the previous year attempting to save a six-hundred-year-old street from the wrecking ball in his hometown of Tianjin, located seventy miles southeast of Bejing. In late 2003, Frances called him, and Feng invited us to visit.

Frances and I exited Tianjin's train station and crossed the iron trellis river bridge, wandering under tree-shaded streets that in the nineteenth century had belonged to foreign legations: Rue de France, Victoria Road, Via Matteo Ricci, Kaiser Wilhelm Strasse. Newer street signs displayed their rewritten names, including People's, Liberation, and Red Flag roads. The European architecture had been preserved: mansard roofs, filigreed balconies, Corinthian columns. From behind these colonial mansions peeked the neglected Chinese-built homes, whose rotting wood frames hunched low.

"I want to let people know that these are not merely old houses," Feng Jicai told a local paper. "They're vehicles for traditional culture. If you regard a city as having a spirit, you will respect it, safeguard it, and cherish it. If you regard it as only matter, you will use it excessively, transform it at will, and damage it without regret."

Before meeting him, Frances and I walked to Guyi Jie (Old Clothing Street), at the heart of Tianjin's old town, to see what his lobbying had managed to preserve. Passersby told us to follow the new landmarks: Turn left at the McDonald's, right at the KFC. Only a short length of the narrow road remained.

"Of course we all wanted the entire street to be saved, but there was nothing to be done," said a woman in front of her cosmetics shop there. "It's none of our business, we can't interfere with government affairs. Even the writer Feng Jicai couldn't do it, and he really tried. Look at how ugly the new street is now."

Only one historic building still stood: a former silk store, since converted into a teahouse. That morning, Frances and I were its only customers. The waitress said, "I wish Feng Jicai could have saved all the street's buildings, not just this one."

I knew that in his youth Feng played basketball for the Tianjin city team, but I was still surprised to see the sixty-one-year-old looking hale and energetic enough to throw elbows on the court. He understood English—in the 1980s he spent a term at the University of Iowa's International Writing Program, where he wrote *The Three-Inch Golden Lotus*, a novel about foot-binding—but in his Tianjin office we spoke Chinese.

"In the 1960s and '70s, we destroyed our culture angrily," he said. "In the 1980s to now, we're destroying our culture happily."

For six centuries, he said, Guyi Jie was known in Tianjin as the place to buy funerary clothing. "Suddenly, one day they announced it would be destroyed—in twenty days. Everything here is a race against time."

Feng organized a group of volunteer photographers and told them to "snap every detail of the street: doorways, faces, lamps, street signs, carvings, every detail." The team also interviewed residents; their memories captioned the pictures, which Feng paid to have printed as postcards.

Next, he organized a press conference at a local post office, autographing the postcards, sold in a set called *The Precious Remains of Guyi Jie*. Police shut down the event. Feng self-published the photographs and interviews in an oversized paperback he titled *Remaining Flavor of the Old City*. He mailed a copy to each civic leader, inscribed: "This is your beloved Tianjin."

"In the end, officials promised they would preserve six of the old buildings on the west side of Guyi Jie. Then I left for France for two months, and they said, 'Feng is gone, so now we can proceed.'" When he returned, the entire street had been razed, save for a sliver of the old silk shop, where Frances and I had sipped thin tea.

I wondered why China's age-old tension between Old and New needed to be resolved so brutally and finally. Why did the government approve the clear-cutting of neighborhoods instead of selectively thinning edifices that had fallen beyond repair?

"It's about time. Speed," Feng replied. "For the officials in charge, the faster they demolish old structures and begin new projects, the faster they can declare to those above them, 'Look what I've accomplished.' There are no paths to career advancement for 'Look what I saved,' because the focus is on economic development."

Globally, municipal preservation campaigns often began as an act of civil disobedience. In China, no matter what its constitution promised, merely organizing a crowd—let alone protesting government-backed development—could mean jail time. Feng had managed to avoid serious trouble, perhaps due to his membership in China's (rubber-stamp) parliament and (feckless) writer's association. I asked if he was tolerated because it was easier for officials to pay lip service to a lone dissenter instead of an organization, but Feng just shrugged.

"For a writer," he said, "the most important thing is not the style in which you write but the attention you pay to social problems. This is China's now: the government is good at protecting cultural relics, like the Great Wall or the Forbidden City, but we have to exercise our rights to protect our culture and what makes us unique. China is really diverse. Look, we're talking about a land with five thousand years of civilization, and only recently has it been transformed into a mutual culture. Now, globalization blurs the remaining differences. In China, this process is being sped up."

Again relying on volunteers, in 2002 Feng launched a campaign called Saving Chinese Folk Cultural Heritage, aimed at cataloging village art, songs, legends, clothing, and traditions before they died off with their practitioners.

"This work is urgent and it must be done now," Feng stressed. "Every minute, folk culture is being lost. In Tibet, traditional architecture is being pulled down to build concrete buildings. In Guizhou province, there are thirty-three ethnicities, but three hundred thousand of their offspring have migrated to cities for work. When they return, they laugh at their own culture, which they see as backward. Last year in Gansu province we met a woman over eighty years old. She sang beautifully, she knew many folk songs no else could sing. We planned to go back to record her. But within a half year, she died. When we returned, her daughter told us that on her deathbed she kept asking, 'Why aren't they here yet? When are they coming?'"

China has a history of appreciating its cultural and intellectual heritage too late; it dates back 2,200 years to the first emperor's order to burn Confucian texts. Before leaving Tianjin, Frances and I stopped at the former Italian legation to see the new museum devoted to Liang Qichao, the Qing scholar-official who at the turn of the twentieth century had advocated Western reforms to strengthen China. In response, the dowager empress Cixi sentenced Liang to death. He escaped to Japan, then returned to China after the collapse of the dynasty that had ignored his suggestions.

Liang's son, Liang Sicheng, became known as the father of Chinese architectural studies and also a staunch defender of its traditional buildings. Part of his training at the University of Pennsylvania had required him to finish designs of damaged cathedrals and draw restoration plans for world monuments. As Japan invaded and occupied parts of China in the 1930s, Liang and his wife, the architect Lin Huiyin, scoured the Chinese coun-tryside to track down and draw ancient structures in the event they were destroyed by the war.

Historically, China had no tradition of architectural preservation: succes-sive dynasties ordered other emperors' buildings razed or converted to their own designs. "Since there existed no guides to buildings important in the history of Chinese architecture," Liang wrote, "we sought out old buildings like a blind man riding a blind horse. My experience was that local people were not interested in architecture. When I told them I was interested in antiquities, they would guide me to their stone stele inscribed in earlier times. They were interested in calligraphy, impressed by the written word, not the carpenter's handiwork."

Liang had posted his book's manuscript to the United States while fleeing the advancing Japanese. The package was lost, before finally surfacing on an American shelf three decades later. A *Pictorial History of Chinese Archi-tecture* was at last published in 1980. Frances and I had carried it like a treasure map across central China. Their chapters led us to covered wood bridges, ancient brick pagodas, and—as the snow piled around us—the 1,200-year-old Foguang Temple at Mount Wutai.

Above all Liang Sicheng loved his hometown of Beijing, whose quilt of courtyard homes he viewed as a world treasure. After the Communists took power in 1949, Liang and his wife returned, designing China's national emblem and the ten-story Monument to the People's Heroes that still sticks like a hatpin in the heart of Tiananmen Square. But their voices were soon drowned by the 1,200 "technical advisers" who arrived from the Soviet

Union. They urged Chairman Mao to raze Beijing's "feudal city" core, just as they had done to Moscow's.

The government shelved Liang's plan to convert the wall into a leafy promenade. He famously said that watching Beijing's city wall being dismantled was like having the skin pulled from his bones. He predicted city leaders would regret its destruction: "Fifty years later," he wrote in 1955, "history will prove that you are mistaken, and I am correct."

His wife died of tuberculosis before the Cultural Revolution, when Liang was beaten and banned from teaching. Unlike the novelist Lao She, he did not commit suicide; cancer killed him in 1972.

Liang characterized Chinese architecture as belonging to one of three phases: Vigor, Elegance, and Rigidity. I wondered how he would categorize the current era.

"Alienation," his son Liang Congjie told me. "I miss my old Beijing. It's gone. Completely gone. Even the *hútòng* I'm living in—everything's been torn down. Sometimes I can't even recognize my own home. Really, at times I can't even find it."

In 2003, Frances and I met the seventy-one-year-old Liang in his Beijing office, where he headed China's first environmental nongovernmental organization, Friends of Nature. Like any NGO in China, it operated under a watchful eye, legally subject to warrantless searches and surveillance. Perhaps that's why its office, tucked in a *hútòng* north of the Forbidden City, was so hard to locate. After crossing the new, six-lane Safe and Sound Boulevard in staggered dodges, *Frogger*-style, we walked in circles in the maze of lanes, passing one of his late mother's few surviving designs, an elegant gray-brick low-rise that still housed the Law Institute.

"I am trying to follow my parents' footsteps," Liang said. "Environmental protection was not in their consciousness during their time. People call us every day with issues to be investigated. The economy is growing so fast, and everyone is trying to get rich in the shortest time. If 1.3 billion people want to get rich, just imagine the pressure—it's enormous upon natural resources. Arable land, forest, grassland, water, all divided between 1.3 billion shares. Chinese want to live the life Americans have."

Did he admire any of Beijing's new architecture? "I can tell you the building I hate the most," he said. "Oriental Plaza." The massive shopping mall anchored Wangfujing, the capital's historic shopping promenade. Liang was part of the group of historians who lobbied for the lowering of the project's height, since its plans contravened a regulation that no new buildings could exceed the Forbidden City's highest point. The developer lopped a few stories off the blueprint, but still the buildings were too tall. The plan was approved anyway.

"If I were a terrorist," Liang said, "I would drive a plane into Oriental Plaza. I would sacrifice my life to destroy it."

He made a face when I said we had visited the new Tianjin memorial hall to his once-exiled grandfather. "They moved fifty or sixty families out of that place to commemorate him. Now it's an empty house. We don't own any of his furniture or papers or calligraphy to put in it: all has been lost or already given to museums." The irony of the state evicting workers it had once assigned to live on the property was not lost on him. "For years, my grandfather was branded a counterrevolutionary, and now he's an example of patriotic education." So, too, was his father. Olympic preparations included rebuilding, in a park near Beijing Station, a short portion of his beloved city wall.

The public, Liang lamented, had no voice in the shaping of the city. "Urban planning is strictly controlled by the government, and as this is the capital, it's really in the hands of the central government. Kant said, 'Because of the subject, so you have the government.' A few years ago, I went to a conference of architects held at Beijing's German embassy. I'd been to Berlin and think it is beautiful, so I praised it to the ambassador. He said to me, 'The presence of Berlin as a city represents and reflects the taste of its residents.' If that's true, I really feel embarrassed, because the presence of Beijing thus also reflects the taste of its residents."*

"What I am trying to do in Beijing is to transport a two-thousand-year-old city into the future," the architect Albert Speer Jr. told a reporter. "Berlin in the 1930s—that was just megalomania."

After drawing Beijing's Olympic axis, the son of the man dubbed "Hitler's

---

*In 2010, Liang—modern China's first environmentalist—died of a lung infection, aged seventy-eight.

architect" reportedly designed the headquarters of China's Ministry of Public Security, standing sentry just east of Tiananmen Square.

One year after being hailed as a patriotic hero for exposing the cover-up of SARS cases, Dr. Jiang Yanyong became a state villain.

In the spring of 2004, the surgeon sent a letter to China's senior leadership, urging it to admit that ordering soldiers to fire on civilians in 1989 had been a mistake. He had worked in a Beijing emergency room that day, operating on casualties who had been wounded around Tiananmen Square.

On June 2, two days before the bloodshed's fifteenth anniversary, police arrested the seventy-two-year-old, a Party member who held an army rank equivalent to major general. Dr. Jiang was held without charges for forty-five days. Punishment, it was said, for violating military discipline.

CHAPTER 17

LEARNING TO SPEAK OLYMPICS

I N MAY 2004, Frances again received the good envelope from Berkeley, this time admitting her to the law school's graduate program in Jurisprudence and Social Policy. Concurrently, I won a fellowship to a Berkeley-administered program that taught advanced Chinese at the capital's Tsinghua University. Like most everything I had learned in China, my grant originated with a chance encounter. A former Peace Corps colleague had been selected the previous year; when I ran into him in Beijing, he suggested I apply.

While we did not relish being temporarily separated, Frances and I were also pragmatic and, as our Chinese friends noted, "very Chinese," since couples long had parted for work, from today's coastal factory migrants back to the gold rushers who sailed to California. We continued the tradition: she wanted to earn a law degree and begin her career; I wanted to write a book about life in Beijing's oldest neighborhood. Still, the separation stung, leading to accusations of selfishness from both sides. Yet neither of us wanted the other to abandon our studies—or each other. The Chinese word for nauseating is *ĕxīn*, whose first syllable sounds like a tummy ache: *uhhhh*. That's the dull thrum we often felt, trying to stay together while still going our own ways.

But I needed to stop relying on Frances to translate written materials, which meant learning to read Chinese, nine years after speaking my first word of Mandarin. For a year starting in September, every weekday morning I rode a new subway line from our apartment at Haiyuncang forty-five minutes north to Tsinghua, whose campus was built in 1911 with U.S.-donated funds that equaled the indemnity China paid America after the Boxer Rebellion. Tsinghua's central buildings include a look-alike of MIT's domed hall designed by the American architect Henry Murphy—a fact unnoted on its explanatory plaque. A short walk away, I sat in a small college classroom to start learning Chinese all over again.

I had picked up the language by imitating the people around me, the way a baby babbles back to its parents. Now I had a one-on-one intensive grammar course whose patient teacher worked to untangle my linguistic knot of incorrect prepositions and auxiliary verbs. By the end of class, she often looked as exasperated as an interrogator who could not get her pris-oner to crack.

Another teacher tried to eradicate my Sichuan-tinged pronunciation by reading words in standard Mandarin. For years I had been telling people I liked chopping down trees—*kǎn shù*—when I thought I was expressing a fondness for reading books—*kàn shū*.

Mimicking the hearing tests I had last taken in kindergarten, the teacher ordered me to hold up one, two, three, or four fingers, indicating the tone of each spoken syllable: first (level), second (rising), third (falling-rising), or fourth (falling). Was it *lǐ* (plum) or *lí* (pear)? Then she would enunciate simple sentences—*Wǒ xǐhuan zhōngguó cài*, I like Chinese food—and make me repeat them slowly, like Eliza Doolittle had to do in *My Fair Lady*. No wonder my Neijiang students loved that film: they sat in compulsory Mandarin classes to learn "proper" pronunciation too. My teacher had her own version of "The rain in Spain stays mainly on the plain": *Māmā qí mǎ, mǎ màn, māmā mà mǎ*. Mom rides a horse, the horse is slow, Mom curses the horse. *Tā mā de!* I cursed, internally.

The reading class used a textbook called *Thought and Society*, which paired short essays about Chinese culture with a gazetteer of new vocabulary. I opened its red cover expecting an illustration and English marginalia. Instead, the first page showed thirty lines of text, whose dense typesetting recalled a White Pages phone book. The lesson, "Modern People's Health Problems," continued for three more pages of tiny characters. The vocabu-lary list featured 152 new words. Sixteen grammar structures followed. Then a list of *chéngyǔ*, or idioms, such as 对牛弹琴, *duì niú tán qín*, "playing the lute to a cow." It meant dealing with a stubborn person, or addressing the wrong audience. I suspected the textbook's author was talking to me.

I worked through one lesson each week. "Chinese Attitude Toward Ghosts" gave way to "College Students Feeling of Responsibility." Some days, late at night, after chatting with Frances over her morning coffee in Berkeley, I sat home making 152 flash cards of new characters and wet the textbook pages with frustrated tears. But *Thought and Society* wasn't even my hardest class.

The teacher of *Tell It Like It Is* required me to listen to a CD recording of the popular Beijing radio talk show of that name and transcribe, in characters, an exchange between the hosts and a caller. I spent hours on those lessons, the side of my left hand smearing the ink as I pressed PAUSE after each sentence, frantically trying to remember how to write simple words such as *car*, *love*, *house*, and *expensive*. I quickly learned how to write the last one—贵, *guì* ("gway"). It was one of Beijing's most-used adjectives.

Chinese has an estimated fifty thousand characters; an educated person will know at least eight thousand. My goal was to read a newspaper, which required about a quarter of this figure. Most characters are combinations of simpler components, and like a preschooler I began learning to write by learning the eight basic strokes, including the horizontal and vertical lines used to write 王, *wáng*, "king." Next came the stroke that looks like a dot, as in 玉, *yù*, "jade." Topping that with a roof made 宝, *bǎo*, "treasure." I saw the logic clearly, just as 木, *mù*, "wood," looked like a tree, and 林, *lín*, looked like woods, and 森林, *sēnlín*, looked like a forest.

But less than 5 percent of a typical dictionary's 20,000 characters are pictograms. Most Chinese characters are instead assembled from semantic and phonetic parts, such as 妈, *mā* (mom), whose left-side "radical" indicates a woman, and whose right-side component indicates how the word should be pronounced. In this case, nearly the same as 马, *mǎ*, horse. The character for *mà*, to curse, put the clue to its meaning above the sound: two 口 (*kǒu*, mouth): 骂. Learning to see characters when I listened to speech made the gibberish of *māmā mà mǎ*—Mom curses the horse—clearly intelligible: 妈妈骂马.

Once I memorized the most common characters—similar to the 100 basic "sight words" children learn when reading English—my comprehension started snowballing. Seeing 请 made my mind recognize both "speech" (its left-side radical) and *qing*, the right side's pronunciation. This must be *qǐng*, "please," or "to ask," and not 清, *qīng*, whose left-side water radical makes it the character for "clear" or "pure." Nor was it 情, *qíng*, "emotion," differentiated by the "heart" radical.

Writing became easier, too, as muscle memory took over. Mastering an unusual character's strokes invoked the same childhood thrill as being able to spell a "hard" word, such as *Mississippi*. I learned the simplified version of characters, taught on the mainland since the 1950s to increase literacy by writing with fewer strokes. Taiwan and Hong Kong still use traditional characters. In the latter system, China, *zhōngguó*, is written 中國. In simplified characters it's 中国. The first character means "middle"; the second "kingdom," or country. I pictured the king and his jade, safe within a border.

Slowly, as the months passed, I could read short articles in the *Beijing Evening News*. Every day I chose one and worked it like a crossword puzzle, riffling through my little red dictionary and marking the newsprint with tone marks and translation. One "sight word" I memorized quickly was 奥运会, *àoyùnhuì*, the Olympics, as the paper's front page counted down the days to the event, less than four years away.

By my second semester I could read actual books, albeit slowly. It took a month to plod through my first selection, Wang Jun's 城记 (*Chéngjì*), a Xinhua journalist's chronicle of Liang Sicheng's losing battle to preserve old Beijing. I also sat in on the urban planning courses being taught at Tsinghua's famed architecture school, which Liang had founded in 1946. In the building's lobby, students touched his bust to pay their respects. His metallic brow had been rubbed shiny-smooth.

After Frances returned on her winter break, we traveled to the central plains town of Pingyao, whose four square miles of four thousand courtyards were surrounded by one of China's last intact city walls. I sent the story of tiny Pingyao's struggle to curb the rising tide of tourist buses to *National Geographic Traveler* magazine. The editor passed, but said that he had just started the National Geographic Society's Center for Sustainable Destinations, a conservation program that aimed to educate tourism officials. I could be its (unpaid) China representative.

Official titles go a long way, and soon an invitation came to speak at a training conference for China's World Heritage Site managers, sponsored by the United Nations Educational, Scientific and Cultural Organization (UNESCO). The writer Feng Jicai had told me that China pursued World Heritage Sites like actors do Academy Awards. Altogether, the country has fifty-two listed sites, trailing world leader Italy by only one.

I flew and bused to Lushan (Mount Lu), located just south of the Yangtze River in central China. Its cloud-shrouded peaks had once been a summer resort known as Kuling, popular with Western missionaries, including Pearl Buck's family. Their gray-brick cottage still stood, as did the small auditorium where Chairman Mao had consolidated his control over China. At a party conference here in 1959, he purged Peng Dehuai, the popular defense minister who had criticized Mao's collectivization policies. Over the next three years, these caused a famine that killed an estimated 20 to 43 million people—an event the Communist Party officially calls *sān nián zìrán zāihài*, "three years of natural disasters."

Lushan had been selected as a World Heritage Site for its landscape, which for centuries had attracted painters and Buddhist and Taoist monks whose temples formed one of ancient China's spiritual centers. When I began my talk on "preserving a sense of place," I mentioned to the assembled room of tourism officials that I could not find a map of Lushan—designated a national park—on sale anywhere, frustrating my morning hike. An official politely interrupted me to say that a map remained on the drafting table; every highlighted place, walking trail, and plaque first had to be approved by the party propaganda bureau to ensure they gave visitors the "correct" interpretation. All historic sites tell stories, but China's tell political ones.

Instead of lecturing the one hundred assembled men and women who oversaw heritage sites such as Lhasa's Potala Palace and the classical gardens of Suzhou, I showed them pictures. On my travels over the past decade I had snapped photos of places, such as Tiger Leaping Gorge, that evinced both the best and worst of Chinese tourism. With the lights dimmed and the audience's faces illuminated by the screen's reflected light, I spoke in classroom-improved Chinese about what I both loved and hated. The room was silent, and I worried that I had miscalculated by being so frank.

But when I finished speaking, the World Heritage Site managers could not wait to vent their frustrations. The man who oversaw daily operations at the Potala Palace said that UNESCO had no power in China: "It's just a lot of people with doctorates, giving us suggestions." Of course the Chinese site managers wanted to be good stewards of China's heritage. Local officials, meanwhile, urged more and more visitors, raising revenues. Museums had to adhere to national regulations such as inflexible opening and closing times; managers wanted to stagger group visits or charge a premium for after-hours visits, like Western museums. No, the government said. Sites must be accessible to all people during set hours. To argue with these officials, one manager said in Chinese, was to play a lute to a cow. He paused to ask, "Do you understand that saying?"

Lushan felt like a summation of all I had learned. The question now was how to apply it.

In August 2005, I moved into a dilapidated courtyard shared by several families on a *hútòng* in Dazhalan (Big Wicker Fence), Beijing's most venerable neighborhood, located just south of Tiananmen Square. Equal in size to Vatican City (population 557), its square half mile of 110 lanes was home to 57,000 people, making it among the world's densest communities. Frances, on summer break from law school, helped me find the rental the new Beijing way: online. After looking at several places—some whose owners refused to rent to a foreigner, some that were about to be torn down—we finally found a musty vacancy at the back of a divided courtyard near Liulichang, the capital's antique street.

As part of the preparation for the Olympics, the Beijing city government promised the Internet could be installed in any home, no matter how old. A technician ran a cable over my courtyard's tiled roof, which needed weeding. So I had broadband but no heat, air-conditioning, hot water, or toilet. I shared the home with a couple who had migrated from the Northeast with their daughter, two painters who migrated from central China, their cousin—who slept in a closet-sized annex—and a woman who had lived in Beijing since the 1940s.

In English I called her the Widow, but to her face addressed her as *dàniáng*, a term of respect for an elderly woman. On my first day in the house, she had narrowed her eyes and said, "In this courtyard, we have one rule: Public is public, and private is private. Repeat it."

In Chinese, I echoed, "Public is public, and private is private."

Before dawn the next morning she opened my door without knocking, and yelled, "Little Plumblossom! Wake up! Eat dumplings!" I squinted, half-asleep, to find her standing beside my bed, extending a steaming bowl of dumplings. A Flying Horse–brand cigarette dangled from her creased mouth.

I mumbled: "I thought public was public and private is private."

"In this house," she snapped, "*everything* is public!"

She was as personable as she was garrulous; as on an enjoyable train ride, I felt I had won the lottery. Eight of us crammed into one subdivided slice of what once had been a large home owned by a traditional medicine merchant. I slept in the farthest back corner, in what had once been his servant's quarters. Still, because it held two rooms, my housemates called me *dà dìzhǔ*: big landlord.

Every morning my neighbors checked if an unseen hand had daubed 拆—*chāi*, raze—in ghostly white on the home's gray walls as we slept. Not yet. Another day in Yángméizhú (Red Bayberry and Bamboo) *hútòng* began.

I was here to research the book I had been planning for the past three years. Earlier that spring, a *Time* correspondent passed my name on to an editor at the *New York Times Book Review* who wanted to assign a story on China's publishing industry. I accepted, knowing next to nothing about the subject, and reported on spec, meaning I would not be paid unless the article was published. The contributor's bio stated that I was writing a book about the destruction of historic Beijing, the only sentence that the fact-checker neglected to confirm. In truth, that week I had sat in a Tsinghua classroom, babbling "*Māmā qí mǎ, mǎ màn, māmā mà mǎ.*" A literary agent—whose first-ever sale had been *Waiting for Godot*—reached out anyway, and sold my book proposal shortly thereafter. I dove right in.

Living in the *hútòng* felt like being back in Neijiang: I was again anchored in one small place, wholly immersed and not on the periphery. Despite being a short walk away from the seat of government power at Zhongnanhai, Dazhalan was really a village.

Most mornings when I stepped inside the public latrine, pint-sized students sagging from the weight of their adult-sized backpacks cried, "Good morning, Teacher Plumblossom!"

I volunteered as a full-time fourth-grade teacher at Coal Lane Elementary, located on the adjacent *hútòng*. My nine-year-old students loved Mocky, the naughty monkey that starred in their English textbook. He and his pals were more fun than the characters in their previous textbook series, Ma Nan and her teacher Miss Zhang. Those primers could have been titled "Hectoring English." A typical dialogue went:

"You're late again, Ma Nan."

"I'm sorry, Miss Zhang."

"When do you get up every morning?"

"At seven."

"Get up earlier. Don't be late next time."

In Beijing, students start learning English in first grade. Every child is enrolled in three forty-five-minute lessons weekly until sixth grade. That sounds impressive, but most instruction is automated: students repeat dialogue spoken by animated characters on a DVD. Although Mocky spoke slowly, he sounded like an inebriated Truman Capote on *The Tonight Show*. Like my students, I followed the subtitles.

On my first day in the classroom, I found blackboards decorated with chalked Olympic mascots, the five-colored rings, and doggerel whose Chinese translated as:

> The Olympics will be held in 2008
> Our civic virtue must be great!
> Spitting everywhere is really terrible
> Littering trash is also unbearable
> To get a "thumbs up" from foreign guests
> Beijing's environment depends on us!

After standing for the national anthem each morning, students were supposed to update the number of days until the start of the games. Only one class kept the correct count. Time had stopped completely in Grade 4, Class 2, where there were always 996 days until the Olympics.

It was a pleasant illusion. My classroom did not have a clock, and the view out the windows looked just as timeless. Waves of sloping, tiled rooftops rolled toward the school. We could see the flying eaves of the

Front Gate and the row of red flags fluttering atop the Great Hall of the People. The wider vista, however, revealed that we lived on an ever-shrinking island. Modern office towers and apartments built on razed *hútòng* squeezed our neighborhood from all sides. I pointed to the golden arches shining in the distance, and the kids shouted, "McDonald's!" Soon we could see a Walmart too.

Mocky was the poster monkey for the drive to have 35 percent of the city's population conversant in English by the Olympics. He originated in a textbook series called *Bingo!*, used throughout Asia, if not always beloved. (This from the blog of a teacher in South Korea: "'*What's wrong with Mocky? He ate his banana too fast.*' Why didn't Mocky choke and die on that big banana instead of just making a mess on the kitchen table, the table of my mind!") My students, most of them from migrant, working-class families, often could not relate to the book's vocabulary.

When Mocky explored careers, he considered becoming a farmer, a doctor, a nurse, a pilot, or a dancer. After injuring himself while trying to juggle, he came to respect veterinarians and decided he wanted to be one. But when I asked my students about their aspirations, the first boy yelled, "When I grow up, I want to be a foreigner!"

The students had difficulty saying what their own parents did for a living. "How do I say 'unemployed'?" one asked. On the blackboard, I wrote the English for *fry-cook, road builder, repairman,* and—for a girl who called herself Cher—*fashion designer*. She pointed at a classmate and said in Chinese, "His father is a prisoner!" The man had tried to rob a bank.

Mocky's creator, a man named Ken Methold, also wrote textbooks featuring a red English-speaking dinosaur named Gogo who could be seen on an endless video loop at China's largest bookstore, asking, "Do you like doughnuts? Do you like burgers?"

Book Mansion, a short bike ride from my courtyard to Xidan, the wide intersection west of Tiananmen Square, displayed 230,000 titles. Textbooks filled one of its five floors, each the size of an Olympic swimming pool. A lane-wide aisle held only English-Chinese dictionaries, including one whose cover featured Garfield. It held no entry for *lasagna* but one for *tofu*. This being China, Mocky faced some new competition, in the form of a new textbook that starred a monkey named Micky.

But for all the piles of language primers, a visitor to Beijing still would have difficulty finding locals conversant in English. Book Mansion categorized its manuals by category: leisure English, phone English, taxi English, job-hunting English, even badminton English. I opened one of the many books titled *Olympic English* and found this: "I have made a reservation for tonight through the telephone. My name is Cable Guy."

The police, 60 percent of whom were supposed to be competent in English in time for the 2008 Summer Games, studied from a book titled *Olympic Security English.* Dialogues called "Dissuading Foreigners from Excessive Drinking" and "Interrogating a Suspicious Foreigner" taught the cops such phrases such as "Don't pretend to be innocent."

The first chapter, "Everyday English," modeled how to stop a reporter from covering Falun Gong. "It's beyond the limit of your coverage and illegal," officers practiced saying. "You're a sports reporter. You should only cover the games."

Foreigner: Oh, I see. May I go now?

Police: No. Come with us.

Foreigner: What for?

Police: To clear up this matter.

The lesson's pattern drills included: It's *illegal*

against the law

banned

prohibited

not allowed

not permitted

I realized I knew each of the words in Chinese, having picked them up not from my own classwork, but from reading Beijing street signs.

Aside from brawling soccer hooligans, the book's only bad guys were Muslims with names like "Mohammed Ali." One fictitious culprit was apprehended while robbing an American's hotel room "because my family was killed when the United States bombed Afghanistan. I became homeless and I hate Americans."

Beijing cops recited this response: "We feel sympathy for your misfortune.

But your behavior to deliberately hurt an innocent American is against our law, and you disrupted our social order, especially during the Olympic games. You caused a disturbance, and damaged the reputation of our country, so you should shoulder the criminal responsibilities."

"Yes, ma'am," the perp replied.

While I laughed at these lessons, the directive to learn English helped my book research. No foreigner had ever registered to live in a Dazhalan courtyard, and Chinese migrant newcomers were eyed suspiciously on arrival: the tight-knit lanes were plastered with police-issued stickers that could have been Beijing's real motto: LOCK YOUR DOORS AND RECEIVE STRANGERS CAREFULLY.

A cop named Officer Li called the school and ordered me to come to the station; I walked there warily, expecting him to order me to move out immediately. Instead, Officer Li wanted a private lesson in English vulgarities, "so I know when a foreigner is cursing me." I agreed; he pulled the red ink pad from his otherwise empty desk drawer and stamped my household registration form. We met regularly over dumplings. As the rounds of beer kept coming and other customers turned to stare, I compared Officer Li to body parts, told him what to do with himself, and appraised his mother. He nodded happily and asked for more.

Frances returned to Beijing to spend a semester observing a city courtroom, since, in the spirit of Olympics-related openness, the public was suddenly allowed inside. She wasn't sure how to get in, exactly: on her first morning at the Dongcheng district criminal courthouse, in a *hútòng* near our old Haiyuncang apartment, she parked her Flying Pigeon bike and stepped through the front door, pretending that she knew where to go. A security guard checked her backpack and asked to see her visitor's pass. She retreated and knocked on the receptionist's window. In a cigarette-singed voice, a man snapped, "What do you want?"

Next he asked what courtroom she wanted to visit. "Number two," she guessed. The man smiled. "There is no courtroom number two."

I should have chosen the first one! Frances thought, her heart jumping like a trapped rabbit. Adhering to the Chinese police maxim, "Leniency to those who confess, severity for those who refuse," she admitted she was a

law student, and lost. The man softened and, after registering her identification, handed her a laminated card whose back held rules, which included
dressing neatly, keeping the courtroom clean, and not carrying "guns,
bullets, gun-powder, knives in a sheath and other dangerous objects." The
courtroom resembled a wood-paneled home library decorated with the
national emblem designed by Liang Sicheng and admonishments not to
take pictures, record, or spit. As Frances took her seat in the last row of
red-linen-covered seats, an elderly woman exited, muttering a complaint
about the court: "There isn't one good fruit on this tree."

Three black-robed judges faced the pair of prosecutors and the lone
defendant from their bench. His lawyer was not present; the twenty-six-
year-old had admitted to stealing the equivalent of $4,000 from his
employer, a state-owned hotel. He stood and read a statement that began,
"I feel deeply regretful for having disappointed the Party and the Country."
Frances noted his chubby cheeks; he looked like a high school student
who had been hauled in to the principal's office for fighting. He had
committed the crime in SARS's aftermath, when visitor numbers to the
hotel had plummeted, and his monthly salary had been halved, to 600
yuan ($75). He could no longer pay his mother's medical bills, he said.
The man pleaded for leniency, noting that he had nearly repaid the stolen
money. The judges withdrew to deliberate.

Twenty-three minutes later, they reentered and sentenced the man to six
months in jail. Two security guards escorted him out of the courtroom.

The next case's defendants were three men who had brawled at a nightclub
and had been held for eight months before their trial. Later, in the administrative courtroom, Frances watched a plaintiff who had sued the district
Land Administration Bureau for demolishing his house. He lost. Next came
the family of a schizophrenic woman suing the Civil Affairs Bureau for
allowing her to file for divorce despite being mentally ill. They won.

As she swapped her visitor's badge for her identification, Frances heard
screaming and crying across the street, at the Petition Office. She noticed
people passing through the dusty iron gate with unkempt hair and
ragged clothes. Graffiti on the building's wall criticized the Party, saying
officials were corrupt and blind to their suffering. Some people signed their
names and wrote their phone numbers, as if they no longer cared about
the consequences so long as they would be heard.

When she walked inside, Frances saw the noticeboard detailing how to file a petition. Two small barred windows faced the room. A middle-aged woman leaned down to yell into one: "I've lost everything, including my house. The officials were corrupt!"

The courtrooms felt humane in comparison; people there were at least afforded the dignity of a quiet room and attentive ears, if not justice. Many cases concerned the demolition of homes, which were futile. One man, who had invented a product he swore to be "diet flour," had lost his court-yard home and storefront near the Forbidden City. He was paid a pittance of the real estate's value, which meant he would have to relocate to the far suburbs. Frances went to see the ruins of his home, a pile of rubble amidst a field of it, looking as if a bomb, not pickax-swinging laborers, had obliter-ated the old neighborhood.

More often the litigants were in court to settle interpersonal beefs: a grandmother whose permed hair reminded Frances of dry instant noodles was being sued by a fellow mah-jongg player who said the woman attacked her while playing the game at a *hútòng* parlor. A bald judge listened to her before snapping, "You are sixty-nine years old. All you do is play mah-jongg from early morning to late at night. This is not the first time that you've sued over this type of dispute. Don't you have anything better to do? Why can't you engage in something more appropriate to your age, instead of gambling all the time. It's not the first time I've told you this. You should start reflecting on what you have done wrong yourself."

The plaintiff's tears streamed wild, as did her words. The judge pounded his gavel but couldn't stop her shrieking. The plaintiff stood and cursed the defendants. The judge rose and screamed at her. Thankfully, no one had a cleaver.

Frances remembered what a judge had admitted when she asked him what had become of his ambition to be a "real" judge, independent of the Party, "respected and just." Like most Chinese judges, the man said, he quickly realized that could never be achieved. "So everyone stopped wanting to be a real judge, and in the end, no one behaves like one."

One morning Frances watched a judge berate a defendant for being late, for chewing gum, for putting his elbows on the table, for not understanding legal terms, for not turning off his cell phone's ringtone, for nodding instead of saying, "Yes." A judge sitting beside her on the bench noticed Frances in the back row, scribbling away.

"You cannot take notes without permission," the judge said, calling her out. "You must turn them over to us."

Frances's stomach sank, as when getting caught passing notes in school. She had been jotting her observations in Chinese, recording the judge's imperious tone and her disregard of procedures. Instead of turning over her entire notebook, Frances thought quickly, tearing off and passing forward only the topmost page. The imperious judge inspected the evidence carefully: it detailed the bench trio's clothing, demeanor, and how they spoke. The judge's face reddened, but Frances noticed that her tone softened when addressing the plaintiffs for the rest of the session.

Her page of notes moved back and forth on the bench, then over to the secretary and then back to the bench for the chief judge to inspect yet again. By now, Frances thought, he must have looked at it four times. She realized that the posted regulations said that judges had the authority to arrest visitors and detain them for an unspecified period time if they did not obey court rules. Frances decided that this would be her last visit to the Dongcheng District People's Court. For Chinese, it is often safer to research their own country from afar.

CHAPTER 18

THE ROAD TO SLEEPING DRAGON

M Y INVITATION TO participate in official Party business did not make Chinese governance look any less opaque. After speaking to the UNESCO World Heritage Site managers training at Lushan, my name was passed to the U.S.-China Environmental Fund, a Madison, Wisconsin–based conservation group that had designed the research and visitor center at China's largest panda preserve in Wolong, "Sleeping Dragon." Its plan to limit development was up against an international firm that proposed transforming the entire valley into a panda-themed amusement park. At the end of May 2006, I took a day off from teaching English in the *hútòng* and flew to Sichuan to lobby the Wolong officials.

The conservation group wanted me to repeat my Lushan presentation, showing slides of environmental attractions around China that had allowed unchecked tourism—"tarnishing their brand." Then, using two hands—the polite way—I would present the officials with an invitation from the National Geographic Society to travel to Yosemite National Park to witness American conservation practices firsthand.

To me, naïvely, this seemed like an easy layup. This group had already designed and funded the research center's previous expansion, turning what had looked like a panda penitentiary into a humane park, with winding cobblestone walkways, bamboo rails, and explanatory plaques in English and Chinese. Visiting a Chinese zoo was a sadist's holiday, and I avoided them. In pictures, at least, Wolong's improved facilities resembled an enclosure at the San Diego Zoo, which regularly sent research teams to collaborate with Chinese scientists.

As I had feared, Wolong's valley was still only accessible via a circuitous two-lane road that teetered above a turbulent, boulder-strewn river. To maneuver around landslides, the bus inched down the embankment. We didn't plunge so much as dipped our tires into the frigid water, driving slowly through its shallows and then climbing back up to the rubble-free road. Covering the eighty-four miles from Chengdu took six hours.

Shortly after arrival, a keeper opened a cage door and asked if I wanted to take a picture with a panda.

"It's OK, just stand there next to it," the man said, leading me inside the cage. The panda looked disinterested, lolling on its back atop a raised platform, munching on a stalk of bamboo.

"I don't know," I protested.

"It's OK, come on," the keeper insisted. Pandas enjoyed some incredibly flattering PR. This was not the cuddly symbol of the World Wildlife Fund that I grew up with. This one's fur was streaked with feces. She languidly waved a paw in my direction. The cage door slammed shut.

"Hand me the camera," the keeper said from the other side of the bars. "One photo only costs 30 yuan [$4]."

I stood in a cage with one of the world's rarest animals. "No picture," I said. Panda drool pooled on the cement floor.

"OK, 25 yuan," the keeper said.

So this was Wolong, the China destination I had long wanted to see.

The panda stretched out its tongue, rolled its eyes, and peed on itself. Then it began emitting bursts of sound that reminded me less of Chewbacca and more of a hungry bird. The keeper, standing outside the cage, said not to worry: "chirping" signaled the onset of estrus.

"Move [CHIRP!] closer, I'll take [CHIRP!] a photo."

"Let me [CHIRP!] out."

"Twenty yuan?" [CHIRP!]

Outside the cage, I looked back at the panda, chewing on a plastic mineral water bottle. *That can't be good.* I turned to tell the keeper, but he had walked away.

*

Later that day, as dusk fell, I watched a panda munching a nutritious "panda pie" of rice and corn, baked at the center—ignoring a female keeper's call to dinner. Leafy bamboo sat stacked high in a wheelbarrow.

"Hurry up, lazy bones!" the keeper yelled, banging metal pots. The rushing river drowned out the sounds. The valley's walls glowed from the setting sun, and a breeze rustled the bamboo, moving like a tidal swell across the mountainside. The keeper grabbed a stalk of bamboo and waved the plant in the air. Six panda cubs ambled toward their dinner.

Pandas are gluttons, but picky ones. Bamboo takes two to three years to mature; the research center paid Wolong's farmers to plant it but also had to buy stalks from outlying villages. "One panda eats the equivalent of $3,000 to $4,000 a year," the keeper told me. "Add in medical care and housing, and one panda requires $12,500 in upkeep annually."

She handed me a baby bottle filled with milk as a panda cub treated my legs like a tree trunk. Surprisingly sharp claws scraped and climbed and slid; I was glad I wore jeans. When I squatted, it wrapped its cute cub paws around the bottle, provoking an involuntary *awwww* to escape from my mouth.

Wolong was the heart of both the giant panda's natural habitat and human-assisted breeding. "We had sixteen births last year," the keeper said, bringing the center's total to sixty. "My job is to train them to be accepting of humans so we can help them reproduce." This work included showing inexperienced males video recordings of mating pandas, what the keeper, in English, called "panda porn."

In 2006, Wolong received more than a half million visitors, mostly domestic tourists—a fivefold increase over the previous decade. The village population had doubled to five thousand, and a large hotel had recently opened. The panda keeper knew the local government planned to lure even more tourists to the valley. However, every visitor made an impact on the fragile environment, and the panda center didn't expect to see a windfall from any additional revenue. I asked her where the money went. The keeper nodded down the cobblestone path at middle-aged men wearing navy-blue Windbreakers. I didn't have to ask who they were; their markings—matching jackets, zippered clutch purses, and dyed-black comb-overs—were as recognizable from afar as a panda's spotted eyes. Local officials.

*

The U.S.-China Environmental Fund's proposal again included drawings by the architect who had designed the panda research center's previous makeover. Anthony Puttnam was Frank Lloyd Wright's last living disciple, having trained at Taliesin West. Recently he had shepherded the construction of Wright's long-tabled lakeside convention center in Madison, where Puttnam lived. The elderly architect traveled from there to Wolong to present his renderings—for which he had again waived his fee. They featured wood-framed buildings built in the local style around existing trees, and kept the valley's village—home to native Qiang people—intact but for a state-of-the-art trash recycling center.

As I sat in the Wolong Hotel conference room, listening to Puttnam pitch to the assembled officials, I glanced a printout of the pep talk the U.S.-China Environmental Fund's president had e-mailed that morning: "Your *convictions* about conserving cultural and natural resources, the importance of interpretation and respect for heritage, will be the difference. Win this one for the home team."

My convictions notwithstanding, our competition was a five-thousand-employee multinational firm known for shiny skyscrapers and glassy airport terminals. Its suit-clad bid team waited in the lobby to present a plan that included an IMAX theater, a chairlift, and a theme park ride that it called the Pandacoaster.

I remembered that Beijing officials had lost interest when Albert Speer Jr. explained to them that his Olympic axis would terminate at a train station. To regain their attention, Speer quickly recast it as *an airport for trains.* How could I make a trash recycling center sound sexier than a Pandacoaster? In Chinese, I mentally repeated saying *high-technology pollution preventer.*

Bottles of unopened mineral water dotted the polished wooden table. Behind each bottle sat a middle-aged official. Each wore a navy-blue Windbreaker and fidgeted as I spoke. One man twirled a pen; another vibrated as he bounced his knee beneath the table. Afterward, Puttnam said he heard the deciding vote would be cast by the man with the comb-over. That narrowed it down to everyone.

With the officials we did not share a banquet, have tea, or even chat. After we finished speaking, there were no questions or even polite, tepid applause. The head of the Chinese nonprofit that partnered with our group told us to go feed the pandas. The sealed bid had been submitted, but now, he said, the real lobbying began.

"You bribe them?"

The man laughed.

"I wish. We don't have any money. I plead with them."

In the end, of course, it did come down to money. The big firm submitted a lowball estimate of construction costs. Wolong officials asked our team to make concessions. A flurry of phone calls and backdoor lobbying occurred offstage; late at night back in the *hútòng*, my e-mail pinged and I, thinking it was Frances, rose from my uncomfortable platform bed to see a note whose subject line said: URGENT. GIVING CONTRACT TO OTHERS! I clicked on it, and the all-caps continued: "I THINK IT IS MOST URGENT THAT YOU CALL AT ONCE." The officials, it turned out, were willing to spend the $100 million our plan had budgeted for construction, but not the $1 million earmarked for its schematic design. Puttnam suggested slashing the cost by outsourcing the blueprints to a local, Sichuan firm. The savings might sway the officials to approve our plan, and not the one featuring the Pandacoaster.

Puttnam submitted less expensive renderings and then, as he wrote me two months later, "after all the hurry it's wait, wait, wait . . ." He also asked if the new buildings really needed air-conditioning in summertime—for Westerners. I thought nouveau riche Chinese tourists would be more likely to demand it, despite the cool mist that usually garlanded Wolong's valley, obscuring its mountaintops.

Three months passed until another late-night call informed me that several Wolong officials had been arrested on suspicion of corruption. I waited to hear the word *Pandagate*, of the cash-for-coaster connection, but no: the men in navy Windbreakers had taken bribes to approve construction of the large hotel where we had pitched to them a plan that left the valley intact.

Perhaps this twist helped the U.S.-China Environmental Fund's coaster-free design win, after all. In 2007, Puttnam wrote from Wolong to say that the low-impact visitor's center teahouse was under construction and that the newly appointed officials had commended its feng shui. He said he was sitting on the Chinese builders: "If you don't specifically identify something that is needed, such as waterproofing or drainage for the kitchen, they don't do anything about it nor will they ask a question." Yet, compared to a kitchen, constructing mega-projects seemed to be a snap: a new tunnel through mountains linked the valley to Chengdu, cutting travel time from six hours to two. However, Puttnam noted with alarm, "the new road is falling apart along the outside lane where the earth fill wasn't stabilized." I expected a bus plunge story to follow, but so far, no one had gotten hurt.

The following year, on May 12, 2008, an earthquake measuring 8.0 on the Richter scale triggered landslides in Wolong, located only eighteen miles from the epicenter in a town named Wenchuan. An estimated sixty-nine thousand people died; remarkably, Wolong's eight-hundred-square-mile nature preserve only had five fatalities, although no one at the research center was hurt. One of its sixty-three captive pandas—Mao Mao, a mother of three—perished after being crushed by a falling wall. Mudslides buried the only road to the center, whose buildings—including those designed by Puttnam and the new hotel—were damaged beyond repair.

Wolong's captive pandas were moved fourteen miles east within the sanctuary. Despite China's booming economy and burgeoning list of billionaires, money for the research and visitor center built there came not from the government or private donors, but from Hong Kong, which channeled $29 million of its $1.3 billion earthquake relief fund to rehabilitate the Wolong National Nature Reserve.

At the center's ribbon cutting in May 2016, a new group of Windbreakers praised Hong Kongers' "selfless" support, and gifted the city two pairs of pandas. The old research base was abandoned, and being reclaimed by nature.

CHAPTER 19

"One World, One Dream" One Year Later

I N 2007, AFTER two years living in the *hútòng*, I retreated from my shared courtyard, whose door held no lock and where privacy was a foreign concept, to write the Beijing book in London, where Frances worked as a summer associate at a British law firm. In a South Kensington hotel room, I emptied a duffel bag filled with lesson plans, newspaper clippings, photographs, students' drawings, and notes. The pile made what archaeologists call a "tell," and slowly I began sifting through the evidence to see what story it revealed. The pile smelled of ashes and age, and every morning I had to remind the hotel's maid to not toss the irreplaceable materials, which looked to her like "rubbish," into the "bin."

The next year, after Frances graduated from law school, the London firm hired her to its New York office. Neither of us had lived on the East Coast, and we were excited for the change of scenery, even if—as we advanced into our thirties—every discussion and argument seemed catalyzed by the question of whether it was time to settle down and become parents. Yes, I said; no, she replied. No, I agreed. Yes, she said. The indecision wasn't surprising: aside from each other, the only constant in our adult lives had been change. Of course it was: we had fallen in love in Beijing.

When I returned in 2009, nine months after the Olympics, to hand a copy of *The Last Days of Old Beijing: Life in the Vanishing Backstreets of a City Transformed* to each person featured in the book, nearly all of them had the same reaction. They flipped through the English-language pages, wondering: *Where is my picture?* I had expected they would not want to be shown for fear of reprisals; instead they posed for portraits to be included in the paperback edition, taken by Mark Leong, a *National Geographic* photographer whom I had also met, years earlier, at the Sunday basketball game.

Secondly, my *hútòng* neighbors asked when the book would come out in Chinese. Not for another four years, after my best graduate student, a Sichuan native named He Yujia, translated its pages on her own—without waiting for permission, or even telling me, initially—and sent the manuscript to Mainland publishers, urging them to take a look. The razing of heritage was no longer deemed a "sensitive" topic; by then, so little would remain of Old Beijing that the book could be classified not as "current affairs" but as "history." Many Chinese publications reviewed *Zài Huì, Lǎo Běijīng* (*Farewell, Old Beijing*) not as a plea for the preservation of neighborhoods, inclusion of local residents in decision making, and transparency in planning but as a book illustrating the need for affordable housing in Beijing and other big cities.

Nevertheless, on the book tour in 2013, the Chinese edition's publisher seized the opportunity to turn my talks into public forums, pairing me with local activists, including a Shanghai conservationist, a Beijing professor critical of city planners, and the bookshop owner Liu Suli, who had spent twenty months in prison for his role in 1989's protests at Tiananmen Square, and had been detained again in 2010 after his friend, the political prisoner Liu Xiaobo, won that year's Nobel Peace Prize.* Audiences had more questions for these men than they did for me, and for once I enjoyed being on a Chinese stage, since I could just listen.

The book's title was not a declaration but a trope: for eight hundred years the capital had cycled through a series of "last days" as dynasties fell and new regimes reshaped the city in their image. Still, when I returned after the Olympics in 2009, I was surprised to see Dazhalan, my old neighborhood, largely intact. A year before the games began, posters commanding BUILD A NEW BEIJING TO WELCOME A NEW OLYMPICS

---

* In 2017, Liu died of liver cancer while serving an eleven-year prison sentence for "inciting subversion of state power" after promoting a pro-democracy charter.

were pasted near my courtyard. One night a hand finally painted 拆 on its wall. But a year later the old house remained—and, remarkably, still stands today.

My former neighbors (wrongly) credit the book. The Great Recession turned out to be a better protector of old Chinese architecture than any heritage conservation campaign. There was far less capital to pay for the resettlement of fifty-seven thousand people, let alone build more malls in downtown Beijing.

At her courtyard home, as her father's pet pigeons flapped in circles overhead, my former student Little Liu, who had advanced to middle school, slowly repeated *global economic crisis* in Chinese. "Interesting" times always taught me new vocabulary: *bàng bàng bàng bàng, raze, U.S.-led NATO, cockfight, honeysuckle, Pandacoaster*. Little Liu had anticipated the Beijing Games the way I once counted down to Christmas Eve, but nine months later the event felt far away. "The Olympics showed foreign countries that China is a friendly and developed country," she said in polished English. "But now it's over." She shrugged and switched to Mandarin. "All the activities about the Olympics at school have been replaced by ones about psychological health, like 'Don't snatch purses' or 'Don't cheat people online.'"

I could not confirm these changes firsthand: fears that foreigners might be carrying swine flu (another new word) meant that I was forbidden to set foot back inside Coal Lane Elementary, the school where for two years I had taught full-time, for free.

"Olympic gold medals, cheap!" called a woman outside Beijing's National Stadium. "Gold medals, buy one now!" The freelance vendor did not sell faux silvers or bronzes. "After all," she said, "people only want a champion's memory."

Buses disgorged visitors—mostly Chinese from outside Beijing—to tour the stadium, known as the "Bird's Nest" for its façade of interlaced steel. The $450 million icon of the 2008 Summer Games had become, like the Great Wall and the Forbidden City, a national symbol. Similarly, the Bird's Nest now lacked a practical purpose, hosting not a home team but a handful of pop concerts and tourists who paid 50 yuan ($7.25) to picnic in the seats and pose for photographs on a mock medal stand.

The state-owned investment company that managed the Bird's Nest had added an amusement park beside Albert Speer Jr.'s axis outside the stadium, but on a searing June afternoon few visitors ventured from the shade of the structure's distinctive steel ribbons, now flecked with scabs of rust and coated in dust. Tourists stared at barren flagpoles, the unlit cauldron, and an empty field. The scoreboard flashed clips of Jamaican sprinter Usain Bolt lunging across the finish line, and fireworks blooming along the capital's imperial axis, and the pigtailed nine-year-old singing "Ode to the Motherland" during the opening ceremonies. Only one of these images was real; the pyrotechnics were partially rendered digitally and the girl lip-synched the song.

What was the legacy of the Beijing Olympics? Western perceptions of China tend to veer between marvel and apprehension: online reactions to the opening ceremonies slid along a continuum of awe at the sight of thousands of drummers and flying sylphs to the uneasy realization that a production of such scale was only possible in a nation with an enormous population and resources, and a government powerful enough to mobilize them. If they could do this, what couldn't they do? Today the Olympic venues looked all but deserted. Crosswalk signals flashed red over empty four-lane roads.

The capital felt the hangover that came after hosting the world's biggest-ever coming-out party. Beijing was learning, as other host cities had, that the Games' good feelings were often extinguished with the torch. (The hangover was not soothed, of course, by the simultaneous near collapse of the world's economy.) A year after the Olympics, Beijing residents still could not drink the tap water, or surf an unfiltered Internet, or exercise in safe air. They had discovered, too, that the "temporary" security measures adopted for the Games, such as metal detectors and X-ray machines at subway entrances and closed-circuit security cameras in neighborhoods—and even, I was told, in my former *hútòng* classroom—were now permanent fixtures.

Across the country, countdown clocks were reset to show the days until the start of Shanghai's 2010 World Expo.

I was not going to attend that or write any more about China's large cities, whose development promised more of the same story. When I told a Beijing official that the city's planners did not have to make the same mistakes America's made, he replied, with great indignation, "We have every *right* to make the same mistakes that America made!"

Because only elementary-school-aged children of migrant workers were permitted to attend Beijing's public schools, nearly half of my class of twenty-four students had left the *hútòng* after finishing the sixth grade. By law, they had to return to their parents' home villages to sit for the middle school entrance exam and continue their studies there. What did they return to? What was daily life like in contemporary China's rural half? I learned that the time to write a book is when the book you want to read doesn't exist. I started thinking about moving to where Frances's grandparents had raised her as a child, in Manchuria, the Northeast, in a rice-growing village named Wasteland.

While walking in my former *hútòng*, I stopped to chat with sixty-two-year-old Auntie Li as she stood beside her flatbed tricycle selling socks and other sundries. She parked the portable convenience store beneath painted characters that spelled ONE WORLD, ONE DREAM over a slogan from a preceding era: NEVER FORGET CLASS STRUGGLE. Auntie Li still wore the blue-and-white polo shirt issued to the one hundred thousand volunteers who staffed the Olympics.

"I worked every day for three weeks out at the Bird's Nest," she said. "It made me feel connected to the event, to the world." Admittedly, her contribution was limited. "Mostly I just smiled at passersby." But for a change she had felt useful.

The Olympics' promotion of volunteerism was a novel change for Beijing. When I was in the Peace Corps, people often felt sorry for me, wondering what sort of nation sent its citizens overseas to work with strangers. In the run-up to the Olympics, however, the government mobilized students, state employees, and retirees to pitch in. Older residents of my neighborhood recruited me to teach them state-approved English phrases such as *Beijing is getting better and better every day*. They laughed knowingly when I added, "But today things will just get worse."

The capital's Olympic legacy didn't follow Seoul's, whose 1988 Games played a part in nudging its one-party government to allow direct elections. No such relaxation of control was evident in Beijing, where plainclothes police were still easily identifiable on Tiananmen Square, still talking into rolled-up newspapers. They patrolled, too, outside the home studio of the artist Ai Weiwei, who had been chosen by the Swiss firm Herzog & de Meuron to collaborate on the design of the Bird's Nest.

We met at his home studio on June 4, 2009, the twentieth anniversary of Tiananmen. "It's good to talk today," the bearded, portly Ai said in English. "Let them see that people aren't scared to visit me." When I admitted that *I* was a little scared, walking past the police parked outside his house, carrying a passport stickered not with a journalist but a tourist visa, his caustic laugh boomed off his modern courtyard's walls. "You're an American! This shitty government can't tell you what you're allowed to write."

During the Cultural Revolution, Ai's father, a well-known poet, was exiled to Xinjiang; the fifty-one-year-old Ai was an avant-garde artist known globally as much for his dissent as his art. I came to praise him, to his face, for what I consider his masterpiece: After 2008's devastating Sichuan earthquake, Ai's popular blog began posting profiles of children who died after their shoddily made schools collapsed, a result, he charged, of local officials misappropriating construction funds. The government shut the blog down, but not before Ai and his volunteers had posted the names of thousands of victims. A year later the government admitted 5,335 children had perished in the quake, mostly in 7,000 poorly built classrooms.

In his courtyard, Ai pointed at a poplar. "When the road was widened, trees were cut down. One day I found a magpie's nest sitting on the ground. I was really worried about the unhatched eggs in it, so I carried it inside here and then placed it in that tree. But of course the mother never returned to the nest. I had ruined it."

No, Ai corrected me: this was not the Bird's Nest stadium's origin story. But it did illustrate what followed its completion.

"I wasn't invited to the opening ceremonies, and I wouldn't have gone," he said. "I have disassociated myself from every act associated with the state. Look at this city now: Beijing is the most inhuman city on the planet. From every aspect I hate it. It's a city for a dictatorship's regime. They took the best location and shamelessly ruined it. Old neighborhoods have been torn apart to be occupied by the people who have made a fortune by taking property from the people. Your Dazhalan is the latest example of government officials and developers shamelessly chasing profit and more profit."

I fished an official Bird's Nest key chain from my pocket, one of the hundreds of trinkets branded with his design on sale at the stadium. "I've never been inside it," Ai admitted with a laugh. "I love the building. I'm Chinese, after all, and it's good for China. Maybe young kids can see there is such a thing as graceful design, that it's OK to have dreams, that they can come true." Ai fingered the key chain and shook his head. "But for now, my name is permanently associated with the country's biggest propaganda item."

CHAPTER 20

A Trans-Siberian Exit

I BOARDED THE TRANS-SIBERIAN expecting sinister, unshaven traders with Peter Lorre leers shouldering lumpy sacks. Instead, my compartment filled with boxes of carefully stacked woks, bundles of Gap sweaters, plastic sacks the colors of a faded French flag, and three women. The goods belonged to two of them, and they swatted me away when I tried clearing a space. The third woman moved a small duffel bag, her only piece of luggage, and motioned for me to sit beside her.

Miss Zhou introduced herself and then interrupted my reply with an exclamation. "We're leaving!" It was an illusion: the train beside us was departing. Miss Zhou swiveled her head from the moving side of the carriage to the still one, realized her mistake, and climbed, embarrassed, into her bunk above mine. Our train remained for now in Beijing Station.

To Miss Zhou it always would. For her and the Chinese passengers, train number three, car fourteen, was really two trains: one speeding away from China and one that never seemed to leave. Over the next six days and 4,887 miles, we rode them together, at once. The twenty-three-year-old was heading for Moscow. I was here to complete a fabled train journey en route to a connection to London, where Frances would be waiting to begin our first-ever vacation free of commitments.

The diesel departed the station, creeping out of the grid before gathering speed and chugging toward the Great Wall. Dried corn stalks piled high beside drying bricks in dried-out fields scrolled past the window. In the hallway a mother held an infant to the glass, naming the sights: "Cow. Crow. Coal."

Miss Zhou swung down from her bunk onto mine, landing with a thud, a bouncing ponytail, and a giggle. She framed crooked gray teeth in bright pink lipstick. Brushstrokes of concealer caked over acne, and her plucked eyebrows had been redrawn with two penciled bolts. Embroidered flowers grew on each flared jeans cuff, while a tight white tank top clung flat to her chest.

She thrust a piece of notebook paper into my face. "Sir, how do I say these in English?"

Through her shaky characters, I made out the months April through September.

"Why do you want to know?"

"I'm going to Russia!" She laughed, as if it were as obvious as the painted propaganda passing by outside. The mother read aloud: "Love My China. Serve the People." The infant giggled and smacked the glass.

At dusk, a fine mist of sand coated the compartment. Outside, an unrestored fragment of the Great Wall stood atop scrubby grass, an Ozymandias now leaned upon by a watchful shepherd in the dusty sunlight. Miss Zhou huddled over my customs form. "What did you write? What should I write?" I filled out her paperwork. Under "Currency" I recorded "$330," the amount of folded dollars she'd bought from a friend who had returned from America. She leaned on me with knees apart, a pose completely innocent on a Chinese train. "We're friends, right?" she asked, offering an apple. She studied my Russian visa, comparing it to hers. Something troubled her. She stood up, opened the compartment door, closed the door, sat down, and stood up again. I crunched through the apple. She fussed, she fretted. Finally she motioned me into the hall. "I've never been out of China before," she whispered. "I'm really nervous about customs. And the police."

Her story tumbled out in a voice more worn than conspiratorial. She worked twelve-hour days, six days a week, making dresses with Italian labels. The job exhausted her. She held up chafed hands and pointed to her raspy throat. "Dirty air." A friend of a friend told her about Moscow, where a factory of a friend of another friend employed seamstresses. Miss Zhou's suddenly awe-filled description of the gig made it sound like Moscow was the magnificent, pulsing heart of the modern world.

I unfolded the map on which I'd been tracing our route and pointed to Beijing and the line we'd thus drawn. "It's too far!" she exclaimed. "That's impossible." She fingered a city in central Mongolia. "Is this Shanghai?" I asked her to find Moscow. She motioned to South America. I asked to see her hometown, Wenzhou, located on the central China coast. She pinned down Beijing, keeping the slippery concept in place, and moved south, stopping in Hong Kong. "Here?"

She asked where I was from. She had never heard of Minnesota. I said that Frances would be in London. "The capital of South Korea?" asked Miss Zhou.

I believe in maps, in scale. At every waking moment, I know where I am in relation to the rest of the planet. Miss Zhou had no use for them. Until now, her entire life revolved around home, from where she knew the way to work, and the way to Moscow. Just hop on the number three, where the PA played Chinese pop songs, the conductors spoke Mandarin, and the canteen sold *mápó* tofu. I asked Miss Zhou where she was. "I'm on the train," she laughed. "In China. Where are you?" I pointed to the border on the map, then out the window. "Mongolia."

At the Erenhot-Zamyn-Üüd crossing, the stern customs agent flipped through Miss Zhou's passport and demanded to know why she had unused visas to Burma, Thailand, and Saudi Arabia. "I changed my mind?" she replied meekly. The ingénue glow faded from her cheeks. The agent led her away after that. I remained on the train, riding to the wheelhouse to watch the undercarriages being changed to fit the five-foot gauge, used on Russian-built rails.

As our car lifted from its Chinese wheels, a Mongolian woman with piercing black eyes asked me for a light. She rolled the *r* and voiced the *qu* when she said her name: Turquoise. At age twenty-six, she remained single. "Marry who?" she asked, sweeping her arm at the vast darkness beyond the tracks.

For the past five years she had lived in Sydney, happy, tan, and lean. Then her mother fell ill. She opened her passport. It belonged to a plump, pale girl in gaudy lipstick, frilly blouse, and pageboy haircut. "This," she said, tapping the picture, "is me when I live in Mongolia."

The train settled back down atop wider wheels.

Depending on the passenger's perspective, the train moved in different directions. It bore us all toward Moscow, but, like the morning's illusion, not everyone felt they were going forward. Turquoise said the train was a lifeline for Mongolians, yet she was heading back to her old self and her mother's death. The Chinese conductors groused that the train was a looping routine, returning them through cities they had already seen. The traders, like those whose woks and sweaters threatened to spill from our compartment into the corridor, made the train a rolling warehouse. They repeated a biweekly ritual, powdering their cheeks, painting their lips, and unbuttoning the tops of their blouses to persuade the officers who searched the train to forget duty. We rolled along tracks that made a century-long time line, revealing its ironic history at every stop: a railroad constructed to send homesteaders east to keep Chinese from encroaching on Russia now brought them in by the trainload.

Flashlights stabbed at the platform's darkness, a whistle trilled, and Miss Zhou returned, exuding anxiety and cradling an armful of items. "They made me buy these pills—230 yuan!" That was equivalent to 10 percent of her savings. "Take what you want. I only need the ones for headaches. Hey, want some grapes?" She held up the bunch she bought from the entrepreneurial customs agents. I wondered if they sold the items they confiscated.

"They also gave me this," she said, tossing me a yellow WHO vaccination card. "I had to pay for a shot. My arm hurts." She stretched it out, revealing a lump. "It hurts when I do this." She did "this" five times, hyperextending her elbow and twisting her wrist, the motion of throwing a screwball, which always hurts. "They said it was for hepatitis A." She lowered her voice. "They also gave me an AIDS test." Her face flushed. "In China, there is no AIDS. How embarrassing." I said that China, did, in fact, have AIDS cases: in some regions it was a public health crisis. Miss Zhou shook her head and buried her face behind the newspaper the customs agents also helpfully sold her. I read the date: yesterday.

After clearing the border, the train for Miss Zhou barreled unimpeded toward her new life in Moscow. Although it was nearly dawn, she was wired, relieved that the $300 she had paid in Beijing to an agent to secure a Russian tourist visa had actually bought a real one. I told her she had only made it to Mongolia. The Russian border loomed a day's journey ahead. Miss Zhou's face fell and she stared at my map, running her seamstress's fingers over the black lines that pattern the world.

*

We followed the route of an ancient tea caravan between Beijing and Moscow. Officially, we rode the Trans-Mongolian line until linking up with the Trans-Siberian railway the next day. The green-felt prairies of Mongolia teemed with wildflowers and birds. I watched a sharp-winged swallow keep pace with the train before banking free toward the unreachable horizon. Miss Zhou and the other Chinese passengers bunched at the windows, laughing and whooping. On a Chinese train, a converse relationship exists between serenity and raucousness. The more peaceful the outside, the louder the inside grows. Soon people turned away to make dinner.

Miss Zhou shared her cache of instant noodles with me while the conductors boiled frozen dumplings, part of the pantry they had stocked in Beijing. Over the PA lilted a Faye Wong ballad, a piece of Chinese culture clinging to the train like a hobo. Miss Zhou knew the words. Other Chinese passengers heard her singing along and joined the chorus: *I only love strangers*. Mongolia's purple sunset rolled past unseen.

After easily clearing customs—no inoculations, no questions—Miss Zhou decided she liked Russia. On our third day she awoke to the steaming, ice-coated shores of Lake Baikal, leaned from the window, and smiled silently. A marker said 5,587 more kilometers—3,471 more miles—to Moscow. The houses had changed from Chinese concrete to Mongolian brick to Siberian timber. These were painted bright green, blue, and yellow, draped in white cooking-fire smoke that hung in the larches like tulle.

At Irkutsk, Miss Zhou bought smoked *omul*, a local lake fish, from a platform babushka. It was her first Russian transaction. "Too oily; it stinks to death," she said, frowning while sniffing the caramel-colored flesh. The fish's head fell off, thumping to the compartment floor. "I love rice," Miss Zhou said. "Do they have rice in Moscow?"

Later she sang with the tinny love song blaring on the PA as the clumping train passed the misting Baikal and entered a dewy birch forest. "*My heart's too soft*," she crooned. For the first time, after seventy-two hours together, I appreciated her voice, felt the cradle-calm rhythm of the steel wheels in my bones, the echo that Thomas Wolfe called the sound of forever. I looked outside to see whom I could say hello and good-bye to forever all at once. A young Russian soldier huddled by a fire. I waved. He flipped me off.

The Mongolians got drunk on vodka and belted out rousing anthems about Genghis Khan. The Chinese crowded into the farthest end of the car and compared prices in their respective hometowns. I soon knew the cost of cooking oil in Wenzhou, in Xuzhou, in Zhengzhou. Then the price of toilet paper, pork, and chives—everywhere, in China, always, this talk of chives. How bad was inflation? Forget government figures; track the China Chive Index. Up another 10 percent in berth five, car fourteen, train number three.

Beside the track, on an open sun-drenched plateau near bright white birches weighted with plump twinkling leaves, Russian girls in billowing dresses picked purple and white wildflowers. "It's just like Wenzhou," Miss Zhou observed. It was nothing like Wenzhou. But the Chinese passengers nodded in agreement.

On our fifth day of travel, and our second day in Russian territory, the Chinese were adept enough in the language to barter on the platforms.

At Perm, the city Chekhov's three sisters wanted so desperately to leave, Miss Zhou spent her last yuan on two eggs and a jar of peach halves. The rest of her Chinese currency had gone to the conductors in exchange for a daily share of their rations, in particular the rice. I envied her: a dining car waitress with hair the color of aortic blood emptied the pantry to serve me a dinner of vodka, Marlboros, Snickers, and sausage. "Ten dollars!"

After a decade of making the excuse that I didn't have time to read all four of its volumes, I had brought along the Chinese classic novel *Journey to the West*, in which characters including the Monkey King travel to India to fetch Buddhist sutras and fight their way back to China. As I neared the end of its 2,300 pages, Miss Zhou said dismissively: "I saw the movie. It wasn't bad." I read aloud my favorite line: "'Every piece of duckweed floats down to the sea; people will always meet each other somewhere.'"

At this, she closed the compartment door. "Can I tell you another secret? My boyfriend doesn't live in China. He left Wenzhou and now he's in Milan. He makes pizzas." I conjured the incongruous image of a Chinese man tossing dough for Italians. "I talk to him every week," she said. "I know one word in Italian." She said the word for *love*. "*Amore.*"

Frances and I planned to hike the Italian Riviera's Cinque Terre and would change trains in Milan. I offered to courier anything to Miss Zhou's boyfriend. On a page torn from my journal she wrote the characters for *I miss you*. "Should I sign it?" she wondered, then laughed, replacing her name with a heart drawn in two careful halves.

She applied fresh lipstick and I snapped a photo of her to deliver with the note. "Give me your address in Wenzhou and I'll send you copies."

Miss Zhou looked at the floor.

I said: "You're not going back, are you."

She raised her head, looking relieved. The story and her plans came out in a rush. "He doesn't know I'm going to Moscow. Please tell him I love him and not to worry about me. My friends are meeting me at the station and will find a job for me. I don't know how much I'll make—I think more than in China. My parents know I'm going. Why go? Because I don't know anything about the world! I've never been outside of Wenzhou until now. I don't want to stay there and make clothes. I can make clothes anywhere and learn about the world. I'm not scared. No, I'm not brave. I'm just Chinese."

Later she asked me to test her again. Three days before, she'd written a list of phrases in Chinese, which I translated into English. Over the past four thousand miles she memorized the lines for her new role far away from home, laughing off my gentle suggestion that learning them in Russian might be more useful.

"Where is the Internet café?" she recited. "I want to call China. How much per minute? Where is the Chinese embassy? Passport. Where is the metro? Taxi. Help! Sorry, I don't speak Russian."

A+. Miss Zhou smiled and tried one more. "How much is a ticket to Milan?"

We awoke to a blizzard. Miss Zhou had never seen snow before. We pressed our faces to the glass. The window reflected her face at the moment of joy and wonder, watching a frozen tempest swirl over feather grass and pine. Then we saw a rainbow. "Russia also has rainbows?" she marveled.

The train slowed around a bend, creeping past a row of chestnut horses facing west. An old Mongolian man leaned from the window and made a gentle cooing noise. All of the animals turned their heads. The man smiled. "Horses know one language."

As we pulled into Vladimir and neared the end of the line, dread overcame me. Miss Zhou stared wide-eyed at a raging garbage fire on the platform, at the defeated faces of pensioners, at kids sentenced to adolescence, buried in Yankees caps, Sex Pistols T-shirts, and baggy jeans. "Hot dog!" one yelled in English while chewing on an empty film canister. "Fuck fuck shit shit." So this was the West.

Miss Zhou had $280, a page of English sentences, and the skill to sew. I imagined the dangers that awaited her. After 107 hours, through seven time zones, our farewell was approaching. I didn't want it to come. I didn't want to get off the train. Inertia had bypassed fatigue and turned into something else.

As the train eased into Moscow, the conductor pulled me aside. He'd also been silently worrying. "Listen, little brother," he said in Chinese, wrapping his arm around my shoulders. "Be careful. Russia can be dangerous. Don't trust strangers. You're a foreigner."

"You're concerned about me? But what about . . ."

"Her?" The conductor chuckled, looking at Miss Zhou. "She's Chinese. She'll be fine."

The train shuddered to a stop. We stepped off it and into the world. A pair of kindly-looking aunties greeted Miss Zhou by name. She waved good-bye and walked away with them, toting her little bag, chattering happily in Chinese. I stood alone on the platform, wondering where I was.

ACKNOWLEDGMENTS

Recording all the people to whom I am indebted in China would fill a phone book. The first entry, in boldface, would be that Sichuan bus driver. Long may he roll.

In Neijiang, I am grateful to Wang Qi, Luo Zaixiang and her husband Emperor, librarian Li Nan, Kevin Nicolette, and Rebecca Wallihan, née Steinle. Also Dave Douglas in Pengzhou, and my fellow Minnesotan Mike Goettig, posted to Leshan. In Beijing, I owe much to the New School of Collaborative Learning's Stephanie and Bob Tansey; Will Bate; the Blakemore Foundation; David Spindler, Kaiser Kuo, Ian Johnson; Kai Yang; Ted Wright; Mark Leong and the Dongdan basketball game; Luke Mines; Ron Gluckman; Jake Hooker; Matt Erie; John Thomson and Tom Gold; editors Maureen Murphy, Catharine Hamm, Randy Curwen, Chris Hill, Rachel Donadio, Jennifer Schuessler, Jonathan Tourtellot, Richard Story, and Terry McDonell; and *Time*'s Susan Jakes and Matt Forney, plus his family: Paola, Roy, Alice, and Cloud. I am especially indebted to my and Frances's parents, who bridged the cultural and bureaucratic divide to enlarge our family on both sides of the Pacific. Cheers, too, Mom and Dad, for saving all of the letters I sent home, both stamped and e-mailed.

Thanks to my agent, Georges Borchardt, and editor, George Gibson, for seeing through this last panel of a China triptych together. As usual, Peter Hessler, Adam Hochschild, and Travis Klingberg provided much-needed feedback on earlier drafts. It never gets any easier.

Frances: twenty years and counting, five of those with Benji. It keeps getting better. As ever, 瓜子, 我爱你.

NOTES

1: A PLUNGE INTO THE MIDDLE COUNTRY

1 *Who will be China's interpreters?* Lin Yutang. *My Country and My People* (New York: John Day, 1936), p. 7. (He dated the preface in which this appears "1935.")

2 *In the next twenty years, the number would soar to $8,000.* Year-to-year per capita income statistics are posted at the World Bank's website: www.data.worldbank .org; poverty statistics are from: http://povertydata.worldbank.org/poverty/country/CHN.

5 *Later I learned that editors laying out newsprint often pulled bus plunge stories.* Jack Shafer, "The Rise and Fall of the 'Bus Plunge' Story." *Slate*, November 13, 2006.

6 *A linguist famously observed.* John DeFrancis. Cited in the chapter "Linguistic Digression #1: Language and Dialect" in David Moser's excellent *A Billion Voices: China's Search for a Common Language* (Beijing: Penguin Books China: 2016).

6 *In English, it's more commonly named Mandarin.* At that time, Mandarin adhered to a southern dialect, which may explain why 北京—Běijīng, Northern Capital—was originally transcribed by Western missionaries as "Peking." Its spelling was officially updated in 1958 with the adoption of *pīnyīn*.

6 *Despite being added to the country's Constitution in 1982.* Article 19, which also enshrines compulsory primary education and the state's development of "educational facilities of various types in order to wipe out illiteracy."

6 *One-third of Chinese citizens, at least 400 million people, do not speak it.*
"One-third of Chinese do not speak Putonghua, says Education Ministry." *South China Morning Post*, September 22, 2014.

6 *In the run-up to the fiftieth anniversary of its introduction.* Ibid.

7 *He wrote on the blackboard in characters but also in pīnyīn.* The current system, developed in the 1950s, replaced the Wade-Giles system, which rendered Sichuan as Szechwan.

18 *Then a fellow rider stressed that the attackers were Yi, an ethnic minority.* The Yí people constitute China's seventh-largest ethnic group. Also called the Lolo, they primarily live in southwest China and northern Vietnam.

2. ON THE STALL-FOR-TIME RIVER

My account of the bus attack, and quotations from letters, all come thanks to my parents, who saved all of my correspondence, including the stamped airmail envelopes. I saved their letters, too, not with an eye to posterity but to prevent them ending up in the hands of Mr. Wang or another colleague or student, since my trash was often picked through with the care of a Kremlinologist.

28 *A newcomer to a city like New York or London.* For this observation, credit an assist to the great Ian Frazier, who in "The March of the Strandbeests" (*The New Yorker*, September 5, 2011) noted how familiar Holland felt to him on arrival, making him realize that he had "habituated myself to the place during long contemplations of Dutch landscapes in American museums."

3. EVERY VILLAGE FACES THE SUN

43 *The simple fact is, Mr. Ambassador, that average Americans.* William J. Lederer and Eugene Burdick, *The Ugly American* (New York: Norton, 1958), p. 108.

44 **Writing in the New York Times Book Review.** Robert Trumbull, "The Ambassador Didn't Read Sarkhanese," *New York Times*, October 5, 1958.

44 *"The American ambassador is a jewel."* William J. Lederer and Eugene Burdick, *The Ugly American* (New York: Norton, 1958), p. 40.

44   *The "ugly" American of the title is not one of these bunglers.*   Ibid., p. 205.

45   *"Whenever you give a man something for nothing."*   Ibid., p. 216.

45   *Perhaps the book's more enduring legacy.*   Ibid., p. 281. The authors also note that American officials had not read the works of Chairman Mao and so did not understand the Communists' appeal to the Chinese masses, especially in rural areas. "We have been offering the Asian nations the wrong kind of help. We have so lost sight of our own past that we are trying to sell guns and money alone, instead of remembering that it was the quest for the dignity of freedom that was responsible for our own way of life. All over Asia we have found that the basic American ethic is revered and honored and imitated when possible. We must, while helping Asia toward self-sufficiency, show by example that America is still the America of freedom and hope and knowledge and law" (pp. 284–85).

45   *America annually allocates more funds to its military marching bands than it does to the Peace Corps.*   In 2016 its annual budget increased 20 percent, to $410 million. Marching bands were allocated $437 million. There were 7,213 Peace Corps volunteers and trainees versus 6,500 military marching band members. https://www .peacecorps.gov/about/open-government/budget-and-performance/ and Dave Philipps, "Military Is Asked to March to a Less Expensive Tune," *New York Times*, July 1, 2016.

47   *In its southern dialects.*   Linguists disagree whether the word comes from the Cantonese for "tomato juice" (*ke-chap*) or the Malay *kechap*, a kind of brined fish sauce produced in China (hence, the usage "tomato ketchup"). See Glynnis Chantrell, *The Oxford Dictionary of World Histories* (Oxford, UK: Oxford University Press, 2002), and Bryan Garner, *Garner's Modern American Usage* (Oxford, UK: Oxford University Press, 2003).

48   *Doubtless all small towns, in all countries.*   Sinclair Lewis, *Main Street* (New York: Collier, 1920), p. 266.

48   *Sure of itself, it bullies other civilizations.*   Ibid., p. 267.

48   *The test of a first-rate intelligence.*   F. Scott Fitzgerald wrote this in an *Esquire* article published in 1936. After his death, it was collected in *The Crack-Up* (New York: New Directions, 1945), p. 69.

50   *SEX—Joining the Party.*   *Newsweek*, March 31, 1996. The magazine's "Sex" issue won an Overseas Press Award for Best Magazine Reporting from Abroad. "China's

emergence as a superpower has provoked all kinds of overheated rhetoric," the magazine wrote in its announcement. "It's gratifying to have our peers recognize *Newsweek*'s cool and lucid approach. Washington and Beijing may not be headed for a new cold war, but there is probably no more important story to watch as we head for the new millennium. *Newsweek* will be out front all the way." Thirteen years later, the magazine's owners sold *Newsweek* to a stereo equipment mogul for $1.

52 **He made observations familiar to anyone.** Bill Holm, *Coming Home Crazy* (Minneapolis: Milkweed, 2000), p. 29. Holm became a frequent guest on Garrison Keillor's radio show *A Prairie Home Companion*. In 2009 he died from complications from pneumonia, age sixty-five.

53 **The authors' aim was not really to portray daily life.** Nicholas D. Kristof and Sheryl WuDunn, *China Wakes* (New York: Vintage, 1995), p. 451. This passage goes on to quote the former U.S. ambassador to China that "'a China expert' is an oxymoron" as well as the authors' observation that "China watching, simply put, is an exercise in humiliation."

53 **China is too big a country, and her national life has too many facets.** Lin Yutang, *My Country and My People* (New York: John Day, 1936), p. xii.

54 **He lamented the trickle of news.** Ibid., p. 3.

54 **It is difficult to deny the Old China Hand the right to write books.** Ibid., p.10.

54 **Minus the sailors' obscenity of language.** Ibid., p.11.

54 **Understanding a foreign country, Lin said.** Ibid., p. 7.

54 **"What do women want? Sexy underwear."** *Newsweek*, February 11, 1996.

4. Sinking In

58 **Dali is a perfect place to tune out for a while.** Robert Storey, *Lonely Planet China*, 4th Edition (London: Lonely Planet, 1994), p. 872.

5. Parting the Cloud of Compassion

80 **The most recent national census.** The figures come from the Sixth National Population Census of the People's Republic of China (2010) and "Who Is Chinese? The Upper Han," *Economist*, November 19, 2016. China restricts naturalization for demographic and political reasons. Its agencies and regulations to handle applicants are nascent; until China's economic rise, few people wanted to emigrate there.

80 **It also rarely grants legal asylum.** Per the Beijing office of the United Nations High Commission for Refugees. See its fact sheet at: http://www.unhcr.org/5000187d9 .pdf. A tip of the cap to the *Economist* story for the billionaires comparison. The figure of 594 Mainland super-rich comes from the annual *Hurun Report*, noted in "China tops U.S. in number of billionaires," BBC.com, October 13, 2016. For a Chinese perspective on refugees, see Cui Jia, "Refugees Look to End Life in Limbo," *China Daily Europe*, December 29, 2015.

80 **By the time I finished the coffee.** This exchange and this trip are recounted in my article "New Year, Old China," *Los Angeles Times*, January 4, 1998, pp. L1 and L8.

82 **Experts unite to push back superstition.** The headlines and stories appeared in *China Daily*, February 21, 1997.

6. Far and Away in Tibet

My story of this trip was published as "The Predicament of Tibet," *Chicago Tribune*, October 18, 1998, pp. T1 and T5–6.

90 **They make a mirror in which, as Jonathan Swift said.** "Satire is a sort of glass wherein beholders do generally discover everybody's face but their own." Jonathan Swift, *The Battle of the Books* (London: Chatto and Windus, 1908), p. lxv.

8. Thought Liberation

124 **In fact, the line built during the Ming.** In 2012, Chinese researchers announced the Wall's various offshoots and remains built across all dynasties in fact stretch thirteen thousand miles, a distance over half the earth's circumference. The claim includes walls that Koreans say are part of their Koguryo kingdom. See Erica Ho, "Is the Great Wall of China Longer Than Previously Thought?," *Time*, July 22, 2012.

9. Beijing Spring

127 **You saw that teacher being slaughtered.** Lao She, *City of Cats* (*Mao Cheng Ji*) (Ann Arbor: University of Michigan Center for Chinese Studies, 1964), pp. 32–33. This edition was translated by James Dew, who, three decades later, would design the introductory Chinese language program for my Peace Corps training.

130 **In fact, trade flowed primarily in the opposite direction.** See the United States Census Bureau's table of year-to-year trade: https://www.census.gov/foreign-trade/balance/c5700.html.

133 **A Party boss called them.** "A Message from Confucius," *Economist*, October 22, 2009.

10. Meet the Parents

160 **In 2017, one out of three international students in the United States were Chinese.** Statistics on Chinese students and revenue come via http://www.iie.org/Who-We-Are/News-and-Events/Press-Center/Press-Releases/2014/2014-11-17-Open-Doors-Data#.WJiQMBDvelV and http://beijing.usembassy-china.org.cn/business/2016-u.s.-china-tourism-year.

11. Signposts

170 **I could not understand why the imperial authorities.** Lao She, *Beneath the Red Banner* (Beijing: Panda Books, 1982), p. 118.

172 **In 2016, a new store opened at the rate of one per day.** https://news.starbucks.com/news/starbucks-2016-annual-meeting-of-shareholders.

173 **"Although it is uncertain where God created paradise."** Evariste Regis Huc, *Annales de la Propagation de la Foi*, Tome XVI (Lyon: M.P. Rusand, 1844) p.359.

12. Three Protests

183 **The khan had ordered them planted two paces apart.** Marco Polo, *Travels in the Land of Kublai Khan* (London: Penguin, 2005), p. 74.

13. ARRIVALS AND DEPARTURES

196   *The document said that all citizens are equal before the law.*   Articles 33, 34, 35, 36, 41, 42, 43, 48, 49, 52, and 53. *Constitution of the People's Republic of China* (Beijing: Foreign Language Press, 1982), p. 29.

197   *I feared I "had the experience but missed the meaning."*   T. S Eliot, from "The Dry Salvages," a poem in *Four Quartets* (New York: Harcourt, 1943).

197   *I didn't want to become the "Old China Hand."*   Lin Yutang, *My Country and My People* (New York: John Day, 1936), p. 9.

200   *It was the cliché "that launched a thousand articles."*   "China's Fitful Sleep," *Economist*, July 17, 1997.

201   *In fact, Napoleon probably never said it.*   Isaac Stone, "Crouching Tiger, Sleeping Giant," *Foreign Policy*, January 19, 2016.

201   *In his 1958 book* Scratches on Our Minds.   Harold Isaacs, *Scratches on Our Minds* (London: Routledge, 2015), p. 209.

202   *He had grown up dirt poor.*   Lao She, *Beneath the Red Banner* (Beijing: Panda Books, 1982), p. 31.

202   *Pearl Buck wrote about hosting Lao She.*   Pearl S. Buck, *My Several Worlds* (New York: John Day, 1954), p. 368.

202   *Now he is an exile of a sort.*   Ibid., p. 367.

203   *"How do you get to our factory?"*   I wrote about the Yanjing brewery visit in "Thirst Come, Thirst Served," *Time Asia*, September 22, 2003.

204   *In fact, China did grow barley.*   Mike Verdin, "Not All Origins Are Equal in China's Booming Barley Import Market," Agrimony.com, June 18, 2005. China trailed only Saudi Arabia in barley imports worldwide.

204   *It is surprising to discover the number of Americans.*   From the essay "China Today," collected in Pearl S. Buck, *China As I See It* (New York: John Day, 1970), pp. 294–95.

14. DIGRESSIONS ON THE NEW FRONTIER

210 **The only bad moment the train passenger has.** Paul Theroux, *Riding the Iron Rooster: By Train Through China* (Boston: Houghton Mifflin, 2006), p. 296.

211 **Often used as flexibly as the f-word in English.** I am grateful to Huichieh Loy for the translation, found here: http://languagehat.com/tamade/.

233 **He spent only 250 words on his stay.** Marco Polo, *The Book of Ser Marco Polo, the Venetian* (Cambridge, UK: Cambridge University Press, 2010), p. 169. This chapter's title follows Polo's preferred way to alert the reader that his main story has paused.

15. COUNTDOWN CLOCKS

For a pieced-together account of Margo Carter's unexplained death, see Michael Woodhead's "The strange life and mysterious death of Margo, Aussie 'queen of Tiger Leaping Gorge'" posted to his blog that recounts his own treks in the footsteps of the 1920s botanist Joseph Rock: http://www.josephrock.net/2010/03/strange-life-and-mysterious-death-of.html. Woodhead says that I was one of the last journalists to interview her. If so, I should add that I enjoyed meeting Margo. She made me laugh, and she exuded a protective love for the gorge and southwest China's nature. As Woodhead notes, "It must be heartbreaking to settle in such a beautiful wilderness and see it slowly transformed into an overdeveloped tourist trap."

239 **When Marco Polo visited the capital at that time.** Marco Polo, *Travels in the Land of Kublai Khan* (London: Penguin, 2005), p. 38.

239 **In the face of modernization, globalization and the 2008 Olympics.** Li Xiguang of Tsinghua University, quoted in Julie Chao, "Goodbye to Old Beijing," Cox Media Group, May 28, 2004.

16. DEFENDING THE GHOSTS

240 **We're even bigger here.** Richard Bernstein, "The House of Speer: Still Rising on the Skyline," *New York Times*, February 27, 2003.

242 **But do the Chinese understand themselves?** Lin Yutang, *My Country and My People* (New York: John Day, 1936), p. 12.

242 *That recalled the contemporary writer.* My interviews with Feng Jicai and Liang Congjie also appear, in different form, in the chapter "Saving the Old Street" in *The Last Days of Old Beijing: Life in the Vanishing Backstreets of a City Transformed.* I am including them here because talking with these two men, remarkable in different ways, set me on the path to researching my first book.

246 *"Since there existed no guides to buildings."* Quoted in Wilma Fairbank, *Liang and Lin: Partners in Exploring China's Architectural Past* (Philadelphia: University of Pennsylvania Press, 1994), p. 65.

247 *"Fifty years later."* Quoted in Wang Jun, *Chengji* [*City Record*] (Beijing: Sanlian, 2003), p. 184.

For a warm remembrance of Liang Congjie, see the *Economist*'s, published November 18, 2010. http://www.economist.com/node/17519870.

248 *"What I am trying to do in Beijing."* Jasper Becker, *City of Heavenly Tranquility* (Oxford, UK: Oxford University Press, 2008), p. 292.

248 *After drawing Beijing's Olympic axis, the son.* Rowan Callick, *The Party Forever: Inside China's Modern Communist Elite* (New York: St. Martin's Press, 2013), p. 5.

17. LEARNING TO SPEAK OLYMPICS

257 *Mocky was a naughty monkey.* My least favorite monkey and some of the students' dialogues, as well as a portion of the police officer's lessons, appear in the chapter "Mocky and Me" in *The Last Days of Old Beijing: Life in the Vanishing Backstreets of a City Transformed.* I am including them here as a snapshot of my life and neighborhood in the run-up to the Olympics.

259 *Dialogues called "Dissuading Foreigners from Excessive Drinking."* From Wang Sheng'an, ed., *Àoyùn ānbǎo fúwù yīngyǔ* [*Olympic Security English*] (Beijing: Chinese People's Police University Press, 2002).

260 *She wasn't sure how, exactly.* Frances's courtroom observations are culled from her fascinating observations and detailed transcriptions of the proceedings, from May 24, 2005, onward. The best lines, including the description of the judges and litigants, are hers. She never returned after being called out by the judges. Such are the dangers academic researchers face when conducting fieldwork in China.

19. "ONE WORLD, ONE DREAM" ONE YEAR LATER

271 **Nevertheless, on the book tour in 2013.** My article about my talks in Taiwan
and on the Mainland, "See You Again Old Beijing," appeared on *Slate*, August 9, 2013.

274 **I was not going to attend that.** A thread throughout this book is how capricious
the very concept of China's "change" has turned out to be. While the country undoubt-
edly transformed over the past two decades, in many ways—politically, for example—it
remains unchanged, or even more entrenched. Trying to understand, let alone explain,
the gradations of change invokes the same sense of whiplash I felt on landing, uttering
an innocuous sentence such as "The Chinese countryside is beautiful." *Yes, but also
harsh.* And it remains so, in terms of access to education and financing. Land rights
reform has stalled, and the household income and schooling gap has widened: From
2000 to 2015 nearly three-quarters of rural primary schools were shut, causing students
to commute longer distances to merged schools. While the average number of years
spent at school has doubled since 1980, less than 10 percent of rural children make it
to senior high school, compared to 70 percent in cities. (For a wealth of readings on
this topic, see Stanford University's Rural Education Action Program: http://reap.fsi
.stanford.edu.)

Another whiplash-inducing sentence: "China has a market economy." *Yes, but* . . . The
reforms launched by then-premier Zhu Rongji resulted in a 63 percent drop of employment in state-owned companies since 1998, while jobs in private companies rose 644
percent. Private enterprise does drive China's economic growth. At the same time, the
state's heavy hand is still felt throughout the economy, especially in manufacturing—
where at least one-third of output is by state-owned firms—and in the banking sector
that keeps loaning money to firms dubbed (politically) too big to fail. (See "Recasting
the Iron Rice Bowl: The Reform of China's State-Owned Enterprises," by Daniel
Berkowitz, Hong Ma, and Shuichiro Nishioka, in *The Review of Economics and Statistics*,
August 24, 2016.)

It terms of China, these days when I hear the word "change," my mind substitutes it
for the "faults" in Philip Larkin's "This Be the Verse,"* which begins, "They fuck you
up, your mum and dad./They may not mean to, but they do./They fill you with the
faults they had/And add some extra, just for you."

Collected Poems (New York: Farrar Straus and Giroux, 2001.)

A NOTE ON THE AUTHOR

Michael Meyer went to China in 1995 as one of its first Peace Corps volunteers. The author of *The Last Days of Old Beijing* and *In Manchuria*, Meyer has won two Lowell Thomas Awards for travel writing, a Whiting Writers' Award for nonfiction, and a Guggenheim Fellowship. His stories have appeared in the *New York Times*, *Time*, *Smithsonian*, *Sports Illustrated*, *Slate*, the *Financial Times*, *Foreign Policy*, *Architectural Record*, the *Los Angeles Times*, and the *Chicago Tribune*, as well as on National Public Radio's *This American Life*. As an associate professor of English, Meyer teaches nonfiction writing at the University of Pittsburgh. Visit his website at www.road tosleepingdragon.com.

47